W9-AXO-735

CHEZ PANISSE CAFÉ COOKBOOK

ALICE WATERS

and the

COOKS *of* CHEZ PANISSE

in collaboration with

DAVID TANIS *and* FRITZ STREIFF

illustrations by

DAVID LANCE GOINES

WILLIAM MORROW

An Imprint of HarperCollins*Publishers*

ALSO FROM CHEZ PANISSE

Chez Panisse Vegetables
Fanny at Chez Panisse
Chez Panisse Menu Cookbook
Chez Panisse Pasta, Pizza, and Calzone
Chez Panisse Desserts
Chez Panisse Cooking

Chez Panisse Café Cookbook
Alice Waters and the Cooks of Chez Panisse
HarperCollins*Publishers*

CHEZ PANISSE CAFÉ COOKBOOK. Copyright © 1999 by Alice Waters. Illustrations copyright © 1999 by David Lance Goines. All rights reserved. Printed in China.
No part of this book may be used or reproduced in any manner whatsoever without written permission except in the case of brief quotations embodied in critical articles and reviews. For information address HarperCollins Publishers, Inc., 195 Broadway, New York, NY 10007.

HarperCollins books may be purchased for educational, business, or sales promotional use. For information please e-mail the Special Markets Department at SPsales@harpercollins.com.

Designed by David Lance Goines
Typeset by Wilsted & Taylor Publishing Services

Library of Congress Cataloging-in-Publication Data
is available.

ISBN 978-0-06-017583-2

20 SCP 20 19 18 17 16 15

FOR CATHERINE BRANDEL,
CHEF, MENTOR, AND FRIEND.

Acknowledgments

This cookbook could not have happened without the collaboration of three dear friends: David Tanis, former Café chef and the most wonderful cook, who helped plan and write the book, gathering all the recipes, testing, and rewriting them; Fritz Streiff, former Chez Panisse cook and Café host and my faithful word processor, who went over the manuscript checking grammar, typography, and style; and David Lance Goines, the artist whose illustrations and design for this book so perfectly express its spirit—and who has eaten in the Café since the day it opened.

We were inspired by two unforgettable past Café chefs, Catherine Brandel and Peggy Smith; the two extraordinary Café chefs at present, Gilbert Pilgram and Russell Moore; and by my partner Lindsey Shere, who continues to encourage and enlighten us. Alan Tangren, currently pastry chef and formerly our first full-time forager, provided invaluable support by researching and writing most of the material in the chapter introductions; and Kelsie Sue Kerr, another former chef, pitched in with additional knowledge and recipe testing.

The other contributors to the book are the following Chez Panisse cooks and friends: Tracy Bates, Diane Bouma, Phillip Dedlow, Amy Dencler, Anne Dickey, Jenny Emanuel, Michael Emanuel, Brian Espinoza, Niloufer Ichaporia, Sharan Ikeda, Anna Kovel, Christopher Lee, David Lindsay, John Luther, Scott McGehee, Jean-Pierre Moullé, Michael Peternell, Gayle Pirie, Tasha Prysi, Charlene Reis, Mary Robida Canales, Jennifer Sherman, Anthony Tassinello, David Visick, and Samantha Wood. I want to thank them all for their dedication to the philosophy of Chez Panisse. I also owe a debt of thanks to all the other cooks, past and present; the hardworking and devoted floor staff; and our loyal customers, who have continued to give us the enthusiasm and criticism we need to help us change and grow.

Finally, my gratitude to our editor, Susan Friedland, for believing in us and our idiosyncratic method of designing and writing cookbooks.

CONTENTS

PREFACE

WHEN my friends and I started Chez Panisse, in 1971, in a cozy little two-story house in Berkeley, California, our signs and menus and matchbooks all said "Café & Restaurant." I believed, naïvely, that our new establishment could be all things to all people. Chez Panisse, I thought, could have a flower-bedecked dining room with white linen and candlelight and soigné cuisine and, at the very same time, it could be a bustling neighborhood bistro, with butcher paper on the tables and old-fashioned, straight-ahead fare, where you could get as much or as little as you wanted. I must have known at some level that these were irreconcilable fantasies, but that didn't stop me. We were open seven days a week, from seven-thirty in the morning until two in the morning. In the daytime, we tried to be a café: We offered a chalkboard menu of simple dishes à la carte, and we encouraged people to hang out for hours at tables covered with checkered oilcloth. Then, at dinnertime, we got out the linen tablecloths, dimmed the lights, and served an ambitious fixed-price dinner of four or five courses. And when the diners went home, we tried to metamorphose back into a café.

It never quite worked. The restaurant was such a huge success that people started making reservations weeks in advance, and we didn't have enough tables. Discouragingly, we found ourselves displacing the café regulars (many of whom were students and bohemians who couldn't afford the fixed-price menu, which had climbed to a dizzying $12.50 per person) in order to make room for an increasingly homogeneous clientele of well-heeled people dressed up for a fancy occasion. We tried to keep our café side alive: we opened for coffee and croissants in the morning; and after the dinner service, our friend Bob Waks, who worked at the Cheeseboard collective across the street, would come in to fry potatoes and grill steaks with garlic and black pepper. The trouble was that all of us on the restaurant staff would hungrily eat up Bob's late-night suppers as fast as he could cook them, so we never made any money.

Around this time we started thinking seriously about enlarging our premises, and I went off on vacation to Italy with my friends Jay Heminway, Bob Waks, and Jerry Budrick, who was one of my partners and a waiter in the restaurant. We ended up in Torino one freezing November night, outside a little restaurant. We could see a fire burning inside and it pulled us in. And there I had my first pizza out of a wood-burning oven. We all thought it was the best thing we had eaten on the whole trip. We shared several pizzas and a few bottles of wine, and by the time we left we had it all figured out: we would turn upstairs at Chez Panisse into a café open day and night, with an exposed kitchen, a grill, and a big brick wood-burning pizza oven, and downstairs would remain a restaurant with a single carefully composed, fixed-price menu.

Back in California, I enlisted the help of our friend Cecilia Chiang, who owned The Mandarin, a San Francisco restaurant. She introduced me to her good friends Lun Chan, an architect, and Bumps Baldauf, a kitchen design expert, who laid out the plans for the new upstairs café. Somehow we located a cantankerous German bricklayer who claimed to know how to build a pizza oven, and work began. Kip Mesirow, a master craftsman and old friend, recruited a team of superb carpenters who were skilled in Japanese-style joinery. Together they built the café in Kip's inimitable hybrid style, combining elements of traditional Japanese architecture with the California Craftsman redwood interiors of Greene & Greene and Bernard Maybeck, and the Art Nouveau decor of Charles Rennie Mackintosh. We hung the walls with old French movie posters advertising the films of Marcel Pagnol, films that had already provided us with both a name and an ideal: to create a community of friends, lovers, and relatives that spans generations and is in tune with the seasons, the land, and human appetites.

Perhaps appropriately, the Café opened on April Fools' Day, 1980, with Jerry Budrick as the maître d'hôtel, Steve Crumley (now a maître d' himself) as bartender, and a colorful crew of cooks and waiters, some of whom are still at their jobs. Over the years, the Café has employed a number of other memorable hosts in addition to Jerry and Steve, including my old college roommate, Eleanor Bertino, the brassy journalist Kate Coleman, the affable Fritz Streiff, and our loquacious tea authority, Helen Gustafson. From the start, the place was a hit. We decided not to take reservations in advance, and people started crowding in and waiting hours for a table. Wolfgang Puck came to dinner, loved what he saw, looked up our bricklayer, and designed and built his own open kitchen and pizza oven at Spago in Los Angeles. (Little did he

know that our bricklayer didn't really know how to build a proper Nea-
politan pizza oven at all. In fact, it was years before we were able to im-
port and install the Italian insert that now makes our oven fuel-efficient
and sufficiently hot.) The concept of an open kitchen is a simple one:
cooks and diners should interact and cooking smells should fill the
room. And in the Café, they do.

Just two years after the Café opened, early one Sunday morning after we had all gone home, a fire started in the downstairs kitchen. No
one was hurt, but before it was put out, the Restaurant was gutted and
the Café was seriously damaged. We had to close for months to regroup
and rebuild, and that time was a turning point for me. As sympathy
poured in, I began to understand that we had, indeed, created a community—not just for ourselves, but one that included our customers.
People wrote telling me that they had fallen in love in the Café, that
they celebrated all their anniversaries in the Restaurant, that they had
written their graduate theses on the little tables by the bar. I began to
understand that all these events had become part of Chez Panisse and
we needed to be considerate in ways I could never have predicted before then. We couldn't go on doing anything we wanted without trying
to be more hospitable and accommodating. We had to offer a few more
choices, and stay informal enough that customers could get to know us
and identify with us. We had to keep changing, too: it is much more
important that the food be consistently delicious than that it always be
the same.

To achieve that goal, we now have two chefs in the Café instead of
one. Three days a week, one chef writes both daily menus and oversees
the kitchens; on the other three days we are open, the other chef takes
over. The chef not in the kitchen labors in the office or at home, plan-
ning menus, ordering provisions and supplies, scheduling personnel,
creating new recipes, and performing other administrative and mana-
gerial duties. I think this is one of the best organizational moves we ever
made. The line cooks, prep cooks, and interns who work under the
chefs learn twice as much, and the food is twice as good, and always
different.

The Café menus are constantly changing and evolving, but two
dishes are always on the menu, and have been since the night we
opened: one is a garden salad with baked goat cheese and the other is a
variation on the calzone, a sort of pizza turnover (now called Crostata
di Perrella, after our senior *pizzaiolo*, Michele). Recipes for both have

been published before, but we had to include our current versions in this book. We have revisited a few other old favorites, and included over a hundred new recipes from our recent repertoire.

Except for a chapter of desserts, this cookbook is organized by ingredients, rather than by type of dish, so in the same chapter you may find appetizers, pizzas, soups, and main courses. We have paid special attention to the ingredients we left out of our last book, *Chez Panisse Vegetables*: fish and shellfish, meat and poultry, eggs and cheese. Because I want this book to be an inspiration as well as a reference, each chapter has an introduction describing the sources of the foods we cook—farmers, foragers, and artisans who care deeply about what they are doing, and who are constantly opening new avenues in our work and giving us new ways of seeing things. Our search for fresh and pure ingredients is a work in progress, and by the year 2000, we want all of our ingredients to be certifiable as organically grown. We hope our descriptions of some of our suppliers will inspire you to seek out similarly dedicated farmers, foragers, fishermen, and other purveyors who practice and support the sustainable, ecologically sound harvest of nature's bounty.

Some dishes in this book are utterly simple, while others are complex, in some cases requiring days of preparation. I hope the cook will feel free to improvise in the spirit of the recipes. Seek out and experiment with the products you find at your local farmers' markets. Go to the market *before* you decide what you want to cook. Learn to use all your senses and, especially, how to taste—the best skill a cook can cultivate.

You will need no special tools or equipment to cook these recipes other than a good sharp knife and a few basic pots and pans. A large heavy mortar and pestle is useful and far more satisfying to use—and better exercise!—than a whirring electric food processor. An inexpensive Japanese mandolin for slicing vegetables paper-thin is another helpful tool. If you have a fireplace, consider using it to bake, say, potatoes under the burned-down coals, or to grill a steak over vine cuttings. At home I have a marvelous, very simple fireplace grill I found in Tuscany. My friend Alta Tingle now imports them at her Berkeley store, The Gardener. They are great because they are adjustable, sturdy, and portable, and can be used both indoors and outdoors.

A garden can help make the kitchen the sensual center of your house. A small lettuce patch is easy to sow and cultivate, and you will never regret the time you spend there. If there is no room for a garden at your house, at least try to make room for a few pots of herbs. Often you only need a few sprigs of thyme to flavor a pot of beans, or a few leaves of basil and mint for your cucumber salad.

A word about salt: we use kosher salt, mild-flavored and additive-free, in the Café kitchen; all the recipes in this book have been tested using it (except for Jean-Pierre's Cured Salmon on page 70, which requires rock salt). There are many interesting unrefined sea salts available, with wonderful, complex mineral flavors. They tend to taste much saltier than ordinary table salt or kosher salt. By all means experiment with them: you may find yourself using less salt. At Chez Panisse, we sometimes use the remarkably tasty though expensive *fleur de sel* from France, to sprinkle over a salad of perfectly ripe late-summer tomatoes.

Good olive oil is indispensable. We use far more olive oil than butter in our cooking these days. Not only is it healthful, it is the best-tasting cooking and salad oil. Pure olive oil is fine for a lot of everyday cooking, but extra-virgin olive oil is essential for salads, for seasoning, and for slowly stewed vegetables. Patronize places that will let you taste before buying, and discover which qualities you prefer in an extra-virgin oil. Some are peppery and some are fruity and green-tasting, especially the oil from the first pressings of the fall. Some of the olive oils produced in California now rival the Tuscan oils that we like best.

After almost twenty years, the Café is still a place where people hang out together, and measure out the years from Bastille Day to Bastille Day and from New Year's Eve to New Year's Eve. My old friend, film producer Tom Luddy, still drags in every foreign director and starlet imaginable, holding court with his wife Monique amid film buffs and groupies. Retired professors and Nobel Prize laureates still lunch quietly, and our Saturday lunch regulars are still known by name to cooks and waiters alike. We still have to start work at dawn to make the Café run. And every day still brings its calamities and near-disasters, as we attempt to make the experience special for first-timers while also juggling tables to save room for regulars and cooking a menu that changes daily.

On certain nights, when the place is really humming and smells of fresh garlic, when the customers are "getting it," the waiters are happy, and the cooks are all in synch, all the work and effort seems somehow beside the point. I sigh. It's time for a glass of Bandol rosé.

VEGETABLES

ONE of the first things a customer sees upon coming up the stairs to the Café is an eye-catching basket of vegetables. Every day, a designated cook decides what produce looks the most beautiful and the most nearly as if it had been picked that very morning, and arranges it for display on the counter in front of the salad-making station, next to the bar. New cooks tend to be intimidated by this task because someone is sure to have warned them that I am obsessed with the display. And I am: it's among my very highest priorities, because it demonstrates the quality of the food that we serve.

The display has to look wonderful every day, like a beautiful seventeenth-century Spanish tabletop still life painting—a basket of tiny spiny purple artichokes or purple striped eggplants; a few untrimmed bulbs of fennel with their feathery green tops; an enormous cardoon plant looking like a giant swollen head of celery; a rainbow cornucopia of multicolored glowing tomatoes, some still on the branch; a few huge tumescent boletus mushrooms, or a pile of perfect morels, smelling faintly of the woods. The display is our way of sharing our pleasure in the colors and textures of the raw materials we use in our cooking and hinting at what is on the menu that day.

When the Café opened, we had a limited choice of produce suppliers. Like most restaurants, we got our fruits and vegetables at the commercial produce terminal and a few local markets. We desperately wanted better raw materials, but for years we thought the only way we could get them was by starting a farm ourselves, or by having a farmer grow things just for us. Only gradually have we learned that it takes a network of suppliers, some forty in all, whom we have discovered over the years. This network has become indispensable to us. It is not just a list of purveyors, but a community of people who share our goals of providing fresh, perfectly grown food while promoting a sustainable agriculture that takes care of the earth. Like any community, we find ourselves bound together by mutual dependence and a feeling of responsibility for each other.

These relationships have deepened as we have discovered how central the quality of produce is to our cooking. Because the food we cook is simple and straightforward, every ingredient must be the best of its kind. We have had to learn the right questions to ask growers; whether, for example, the lettuces could be picked younger or the tomatoes could stay on the vine a bit longer. Gradually cooks and farmers have educated each other as we have learned what grows well in our part of California, and how we can best use it at the restaurant.

When a friend sent us some tiny, sweet, seductive green beans he had found at the Chino family's produce stand near San Diego, the door opened to a relationship with a family whose dedication and focus on growing the best continue to inspire us. The Chinos grow a staggering variety of breathtakingly beautiful fruits and vegetables. Thanks to them, we have discovered that carrots are not just orange, but also white, red, and yellow; that beets are white, orange, gold, and pink; that turnips come tapered and long, and white, purple, and pink; and that peppers can be purple, orange, yellow, and brown, as well as red or green.

To visit the Chinos' produce stand at any season of the year is to be utterly astonished by new flavors and diverse colors. In tomato season, you might find fifteen different kinds of cherry tomatoes alone: little round green ones the size of marbles; vivid red Sweet 100s; pink cherry tomatoes; yellow pear-shaped cherry tomatoes; brilliant orange cherry tomatoes; two colors of tiny currant tomatoes; and more. In their uncompromising quest for the best varieties, they have scoured the world, bringing us so many new or forgotten varieties that we sometimes wonder how we ever cooked without them.

We also prize our close relationship with DeeAnn Freitas and Viki von Lackum, the latest in a line of local salad gardeners providing us almost year-round with tender greens grown in backyard gardens and allotments right here in Berkeley, harvested and immediately brought to us for our daily salads. DeeAnn and Viki are part of the immediate Chez Panisse family: DeeAnn started working for us as a bus girl, and Viki is the wife of one of our chefs.

Around the time the café opened, my father retired from a long career in management consulting and moved to California. He wanted to help out, so my partners and I gave him a mission: find us the perfect producer, the farm nearby that will grow us not just salad greens, but all sorts of things! We had been sinking quite a lot of money into failing farming experiments that had fallen victim to bad weather, bad locations, inexperienced gardeners, and our own bad judgment.

But things started looking up when my dad got involved. He developed a list of criteria: the farm had to be no more than an hour from Berkeley by car; it had to be organic; the farmer had to be willing to work with us and plant things that we wanted; and so forth. For months, Dad did research, wrote letters, hunted through databases at the University of California at Davis, and combed the countryside.

Finally he made a presentation of four or five candidate farms and we chose a place in Sonoma County run by a bona fide eccentric named Bob Cannard. Bob is a fanatical biodynamic farmer with his own peculiar idiosyncrasies: he believes that healthy crops need healthy weeds, which Bob sees as "companion plants." Early in the season he may wave his arm toward a field of weeds and say, "Well, there are the carrots." Only after pulling aside the grasses and other weeds can one see the little carrot plants, sheltered from the drying effects of sun and wind and protected from insect pests. Later in the season Bob cuts the weeds to a level just above the tops of the growing carrot plants, which then grow out over the weeds. It may well be that the rich, complex flavor of Bob's carrots and other root vegetables is due to their close association with their companion plants.

Bob also believes in enriching his soil with vast quantities of crushed river rock. He has theories about mineralizing vegetable crops that sound plausible—to be truthful, I really don't understand a lot of what he's talking about. But when he sends us vegetables, I like what I taste.

Bob's farm sits on a wooded hillside above the floor of the Sonoma Valley, an hour's drive from Chez Panisse. Because of its hillside location, the farm is often cooler in the summer and warmer in the winter than other parts of Sonoma County. Bob cultivates about thirty-five acres, and grows a great variety of produce, from tiny watercress and tender baby lettuces to spicy rocket, pungent herbs, earthy potatoes, and succulent apricots, peaches, figs, and raspberries. In the spring he forages for miner's lettuce, which grows abundantly near the woods on one side of the farm. In the winter he grows enchanting radicchios, including the pale yellow-green, maroon-spotted Castelfranco variety. All these ingredients arrive at the kitchen hours after they have been harvested.

We've been working with Bob for over thirteen years. We have both backed away from expecting our relationship to be mostly exclusive—Bob cannot grow everything we want to cook, and we cannot always cook everything he can grow—but we still drive up to his farm for vegetables almost every day in the summer and every other day in the winter.

At the same time Bob grows produce for us, he is growing his soil. He uses lots of compost to improve the soil at the farm, and some of the compost is made from our kitchen scraps. We designate certain garbage containers for composting, and although only fruit and vegetable scraps and leftover bread are supposed to go into these containers, an occasional paring knife or silver fork occasionally turns up in the compost as it is being spread. We take along our compost containers in the van on every trip to the farm, where they are unloaded onto the compost pile. When the driver returns to the restaurant with that day's vegetables, the emptied compost buckets ride back, too.

Access to perfectly ripe, flavorful produce is not the exclusive prerogative of Chez Panisse and a few other special restaurants. A backyard vegetable garden may be the best way to supply yourself with ripe, just-picked produce. The choice of varieties can be almost limitless, and the therapeutic value of gardening is undisputed.

But even those of us without this resource may have access to irresistible produce. Most of the growers we work with at Chez Panisse sell at local farmers' markets, and with the proliferation of such markets around the country, the intrepid home cook can often find beautiful organically grown produce.

At the farmers' market, freshness is judged by hours, not days. Let your growers know that you want vegetables harvested at the peak of ripeness. Ask them which varieties they like, and tell them about your favorites if you don't see them displayed. Tell them you care about how the produce is raised. You'll be surprised at how well they respond to this kind of specific interest in their world, and you'll probably make some good friends.

This kind of information and interaction is nearly impossible to find at the supermarket. The produce displays there often give no clue as to what season it is, because of the easy availability of produce shipped round the world by anonymous farmers. But when you look at what's most abundant at a farmers' market, you'll also learn what's cheapest and best.

Another way for consumers to connect to farms is through community-supported agriculture programs, or CSAs. In exchange for a prepayment at the beginning of the season, a farmer agrees to drop off a box of produce, usually weekly, containing a mixture of the fruits and vegetables the farm has produced that week. This arrangement gives the farmer a source of income at the beginning of the season, when costs are high and other income may be nonexistent, and it encourages the cook to be spontaneous and innovative when she receives a surprise basket of seasonal vegetables. Because many of our suppliers, including Fairview Gardens near Santa Barbara and Terra Firma Farm and Full Belly Farm in the Sacramento Valley, have thriving CSAs, home cooks can use the same produce we do at Chez Panisse. The members of Michael Ableman's Fairview Gardens CSA, for example, have the opportunity to taste the same very special white asparagus we use every day when it is in season, usually in warm salads with shaved Parmesan, a little pancetta and hard-cooked egg, and curly endive.

GARDEN LETTUCE SALAD

It is not an overstatement to say that a restaurant is only as good as its simplest green salad. Our green salad is the important dish on the menu. Judging from the number of salads they order, our customers agree. All our new cooks are taught the nuances of salad making. We stress the importance of handling the greens carefully, choosing an appropriate mixture of lettuces, washing the leaves gently in abundant cold water, drying them and wrapping them in clean linen to await their turn in the salad bowl, dressing them with just the right amount of critically tasted, freshly made vinaigrette. Our preference is for a salad of young greens picked that day, no more than four inches tall, from among the following: red and green oak leaf lettuce, rocket, romaine, curly endive, cress, tender parsley leaves, and chervil sprigs.

Serves 6.

2 tablespoons red wine or sherry vinegar, or a combination
1 small garlic clove, peeled
Salt
6 tablespoons extra-virgin olive oil
Pepper
6 large handfuls salad greens, about ¾ pound

Measure the vinegar into a small bowl. Crush the garlic clove and add it to the vinegar, along with ½ teaspoon salt. After 10 minutes or so, whisk in the olive oil and a little freshly milled pepper. Taste and adjust the seasoning. Make the vinaigrette no more than a couple of hours before serving.

Pick over the salad greens, discarding any tough outer leaves, or any that are wilted or blemished. (If you are using young head lettuces, trim the root ends with a sharp paring knife to free the leaves.) Fill a large basin with cold water and gently submerge the greens, allowing sand and grit to sink to the bottom. Lift the lettuces from the water and drain them in a colander, then dry them in a salad spinner. Wrap the leaves in clean cotton toweling and refrigerate in an airtight container.

To serve, put the greens in a wide salad bowl and season with a small pinch of salt. Remove the garlic clove, whisk the vinaigrette, and toss the greens lightly with just enough dressing to make the leaves glisten. (Your hands make the best salad-tossing tools.) Serve immediately, with garlic toast or croûtons.

Romaine Leaves with Anchovy Dressing

Thanks to our connection with Bob Cannard's farm and our salad growers in Berkeley, we are able to procure very young green and red romaine lettuces picked to order when they are only around four to six inches tall.

Serves 4 to 6.

9 heads baby romaine or 4 romaine hearts
5 salt-packed anchovies, rinsed and boned, to yield 10 filets
1 clove garlic
Salt and pepper
1½ cups extra-virgin olive oil
2 tablespoons Champagne vinegar
2 tablespoons lemon juice
5 tablespoons chopped Italian parsley
¼ cup chopped chervil
¼ cup chopped chives

Slice the baby romaine heads in half lengthwise, leaving the root ends intact. If using hearts of romaine, slice the hearts into quarters or thirds, depending on size. Wash and dry carefully.

With a mortar and pestle, pound 6 of the anchovy fillets and the garlic clove until they form a smooth paste. Add a little salt and freshly milled pepper. Whisk in the oil, vinegar, and lemon juice. Adjust the vinaigrette as necessary; it should be slightly acidic to balance the crisp, juicy romaine leaves.

Slice the remaining 4 anchovy fillets lengthwise into thin slivers.

Just before serving, stir the chopped herbs into the vinaigrette. Taste and adjust. Arrange the romaine halves on a platter or individual serving dishes and season lightly with salt and pepper. Spoon the vinaigrette over the lettuce and garnish with the anchovy slivers.

Variation: For Caesar salad, pound 5 cleaned anchovies and 2 or 3 garlic cloves in a mortar. To the anchovy-garlic paste, add an egg yolk, 1 tablespoon red wine vinegar, 3 tablespoons lemon juice, and freshly milled pepper. Slowly whisk in 1½ cups olive oil to form an emulsion. Stir in ¼ cup grated Parmesan cheese. Carefully dress the romaine leaves, and garnish with garlic croûtons, anchovy slivers, and additional grated cheese.

Dandelion Salad with Mustard Vinaigrette

Spring is the best time for tender young dandelion, delicious in a salad on its own, or mixed with other pleasantly bitter greens like curly endive, radicchio, and escarole. In the bistro tradition, this salad might be the start of a rainy-day lunch, paired with a slice of headcheese or country pâté, or garnished with crisp lardons of bacon, shavings of Gruyère cheese, and chopped egg. The larger, sometimes very bitter dandelion that comes to market at other times of year is better in a wilted salad or added to a mixture of cooking greens.

Serves 6.

6 handfuls young dandelion greens, washed
1 or 2 garlic cloves, peeled
Salt
1½ tablespoons Dijon mustard
1½ tablespoons lemon juice
1 tablespoon red wine vinegar
¾ cup extra-virgin olive oil
Pepper

Pound the garlic to a paste with a pinch of salt in a mortar. In a small bowl, combine the garlic, mustard, lemon juice, red wine vinegar, and a generous pinch of salt. Whisk in the olive oil and taste the dressing with a dandelion leaf. The flavor of the vinaigrette must be assertive enough to balance the bitterness of the dandelion. You may want to add more mustard or acid if the dandelion is particularly bitter.

Just before serving, put the dandelion greens in a large bowl, season with salt and freshly milled pepper, and gently toss with just enough vinaigrette to coat the greens lightly. Serve immediately.

Variation: To make a creamy mustard vinaigrette, add an egg yolk to the vinegar mixture, and slowly whisk in the olive oil for a thicker, emulsified dressing.

AVOCADO AND BEET SALAD
WITH CITRUS VINAIGRETTE

In our temperate climate of Northern California, someone is growing beets all year round, and not just red ones. Golden beets, striped Chioggia beets, rosy pink beets, and ivory beets, lightly pickled, add sparkle to antipasti, grilled fish dishes, or salads like this one.

Serves 6.

6 medium red or golden beets
Salt and pepper
1 tablespoon red wine vinegar
Extra-virgin olive oil
1 large shallot, diced fine
2 tablespoons white wine vinegar
1 tablespoon lemon juice
1 tablespoon orange juice
1 tablespoon chopped chervil
¼ teaspoon chopped lemon zest
¼ teaspoon chopped orange zest
2 firm, ripe avocados
Chervil sprigs

PREHEAT the oven to 400°F.

Trim and wash the beets. Put them in a baking dish, add a splash of water, and cover tightly. Roast the beets in the oven for about 45 minutes, until they are cooked through.

When the beets are cooked, allow them to cool uncovered. Peel and cut them into wedges. Put them in a bowl, season generously with salt and pepper, add the red wine vinegar and 1 tablespoon of olive oil, and toss gently.

Put the shallot in a bowl and add the white wine vinegar, lemon juice, orange juice, and a pinch of salt. Let macerate for 15 minutes. Whisk in ¾ cup olive oil and stir in the chopped chervil, lemon zest, and orange zest. Taste for seasoning.

Cut the avocados in half lengthwise and remove the pits. Leaving the skin intact, cut the avocados lengthwise into ¼-inch slices. Scoop out the slices with a large spoon and arrange them on a platter or individual dishes. Season with salt and pepper. Arrange the beets over the avocado slices and drizzle with the vinaigrette. Garnish with a few chervil sprigs.

Variation: Blood orange, grapefruit, Meyer lemon, and kumquat go well with the roasted beets and citrus dressing—with or without the avocados—as do watercress and Belgian endive.

SHAVED ASPARAGUS AND PARMESAN SALAD

During asparagus season, in April and May, we serve asparagus every day in one form or another. This delightful raw spring salad is best only if the asparagus is very sweet and crisp, like the beautiful purple-tinged asparagus we get at the San Francisco farmers' market. Look for very fresh, large purple or green asparagus with tight buds. (White asparagus is better cooked.) Look at the butt ends of the asparagus where they have been cut: If they're fresh, the flesh will look moist and white.

Serves 4.

2 shallots, diced fine
2 tablespoons Champagne vinegar
2 tablespoons lemon juice
Salt
⅓ cup extra-virgin olive oil
12 large asparagus spears
Pepper
Wedge of Parmigiano-Reggiano cheese, for shaving

To make the vinaigrette, macerate the shallots for 15 minutes in the vinegar, lemon juice, and a little salt. Whisk in the olive oil.

Snap off the tough bottom ends of the asparagus spears. With a Japanese mandolin, very carefully shave each asparagus spear into long, paper-thin ribbons. Put the shaved asparagus in a salad bowl; season with salt and pepper, and dress lightly with the vinaigrette.

Divide the salad among 4 plates. With a sharp vegetable peeler or paring knife, shave large curls of Parmesan over each serving.

Variation: Alongside this one, serve another asparagus salad of cooked white asparagus dressed in mustard vinaigrette (with or without black truffle).

Artichoke, Cardoon, and Endive Salad

These are the winter vegetables we love, slightly bitter but with an underlying sweetness. (Always be sure to taste bitter vegetables after they're parboiled, however. Sometimes they are *too* bitter.) Grilling the cardoons and endives adds an appealing smokiness.

There are so many recipes for Italian vegetable dishes with cardoons that we are happy to see that this cousin of the artichoke is now turning up in farmers' markets across the country. Cardoons resemble giant, gray-green heads of celery.

Serves 4 to 6.

Vinaigrette
1 large shallot, peeled and sliced
1 tablespoon Champagne vinegar
1½ tablespoons lemon juice
1 tablespoon Dijon mustard
Salt
1 cup olive oil

Vegetables
4 medium artichokes
1 lemon
Splash of white wine
A few thyme sprigs
1 bay leaf
2 tablespoons olive oil
Salt
1 pound cardoons
4 Belgian endives
Pepper
Small handful chopped parsley or chervil

Prepare a charcoal or wood fire.

To make the vinaigrette, macerate the shallot in the vinegar and lemon juice for 15 minutes. Stir in the mustard, add a pinch of salt, and whisk in the olive oil. Taste and adjust for acid and salt.

Pare the artichokes down to their hearts, cut off the tips, cut in half vertically, and scoop out the chokes. Cut again into quarters and drop into water acidulated with the juice of half a lemon.

Bring a quart of water to a boil. Add the white wine, thyme, bay leaf, 2 tablespoons olive oil, and 1 tablespoon salt. Add the artichokes to this broth and simmer until just cooked, about 10 minutes. Remove and set aside, discarding the cooking liquid and herbs.

Trim the cardoons into 4-inch lengths. Cook them at a bare simmer in a quart of salted water with a slice of lemon until tender, about 20 minutes. Remove and cool. Discard the outer leaves of the endives and cut them into quarters lengthwise. Lightly coat the cardoons and endives with olive oil and season with salt and pepper. Grill the cardoons and endives over a medium fire till nicely colored, about 5 minutes per side.

Cut the cardoons into ½-inch strips, combine with the artichokes, and dress lightly with vinaigrette. Dress the endives separately. To serve, mound the artichokes and cardoons in the center of a platter and surround with the endive spears. Garnish with the chopped parsley or chervil.

HEIRLOOM AND CHERRY TOMATO SALAD

We dream about tomatoes all year long. When summer finally arrives, we dream some more—the really good, sweet tomatoes aren't ready until late July. August and September menus feature tomato salads every day, making use, in a good year, of a long harvest of an incredible variety of heirloom tomatoes, all perfectly ripe. Big red Beefsteaks, small red Stupices, medium-size red Early Girls (usually the first on the scene), big Golden Jubilees, yellow Taxis and Lemon Boys, small striped Green Zebras, big brownish Brandywines, striped red and gold Tigerellas, big red and gold Marvel Stripeds, red cherry Sweet 100s, tiny red Currants, and delicious cherry Sungolds are all among our favorites.

This kind of salad can only be made with good vine-ripened tomatoes. At the farmers' market, look for as many kinds as possible. In season, our San Francisco Ferry Plaza Market displays mountains of organically grown heirloom tomatoes, all from local growers. All the beautiful and varied colors, flavors, and textures in a salad like this generate lots of excitement in the dining room. By the time the harvest has begun to wane in October, we are ready to start waiting again for the next summer's crop. Is there a better example of the joy of eating seasonally?

Serves 4.

One ½-pint basket assorted cherry tomatoes
2 pounds heirloom tomatoes, different colors and sizes
1 shallot, diced fine
2 tablespoons red wine vinegar
1 garlic clove, smashed
Salt
½ cup extra-virgin olive oil
Pepper
Green and purple basil leaves, chopped
Optional: lemon cucumbers, torpedo onions

STEM the cherry tomatoes and cut them in half. Core the larger tomatoes and cut them into slices or wedges.

For the vinaigrette, macerate the shallot in the vinegar with the garlic and a little salt. Whisk in the oil. Taste and adjust the acidity and salt as necessary. Put the tomatoes in a shallow salad bowl or on a platter. Season with salt and pepper, strew on the chopped basil leaves, and carefully dress with the vinaigrette.

Thin slices of peeled lemon cucumber and torpedo onion are wonderful additions to the salad.

Variation: For a more elegant tomato salad, slice perfectly ripe heirloom tomatoes and arrange them on a platter. Season with salt and pepper, a splash of good Champagne, and a generous drizzle of extra-virgin olive oil.

Spring Vegetable Bagna Cauda

Although nothing more than a few raw vegetables with a simple anchovy sauce, bagna cauda, if prepared with great attention to every detail, can be a wonderful way to begin a meal. It is the kind of light appetizer perhaps best eaten informally with a glass of rosé.

Choose vegetables in perfect condition, straight from the garden. In the spring, we use tender fennel, tiny artichokes, sweet carrots, young cauliflower, Belgian endive, small heads of radicchio, little turnips, fava beans, asparagus, spring onions, and multicolored radishes. Everything is cut into thin slices or manageable pieces (some vegetables with their tops still attached), sprinkled with sea salt, and piled into a colorful mound. The warm anchovy sauce is offered for dipping or spooning, at the diner's discretion.

Besides the undeniable beauty of it all, bagna cauda provides an opportunity to taste raw vegetables in their prime, whatever the season. Strive for variety in texture and color. Try peppers, grilled eggplant, and cherry tomatoes in the summer. In the winter, add a little walnut oil and chopped toasted walnuts and serve vegetables like celery root and roasted golden beets.

Serves 6 to 8.

2 small heads fennel
6 tiny artichokes
4 small carrots
1 small cauliflower
1 Belgian endive
2 small heads radicchio (or radicchio di Treviso)
8 small asparagus spears
1 bunch baby turnips
1 bunch multicolored radishes
1 bunch spring onions
Handful peeled fava beans
Sea salt

10 to 12 salt-packed anchovies
6 cloves garlic
Salt and pepper
1 cup extra-virgin olive oil

4 tablespoons (½ stick) unsalted butter
A few drops red wine vinegar
Optional: lemon zest

Wash the vegetables in a large bowl of cold water and blot dry. Trim the fennel of any stringy layers, and slice thinly crosswise. Peel the outer leaves of the artichokes to reveal the pale green hearts, and slice into thin wedges. Peel the carrots, and slice lengthwise. Cut the cauliflower into thin slices, or break it up into small florets. Separate the leaves of the Belgian endive and radicchio or Treviso. Snap off and discard the tough bottom ends of the asparagus, and slice the spears into quarters lengthwise. Cut the turnips and radishes into quarters, leaving the tops attached, or leave whole if they are small enough. Clean the spring onions and slice in half lengthwise. Sprinkle everything lightly with sea salt and arrange the vegetables on a platter, tossing them together to create a colorful display. Scatter the fava beans over the top.

Rinse and fillet the anchovies. In a mortar, pound the garlic to a paste with a little salt and pepper. Add the anchovies, and pound until roughly mashed. Warm the olive oil and butter over medium-low heat. Add half the anchovy mixture, the red wine vinegar, and lemon zest if you like, and gently simmer for 2 minutes. Stir in the remaining anchovy mixture, taste for salt and pepper, and transfer the sauce to a warmed bowl or individual ramekins.

Grilled Endives with Sauce Gribiche

We use various chicories nearly every day during the cooler months when they are in season. Wonderful Belgian endives are now grown in California, both the traditional blanched kind and a red-tinged endive that is beautiful in autumn salads. Radicchio, curly endive, and escarole generally end up in salads, but Belgian endive is the chicory we cook most often. Cooking endive shows off its sweetness, and a little smoke from the grill enhances the slight bitterness characteristic of all chicories.

In this recipe, a zesty herb sauce adds brightness, both visual and culinary. Fresh herbs are essential. If you don't have all the different kinds, it's fine—the sauce is delicious even when made only with good fresh parsley.

Serve grilled endives as a first course, perhaps with a few sprigs of watercress, or as the vegetable accompaniment to grilled fish or chicken.

Serves 4 to 6.

Sauce Gribiche
1 Hard-Cooked Egg (page 44)
1 medium shallot, diced fine
2 tablespoons chopped parsley
2 tablespoons chopped chervil
2 tablespoons thinly sliced chives
1 teaspoon chopped tarragon
Zest of ½ lemon, chopped fine
1 tablespoon capers, rinsed and chopped
3 gherkins, diced fine
¾ cup extra-virgin olive oil
Salt

6 Belgian endives
Extra-virgin olive oil
Salt
1 tablespoon lemon juice

For the hard-cooked egg, follow the instructions on page 44, but cook for 9 minutes. Combine the shallot, parsley, chervil, chives, tarragon, lemon zest, capers, gherkins, and olive oil, and season with salt to taste. Chop the egg yolk, dice the white, and stir into the herb-oil mixture.

Trim the discolored root ends of the endives, pull off any unattractive outer leaves, and cut the endives lengthwise in half. Brush the halves with olive oil and sprinkle with salt and a bit of water. (The water helps keep the endives from burning before they are cooked through.) Grill over medium coals until well browned and tender, about 10 minutes per side.

Arrange the endives on a platter. Add the lemon juice to the sauce, taste, and adjust with more lemon juice and salt, if necessary. Spoon the sauce over the endives and serve.

Variation: Another way to grill endives is to steam the halves until just done. Oil and season as above, and grill them until colored over medium coals. This way they will take a much shorter time on the grill. You can also put the steamed endives under the broiler, or bake them in a hot oven. Don't be afraid to let the edges get brown and crisp—that's the best part.

Minestra Verdissima (A Very Green Soup)

We make this beautiful bright green soup in the Café from early spring to early autumn. It is not too filling to be a first course, but it can make a satisfying light main course, too. This is a summer version with green beans, zucchini, and spinach. As they become available, substitute other green vegetables, such as asparagus, peas, fennel, or escarole. It is important to season and taste the soup during every step of the process. Chopped fresh green herbs—basil, parsley, chervil, or chives—are good added just before serving.

Serves 4 to 6.

½ pound spinach, washed
½ pound rocket, washed
Extra-virgin olive oil
Salt
1 yellow onion, diced
2 small celery stalks, diced
2 medium leeks, well washed and diced
2 green zucchini, diced
½ pound green beans, trimmed and cut into ½-inch lengths
9 cups Basic Chicken Stock (page 206)
Bouquet garni of parsley, thyme, and bay leaf
¾ cup shelled fresh English peas
A few drops lemon juice or vinegar
Pepper

Wilt the spinach and rocket briefly in a sauté pan over medium-high heat with a little olive oil and a pinch of salt. Drain in a colander. When the greens are cool, squeeze out the excess moisture and chop them roughly. Reserve.

Sauté the onion and celery in 2 tablespoons olive oil over medium heat in a wide, heavy-bottomed saucepan. When they are just tender, add the leeks, zucchini, and green beans. Season with salt and sauté briefly. Add the chicken stock and the herb bundle and bring to a simmer. Taste the broth and adjust the seasoning. When the leeks, zucchini, and green beans are about half cooked, add the peas. Turn off the heat when the vegetables are just cooked. Remove and discard the herb bundle, stir in the spinach and rocket, and check the seasoning once more. Add a few drops of lemon juice or vinegar and a little freshly milled pepper. Garnish each bowl with a little fruity extra-virgin olive oil.

Note: The soup will be more substantial with the addition of cooked rice or pasta, or by adding a slice of grilled bread and shavings of Parmesan. If you are not serving the soup immediately, chill it and add the wilted spinach and rocket after reheating.

TUSCAN BREAD, BEAN, AND VEGETABLE SOUP

This is a very hearty soup, a classic Tuscan peasant dish, perhaps most delicious in the fall, when fresh shell beans and garden tomatoes are still available. Cavolo nero, a loose-headed variety of cabbage, is an omni-present cooking green in Tuscany. With its long, crinkled dark green leaves and deep flavor, it makes a wonderful addition to this soup. Various kinds of kale, mustard greens, or chard make good substitutes when cavolo nero is not available.

Serves 6.

1 pound fresh cranberry beans
Extra-virgin olive oil
Salt
3 stalks celery
2 carrots
2 medium onions
¼ teaspoon chopped rosemary
1 teaspoon chopped sage
1 bay leaf
5 cloves garlic, chopped
1 pound cavolo nero, or other greens, washed
3 ripe tomatoes, peeled, seeded, and chopped
1 quart Basic Chicken Stock (page 206) or water
1 loaf day-old Italian-style bread, crust removed
Pepper
Parmigiano-Reggiano cheese for grating

SHELL the cranberry beans and simmer them in water to cover by 1 inch, with a splash of olive oil and some salt to taste. Cook until soft but not falling apart, about 30 minutes. Reserve in the cooking liquid.

Dice the celery, carrot, and onions. Warm ½ cup olive oil in a heavy-bottomed soup pot. Sauté the diced vegetables, stirring occa-sionally, until softened, about 10 minutes. Add the rosemary, sage, bay leaf, garlic, and 2 teaspoons of salt and cook for a couple of minutes. Coarsely chop the cavolo nero; add this and the tomatoes, and cook for 5 minutes. Cover with 3 cups of stock or water and simmer for half an hour. Add the beans and 1 cup of their cooking liquid—save any extra bean liquid in case more is needed later—and taste for salt. Cook gently for another 15 minutes.

Meanwhile, cut the bread into ¾-inch dice—you will need about 6 cups loosely packed cubes. Day-old (or several days old) bread is best; otherwise dry the cubes in a low oven. Add the bread cubes to the soup, stir well, and let sit for 15 minutes. The bread will absorb the liquid and become soft. Stir the soup again to amalgamate the mixture. It should be quite thick but not stodgy. To thin, add stock, bean-cooking liquid, or water. Taste for salt and pepper and remove the bay leaf. Serve with grated Parmesan and extra-virgin olive oil to garnish.

Note: Use dried beans and home-canned tomatoes to make this soup during the winter. For more flavor, add a piece of meaty prosciutto bone or a thick slice of pancetta to the beans. The soup improves if made a day ahead, but it must be reheated carefully or it will scorch.

Garganelli Pasta with Fava Beans

It's not uncommon in informal cafés in Europe to see waiters peeling garlic during a quiet time. At Chez Panisse, they peel fava beans—lots of them. Sometimes the customers standing at the bar help out. It is a time-consuming process, to be sure, shucking and peeling all those beans, but rewarding when you taste a dish like this one. The combination of pasta, fava beans, and sheep's-milk cheese is especially delicious when the favas are young and tender. Young fava beans are also good served Tuscan-style, eaten raw with salami.

Serves 4.

   1 pound garganelli pasta
   Salt
   Extra-virgin olive oil
   3 cups parboiled and peeled fava beans, about 2 pounds in the pod
      (see Note)
   1½ cups thinly sliced spring onions
   1 tablespoon finely chopped garlic
   1 teaspoon chopped rosemary
   1 teaspoon chopped savory
   Pepper
   A few drops lemon juice
   2 tablespoons chopped parsley
   4 ounces ricotta salata cheese

Bring a large pot of salted water to the boil. Cook the pasta in the salted water until it is al dente.

While the pasta is cooking, prepare the fava bean ragout. Heat 3 tablespoons of olive oil in a large skillet over moderate heat. Add the fava beans, onion, garlic, rosemary, and savory, and season generously with salt and pepper. Gently cook the mixture until the onions are soft and the fava beans are tender, about 5 minutes. Do not let the vegetables brown much; add a splash of water as needed. The ragout should be a bit moist by the end of cooking.

Drain the pasta, reserving a cup of the cooking water. Return the pasta to the pot and add the fava bean ragout. Stir over low heat until the pasta is thoroughly coated, adding a bit of the reserved pasta water if the mixture seems dry. Add a squeeze of lemon juice to the mixture and taste for seasoning.

Transfer the pasta to a warmed bowl. Sprinkle the top with chopped parsley. Use a sharp vegetable peeler to cut shavings of the ricotta salata over the top. Drizzle with extra-virgin olive oil and serve.

Note: To prepare the fava beans, shell them and parboil very briefly in boiling water (30 seconds to 1 minute). Plunge the favas into cold water to stop the cooking. Pop each bean out of its pale green outer skin by pinching with thumb and forefinger.

Morel Mushroom Toasts

In the early days of the Café, a few hardy foragers would show up at the back door with baskets full of freshly picked mushrooms for sale. All the cooks would stop work to admire the mushrooms and banter about the best places to pick them, although no forager worth his salt ever told the truth about where to look. These days, even though the wild mushroom business has burgeoned, and mushrooms fly around the country on airplanes, it's still exciting to see mushrooms at the back door—and we still have our favorite foragers.

We serve wild mushrooms all year round—porcini in the winter, morels in the spring, and chanterelles in the summer and fall. A favorite way to cook them is in the wood-burning pizza oven. The wood smoke perfumes them magically and the intense heat captures all the juicy flavors. At home, you can improvise by roasting them next to a hot fire in the fireplace or outside, in a covered grill. Try these warm mushroom toasts for a savory first course, or served with a simple green salad for a fine lunch.

Serves 4.

2 shallots, peeled and finely diced
2 tablespoons unsalted butter
1 tablespoon Cognac
1 tablespoon Champagne vinegar
Juice of ½ lemon
Salt and pepper
¼ cup crème fraîche
1 pound fresh morel mushrooms
1 tablespoon extra-virgin olive oil
2 teaspoons finely chopped fresh thyme
2 teaspoons finely chopped fresh savory
3 cloves garlic, sliced
4 slices rustic country bread
Salt and pepper

Preheat the oven to 400°F.

Sauté the shallots in butter over medium heat until nicely browned. Add the Cognac and reduce for 30 seconds. Remove the pan from the heat and add the Champagne vinegar and lemon juice. Season with salt and pepper. Stir in the crème fraîche and set aside.

Pick over the mushrooms, discarding any that are moldy and trimming the ends and any discolored spots. If the mushrooms are especially gritty, give them a quick rinse in a bowl of warm water and blot dry. Slice into ¼-inch pieces crosswise, or lengthwise into strips. Toss the morels in a bowl with the olive oil, thyme, savory, garlic, and salt and pepper. Transfer to an earthenware baking dish large enough to hold the mushrooms in one layer.

Roast the mushrooms, uncovered, until they are tender, about 20 minutes, stirring every few minutes. By the end of the cooking, there will be lovely juices to incorporate into the sauce. Add the shallot mixture to the mushrooms, stir well, and continue cooking for 3 to 4 minutes. Taste the sauce and adjust the seasoning.

While the mushrooms are roasting, brush the bread slices with olive oil and toast them over a fire or under the broiler. Spoon the mushrooms and sauce over the toasts and serve.

Wild Mushroom Pasta Handkerchiefs

Over the years, we have learned to use our wood-burning brick oven for much more than pizza, and now a range of savory appetizers and main courses are baked in it. Ingredients in many more Café dishes spend at least some time in the oven, invariably gaining flavor from the hot fire and smoky atmosphere. We use the wood oven for this dish to brown and crisp the handkerchiefs—large, floppy squares of home-made egg pasta—but a hot home oven will do as well. When the hand-kerchiefs are baked, we nestle the pasta in a bed of curly cress, the perfect foil for the rich and juicy wild mushroom sauce hiding inside. If curly cress is not available, use young rocket, tiny mustard greens, or watercress.

Serves 4.

½ pound mixed wild mushrooms (chanterelles, porcini,
    hedgehogs, black trumpets)
4 tablespoons (½ stick) butter
Salt and pepper
1 medium onion, diced fine
1 teaspoon chopped thyme
3 cloves garlic, chopped fine
½ cup crème fraîche
½ cup Basic Chicken Stock (page 206)
½ pound Pasta Dough (page 30)
¼ cup grated Parmigiano-Reggiano cheese
4 handfuls curly cress, washed and dried
A few drops lemon juice
Extra-virgin olive oil

CAREFULLY clean the mushrooms by brushing off the dirt and leaves; or if they are very dirty, quickly swish them in warm water, then immediately drain and blot dry. Trim the ends and chop the mush-rooms into rough quarters and slices.

Melt 1 tablespoon of the butter in a heavy-bottomed pan. Sauté the mushrooms over medium heat, seasoned with salt and pepper, until lightly browned. If the mushrooms give off a lot of liquid, cook until it is evaporated, then brown. Remove from the pan and set aside.

In the same pan, melt another tablespoon of butter, and sauté the onion over medium heat until translucent, about 4 minutes. Add the thyme, garlic, a little salt, and the cooked mushrooms. Lower the heat and cook for 5 minutes more. Stir in the crème fraîche and chicken stock, and simmer for 3 minutes, until slightly reduced but still quite juicy. Taste for salt and pepper.

Preheat the oven to 500°F.

Roll out the pasta and cut into eight 4½-inch squares. Cook a few squares at a time in salted boiling water until barely al dente. Cool them in a cold water bath and lay them flat in one layer on a clean cloth.

Butter four 6-inch earthenware baking dishes. Put 2 cooked pasta squares side by side in the bottom of each dish, overlapping them slightly at the center, so the pasta edges hang over the sides. Divide the mushroom sauce among the 4 pasta-lined dishes. Fold the pasta edges loosely back toward the center over the sauce, leaving a wrinkled, dimpled surface. Brush with melted butter and sprinkle with grated Parmesan cheese.

Bake for 6 to 8 minutes, or until the edges and peaks of the handkerchiefs are crisp and brown. While the pasta is baking, lightly dress the curly cress with a pinch of salt, a few drops of lemon juice, and a drizzle of olive oil. Carefully slip the pasta out of the baking dishes onto 4 plates; pour any remaining juice over the top. Tuck the curly cress around each portion.

Variation: For a more lavish version, cook ½ cup finely diced celery root with the onion until soft, and add some finely chopped black truffle along with the crème fraîche and chicken stock.

PASTA DOUGH

Making good pasta dough gets easier with practice. As one learns about the physical properties of the dough and how to let it rest to relax the gluten, one's pasta-making becomes more intuitive and less mechanical.

Serves 4 to 6; makes 1 pound pasta dough.

2½ cups flour
1 teaspoon salt
3 whole eggs
3 egg yolks
1 tablespoon olive oil

Mix together the flour and salt, and place in a mound on a work surface. Beat together the eggs, egg yolks, olive oil, and 1 tablespoon water in a bowl. Make a well in the center of the flour and pour in the egg mixture. Begin stirring the eggs with a fork, slowly incorporating the flour from the inner rim of the well. When the mixture has thickened, use a bench scraper (the pastry cook's dough scraper, or chopping block scraper) to scrape the board and to help combine all of the ingredients. Slowly begin kneading the dough, using a pushing and squeezing motion. (Alternatively, mix the dough in the bowl of an electric mixer, using the paddle attachment.)

The mixture should appear fairly dry and crumbly. If it is too crumbly, add more water 1 teaspoon at a time. If the dough is slightly sticky, slowly incorporate more flour as you knead. In general, the dough should contain just enough moisture to bring the flour together.

Knead the dough until it has absorbed all of the flour and you can form it into a rough ball. It will not appear smooth and elastic at this point; additional kneading will be done with the pasta machine. Flatten the dough ball, wrap it tightly in plastic, and let it rest for 45 minutes.

Divide the dough in half. Flatten the dough with a rolling pin and pass it through the rollers of a pasta machine at their widest setting. Sprinkle the resulting sheet of dough lightly with flour, and fold it into thirds. Press the dough down with your fingertips and pass it through the rollers again. Repeat the rolling and folding process at the same setting until the dough is very smooth. Wrap the dough tightly in plastic and let it rest for 5 to 10 minutes, to relax it.

The dough is now ready to be stretched. Adjust the rollers to the next setting and pass the dough through. Gradually stretch it to the desired thickness, passing the dough through successively narrower settings, sprinkling very lightly with flour if necessary. (To adjust the thickness only slightly, pass the dough through the rollers two or three times at the same setting.) Test for thickness by cooking a piece of pasta in boiling salted water.

For cannelloni or lasagna, cut the sheet of pasta into 6-inch lengths. For hand-cut noodles, cut the pasta sheet into thirds, sprinkle them with flour, stack them, and roll them up lengthwise. With a sharp knife, cut the dough into noodles about 1 inch wide. Unroll them and spread them on a baking sheet until you are ready to cook. For fettuccine, follow the same procedure, cutting the dough into noodles about ¼ inch wide, or use the cutter on the pasta machine.

Variation: To make herb noodles, mix ¼ cup chopped herbs with the flour and salt before incorporating the egg mixture. We often use a combination of parsley, thyme, rosemary, and sage, but other combinations will work as well.

To make spinach noodles, put 2 egg yolks, 1 whole egg, and a bunch of washed spinach (about ¾ pound) in a blender and process until liquefied. The mixture should measure about 1 cup. Follow the above recipe, using this purée in place of the egg mixture.

WOOD OVEN–BAKED PORCINI MUSHROOMS

Boletus edulis mushrooms, also known as cèpes or porcini—"piglets" in Italian, so named for their meaty flavor, presumably—are the most exciting mushrooms to forage, and are among the most delicious of all wild mushrooms. On the West Coast, porcini appear in the fall and spring, the exact time depending on the temperature and rainfall. We love them in ravioli and risotti, but perhaps the way we like them best is baked in the Café's wood-burning oven, which adds a desirable smoky accent. At home, bake the mushrooms in a very hot oven or roast them next to a wood fire in the fireplace or over mesquite charcoal in a covered grill. Serve as a first course, with garlic toasts, with fresh pasta, or to accompany grilled or roasted meats. Chanterelles are also delicious prepared this way.

Serves 4 to 6.

3 to 4 medium porcini mushrooms, about 12 ounces
Extra-virgin olive oil
Salt and pepper
A few drops lemon juice

PREHEAT the oven to 500°F.
Trim the porcini, cutting away any dirt or pine needles embedded at the base of the stems, and brush or wipe the caps clean. Cut the mushrooms lengthwise into ¼-inch-thick slices, brush them with a little olive oil, and season with salt and pepper on both sides.

Heat 2 tablespoons of olive oil in a wide cast-iron skillet over medium-high heat; add the porcini in one layer. When they begin to sizzle, put the skillet in the oven. Bake 10 to 15 minutes, until the mushrooms have browned beautifully.

Return the skillet to the stovetop. Carefully add about ¼ cup water, and, over medium-high heat, reduce the liquid until the oil and liquid emulsify somewhat, about 2 minutes.

Spoon the mushrooms onto a warm platter. Finish with a few drops of lemon juice.

Variation: Finish the mushrooms with a gremolata of chopped parsley, marrow, pine nuts, garlic, and lemon zest; or serve with shavings of Parmigiano-Reggiano and a salad of rocket leaves.

VEGETABLE SIDE DISHES

Spicy Broccoli Raab

Broccoli raab, or rapini, is among the most delicious greens we know, with a mysterious, almost almondlike flavor and the slight bitterness characteristic of so many Italian cooking greens. Cooked broccoli raab can be served as a vegetable side dish, combined with orecchiette for a simple pasta, or used to garnish crostini or soups.

Serves 4 to 6.

3 bunches broccoli raab, about 2 pounds
Extra-virgin olive oil
Salt
3 cloves garlic, finely chopped
Red pepper flakes
Red wine vinegar

Wash the broccoli raab and chop the leaves and sprouts coarsely. Heat a large sauté pan and coat the bottom of the pan with olive oil. Add the broccoli raab, season with salt, and cook over high heat, tossing frequently, until the raab starts to brown a little. Reduce the heat, add a splash of water, and cook until tender, stirring frequently. When the raab is cooked, remove it from the pan and set aside. While the pan is still hot add a drizzle of olive oil, the garlic, and a generous pinch of red pepper flakes; warm briefly. Add the cooked raab, a splash of red wine vinegar, and toss. Correct the seasoning. Serve hot or at room temperature.

Variation: Add pounded anchovy and/or chopped olives to the cooked broccoli raab. Serve at room temperature as part of an antipasto platter.

Artichoke Mashed Potatoes

These mashed potatoes are just as good when we substitute celery root or parsnips for the artichokes. And they are also just as good with olive oil and Parmesan instead of butter.

Serves 6.

6 large artichokes
Juice of 1 lemon
3 garlic cloves
Thyme sprigs
Extra-virgin olive oil
Salt
5 pounds russet potatoes
4 tablespoons (½ stick) butter
½ cup half-and-half
White wine vinegar
Freshly ground black pepper

PULL off the outer leaves of the artichokes until you reach the tender yellow central leaves. Cut crosswise through the leaves about 1½ inches above the base, and cut off all but an inch of each stem. With a paring knife, cut away all the deep green, down to the heart. Scoop out the chokes with a teaspoon. Drop the trimmed artichokes into water acidulated with lemon juice as you work.

Cut the artichokes lengthwise into slices about ½ inch thick. Peel and smash the garlic. Put the artichokes, garlic, and a few thyme sprigs in a sauté pan with a generous amount of olive oil and season with salt. Stew over medium heat until quite tender; the artichokes should brown slightly. Drain and save the oil; remove the thyme sprigs. Roughly chop the artichokes and set aside.

Peel the potatoes and cut them into cubes. Boil in generously salted water until soft. Put the potatoes through a ricer or food mill with the butter, reserving the cooking water if you like. Stir in the artichokes, the reserved oil, the half-and-half, and a splash of vinegar. Taste for seasoning and correct with salt and freshly milled black pepper. To adjust the consistency, add more half-and-half or a little of the potato cooking water. Keep warm in the top of a double boiler until serving time.

Creamy White Beans

Serves 6 to 8.

3 cups cannellini beans
Bouquet garni of celery, parsley, thyme, and bay leaf
2 medium onions
2 carrots
Salt
Extra-virgin olive oil
2 cloves garlic, chopped fine
Red pepper flakes
1 teaspoon finely powdered fennel seed
Optional: 2 teaspoons rosemary, chopped fine

SOAK the beans overnight in water to cover. The next day, drain the beans and put them into a large heavy-bottomed pot. Add the bouquet garni; 1 onion, quartered; and 1 carrot, peeled and cut in chunks. Cover with water and bring to a boil. Reduce the heat to a simmer and skim any foam that has risen to the surface. When the beans begin to soften, after an hour or so, add a generous amount of salt and continue to cook gently until they are very tender. When they are fully cooked, remove from the heat.

While the beans are cooking, cut the remaining onion and carrot into fine dice. Heat a sauté pan and add enough olive oil to coat the bottom of the pan. Add the onion and carrot, season with salt, and cook over medium heat until tender. Set aside.

Purée 1 cup of the cooked beans in a blender with a little of their cooking liquid. Drain the remaining beans, reserving the liquid, but discarding the onion, carrot, and bouquet garni. Heat a large sauté pan and coat the bottom with olive oil. Add the garlic and a pinch of red pepper, and warm briefly before adding the diced onion and carrot, the bean purée, beans, powdered fennel seed, and rosemary, if you wish. Cook over medium heat, stirring occasionally, until the beans are hot. If the consistency seems too thick, thin with some of the reserved bean cooking liquid. Taste and season with salt as necessary. Finish with a generous drizzle of extra-virgin olive oil and serve.

Variation: To make white bean purée for crostini, put 2 cups of cooked beans and a little of their cooking liquid into a large sauté pan. Cook over medium heat, stirring and mashing frequently with a wooden spoon, until the beans begin to form a rough paste. Taste for seasoning and adjust; thin with more water or cooking liquid if necessary. If you prefer a smoother consistency, purée the beans in a food processor. Serve immediately on thick garlic toasts, drizzled with extra-virgin olive oil.

Celery Root Rémoulade

Celery root rémoulade is a French classic—a comforting dish, rather like a potato salad. We often serve it as part of an hors d'oeuvre plate, with beets, carrots, and leeks vinaigrette, but the way I like it best is alongside some crispy duck confit with watercress.

Serves 6.

1 large celery root
1 tablespoon lemon juice
Salt
½ cup homemade mayonnaise
2 tablespoons Dijon mustard
1 tablespoon chopped capers
Pepper

Peel the celery root and cut into thin julienne strips with a sharp knife or with the help of a mandolin or a food processor. Toss the celery root with the lemon juice and a pinch of salt. Add the mayonnaise, mustard, and capers. Toss again to combine thoroughly. Taste for salt and pepper, and adjust the seasoning. Allow to stand for at least 15 minutes before serving.

CRISPY PAN-FRIED POTATOES

Fried potatoes like these are irresistible, especially when sweet golden Yellow Finn potatoes are used. We serve these potatoes to accompany all sorts of main course dishes, invariably adding a sprinkling of chopped parsley and garlic.

Serves 4 to 6.

3 pounds medium-size Yellow Finn or russet potatoes
2 cups clarified butter, duck fat, or peanut oil
Salt and pepper
1 garlic clove, peeled
Small handful parsley sprigs

PEEL the potatoes and cut them into ¾-inch cubes. Boil them in a large pot of generously salted water until they are tender when pierced with a knife, but still retain their shape. Drain and cool.

Warm an 8-inch cast-iron pan over medium heat. When the pan is hot, add 1 cup clarified butter and heat until the surface of the butter just begins to ripple. Add enough potatoes to cover the bottom of the pan and fry them undisturbed until they begin to brown. Carefully turn the potatoes and continue to cook, shaking the pan occasionally, until they are golden on all sides, about 10 minutes in all. Drain on absorbent paper and keep warm in a low oven. Repeat the process for the second batch of potatoes. Just before serving, finely chop together the garlic and parsley. Pile the potatoes onto a warm platter, sprinkle with salt, freshly milled pepper, and the garlic and parsley, and serve.

Garlicky Kale

Traditionally used in eastern Mediterranean, Northern Italian, and Portuguese cuisine, kale is available in many varieties. Deep blue-green lacinato, or dinosaur kale, is a favorite. Kale is delicious served with pork chops, added to potato dishes, or tucked into a roast beef sandwich. In California, kale is grown all year. Surprisingly, we've found that kids particularly like the strong flavor of kale.

Serves 4 to 6.

2 pounds kale
Extra-virgin olive oil
Salt
4 or 5 garlic cloves, finely chopped
Red pepper flakes
Red wine vinegar
Pepper

REMOVE the stems from the kale and chop the leaves coarsely. Wash and drain well, but do not dry. Heat a large sauté pan, add ¼ cup olive oil and enough kale to cover the bottom of the pan, and cook over high heat while stirring to rotate the leaves. Add more kale as the leaves wilt. When all of the kale has been added, season with salt, cover, and reduce the heat to medium. Cook, stirring occasionally; the cooking time will depend on the maturity of the kale. Young kale will be tender after 4 or 5 minutes. It may be necessary to add a splash of water if the leaves begin to scorch. When the leaves are tender, remove the lid and allow any excess water to cook away. Push the kale to one side of the pan and add an extra drizzle of olive oil, the garlic, and a pinch of red pepper flakes to the bare spot. Just as you smell the aroma of the garlic, stir to combine it with the kale. Turn off the heat, add a splash of vinegar, and correct the seasoning with salt and pepper as necessary. Serve warm or at room temperature.

Pickled Beets

Roasting beets preserves their color and concentrates their flavor. The skins slip off easily when the beets are still warm. Be careful not to overcook them.

Serves 6.

12 small beets, Chioggia, red, or golden
¼ cup red wine vinegar or Champagne vinegar
Salt and pepper
Extra-virgin olive oil

Preheat the oven to 400°F. Trim and wash the beets and roast them with a splash of water in a tightly covered baking pan for 45 minutes to an hour, until they can be easily pierced with a knife. Allow the beets to cool slightly, then peel and cut them into quarters or rounds. Gently toss the beets with the vinegar and season with salt and pepper. Allow the beets to sit awhile in order to absorb the flavor of the vinegar. Balance the flavor with olive oil and adjust the seasoning.

EGGS & CHEESE

Oeuf

We are very fortunate to have located two farms near Chez Panisse that produce eggs from small, free-ranging flocks. New Life Farm, near Stockton, counts their chickens by the hundreds, not the thousands, as most commercial producers do. In fact, Nancy Warner and her family used to sleep with the chickens to protect them from attacks by coyotes and roaming packs of dogs. She and her workers still keep a close eye on the hens when they are let out of their coops and into the pasture in the morning. There the hens forage on grass and insects. It is the grass in their diet that gives the yolks of the eggs from these brown hens such an intense orange color, which makes a noticeable difference in the deep ivory hue of our vanilla ice cream and pasta doughs.

The hens' diet is supplemented with grains, and they are given oyster shells to help build strong eggshells. They are never given drugs in their feed. Diseases are kept to a minimum because the hens are given plenty of room and fresh air. At dusk the hens gather inside their coops, relatively safe from predators. The sizes of the eggs from New Life Farm vary in size, according to the age of the hens, from tiny pullet eggs when they first start laying, to the jumbos produced by the older hens, who may be as much as three years old. Chickens in commercial egg factories usually give out after eighteen months.

Sky High Ranch, near Winters, California, does not always have enough eggs to bring to us, but when they do, it is an exciting event; when we open a carton we find white eggs, dark brown eggs, brown speckled eggs, beige eggs, and—most beautiful of all—the small blue-green eggs from Araucana hens. The eggs are equally beautiful inside, with clear, thick, clinging whites and deep orange yolks. These hens also forage in pastures for greens and grubs, and love to eat leftover greens from the farm garden and kitchen.

Eggs from farms like these are more expensive to produce because a lot of the chickens' energy goes into foraging and other social activities, so the number of eggs each hen lays is lower than in egg factories. And some eggs are laid but never found, lost somewhere out in the pasture. But the chance to enjoy delicious eggs from healthy hens outweighs these concerns.

Eggs are ubiquitous on the Chez Panisse Café menu. During truffle season, we like to make scrambled eggs with truffles. In late spring, when sorrel is tender and flavorful, we chop it and make omelets. In the winter, we wilt greens such as broccoli raab and kale with lots of minced garlic and make frittatas. Hard-cooked eggs are sliced onto anchovy pizzas and antipasto plates and add body and flavor to herb sauces (see Sauce Gribiche, for example, on page 18).

Soft-boiled or poached eggs are required for authenticity when making such dishes as the classic *frisée aux lardons*, the Lyonnaise salad of curly endive, bacon, and eggs. Egg yolks are essential for all kinds of mayonnaise, as well as for hollandaise and béarnaise sauces. Eggs make the breading stick to fried food and enrich pasta and pastry dough. And of course, without beaten egg whites, soufflés and cakes will not rise.

Because eggs are so essential, it is important to know where your eggs come from. Eggs produced in large factory farms can never be as good as those raised by smaller growers.

Most cheeses today are factory-made, which vitiates the flavor of the cheese. Furthermore, most mass-produced cheese is not made with organic milk. Fortunately, there has been a great renaissance of artisanal cheese-making in the United States, and handmade cheeses can often be found at farmers' markets.

Among the cheeses for general use we keep on hand are certain long-keeping cheeses such as aged Parmesan, for grating and shaving over a salad; pecorino (aged sheep's-milk cheese), usually used in combination with Parmesan to add sharpness (a favorite pecorino is Sardo, from Sardinia); Swiss or French Gruyère, for flavoring soufflés and panades and with dandelion or chicory salads; ricotta salata (aged ricotta) to be grated over pasta and salads; fontina, which is useful in baked polenta dishes or on pizzas; local chèvre, or goat cheese, used in salads, pastas, and pizzas; Roquefort, used in fall and winter salads, especially with pears, apples, and nuts.

The fresh local cheeses we find indispensable are ricotta and mozzarella. In Italy, these cheeses are made in the morning and consumed the same day. They both have exquisite flavor and texture when truly fresh. Fresh ricotta is used for stuffed pastas and served both fresh and baked on antipasto plates. Fresh mozzarella is essential for salads, antipasti, and pizzas.

The Perfect Hard-Cooked Egg

Odd as it may seem, a good hard-cooked egg is hard to find. Most have been overcooked to a chalky green afterthought. But a fresh egg cooked until just set is a delightful addition to a whole range of dishes. We use hard-cooked eggs to add richness and flavor to all sorts of things: halved or quartered, as a classic element of a Niçoise salad or as garnishes for simple plates of grilled fish, lettuces, and tapenade croûtons; sliced, over an anchovy pizza; or chopped, over vegetables such as asparagus and green beans or in sauces like salsa rustica and sauce gribiche.

Over high heat, bring to a full boil enough water to cover the eggs. Lower the eggs gently into the water with a slotted spoon, turn down the heat slightly, and cook for exactly 8 minutes. (For firmer yolks, cook for 9 to 10 minutes.) Prepare a bowl of water and ice.

When the time is up, remove the eggs and immediately plunge them into the ice bath to cool. After a minute or so, when the eggs are cool enough to handle, crack them all over on the tabletop and return them to the ice water for another 5 minutes. This will make peeling easier. Remove from the ice bath and peel away the shells under cold water.

The yolks will be a deep golden orange and slightly moist at the center, and the whites will resemble a firm custard.

SCRAMBLED EGGS PANISSE

These are a wintertime favorite on the lunch menu. Laced heavily with fresh black truffles, scrambled eggs are our kind of comfort food on drizzly gray Berkeley days. We store fresh farm eggs and black truffles together in a closed container for two days, so the eggs absorb the truffles' aroma; then we scramble them softly—with more black truffle! It may seem extravagant, but served with garlic toast and a green salad, this dish exemplifies the best peasant cooking: seasonal wild foraged ingredients united with the simplest fresh farm-produced ones.

Serves 4.

    1 black truffle, about 1½ ounces
    8 extra-large eggs
    Salt and pepper
    3 tablespoons butter
    ¼ pound salad greens, washed
    Extra-virgin olive oil
    A few drops lemon juice
    4 slices levain bread
    1 garlic clove, peeled

Brush the truffle with a damp cloth and scrape away rough spots and dirt with a paring knife. Slice the truffle into very thin rounds with a truffle shaver or Japanese mandolin; then stack the rounds and cut crosswise into thin sticks.

Beat the eggs lightly with half the julienned truffles, ½ teaspoon salt, and freshly ground pepper. Melt 1½ tablespoons of the butter in an omelet pan over medium heat. Add the eggs, stirring with a wooden spoon to create soft curds. Stir in the remaining 1½ tablespoons butter. Remove the pan from the flame when the eggs are still a bit too soft—they will continue to cook off the heat.

Divide the eggs among 4 warmed plates and garnish with the remaining slivered truffle. Quickly dress the salad greens with a little olive oil, lemon juice, and salt, and put a handful of dressed greens alongside the eggs on each plate. Serve with toasted levain bread, drizzled with olive oil and rubbed with garlic.

Wild Nettle Frittata

In the drizzly late autumn and early winter, when cultivated vegetables and sunshine are in scarce supply, it's tempting to forage in the wild. Wild mushrooms are always tantalizing, but wild greens also have astonishing flavor and appeal. Tender young nettles are delicious in many ways: in ravioli with sheep's-milk ricotta; simply sautéed with garlic; or in a simple soup with leeks and potatoes. This frittata can be the centerpiece of an easy antipasto garnished with a few slices of prosciutto, some olives, and a few radishes, or served in little sandwiches. If you can't find any wild nettles, use a combination of greens such as rocket, watercress, and escarole instead.

Serves 4 to 6 as an appetizer.

1 pound wild nettles
1 medium onion, peeled and thinly sliced
Extra-virgin olive oil
Salt
3 cloves garlic, peeled and minced
¼ cup grated Parmigiano-Reggiano cheese
¼ cup grated young pecorino or Sardo cheese
6 eggs
Freshly ground black pepper

Wash the nettles thoroughly in two changes of water and drain in a colander. Use gloves to handle them: they sting when raw.

Sauté the onion in olive oil over medium heat in a sauté pan large enough to hold the greens. Season lightly with salt and cook until tender. Add a little more olive oil and the garlic and cook a minute more. Add the nettles and a pinch of salt, turn the heat to high, and cook until the nettles are completely wilted and most of the water has evaporated. Drain in a colander until they are cool enough to handle.

Coarsely chop the greens and mix them in a bowl with the grated cheeses and about ¼ cup olive oil. Lightly beat the eggs in a separate bowl and add them to the greens. Season well with salt and pepper.

Warm 1 tablespoon of olive oil in a large nonstick skillet, pour in the egg and greens mixture, and stir briefly. Cook over medium-low heat until just set around the edges and on the bottom. Slide the frittata onto a large plate. Wipe the pan clean and lightly brush with oil. Invert the pan over the frittata and, holding the plate and pan together, flip them over so the uncooked side of the frittata is down. Return to the heat and cook gently until just set, then slip the frittata onto a serving plate. Cool and serve in small wedges at room temperature.

Green Garlic Pudding Soufflé

If there is a recipe for some kind of twice-cooked pudding soufflé in nearly every Chez Panisse book, it's for this simple reason: this type of soufflé has become a versatile mainstay of our repertoire. Easier to execute than a regular soufflé, it has the great advantage that it can be prepared ahead of time—a boon to restaurant and home cooks alike. Actually, these puddings have their genesis in a recipe by Richard Olney, a long-time friend and mentor, that was first published in 1974 in his *Simple French Food*. We still look to Richard for inspiration whenever the task of menu-making becomes too challenging.

Green garlic is available at farmers' markets in the spring. It is harvested before the individual cloves have formed, so it resembles a green onion or small leek. Green garlic has a sweet pungency and a pure, clean flavor best brought out by gentle simmering. You can serve the pudding soufflé as a simple first course, unadorned, or as a meatless main course, paired with a spring vegetable ragout of peas, onions, and spinach.

Serves 6.

4 tablespoons (½ stick) butter
¼ cup flour
1½ cups milk, slightly warmed
Salt
2 branches thyme
1 medium onion
½ pound green garlic, sliced (about 1 cup)
A pinch cayenne
½ cup grated Gruyère cheese
Pepper
3 eggs, separated
⅓ cup heavy cream

MELT 3 tablespoons of the butter over medium-low heat in a heavy-bottomed pan. Add the flour and cook for a few minutes, stirring to keep the flour from browning. Slowly pour in the milk, a little at a time, whisking each addition until smooth before adding more. Add ½ teaspoon salt and the thyme branches. Cook over very low heat for 20 minutes or so, until this béchamel sauce is medium-thick and lump-free. Stir frequently to be sure it is not sticking. Cool to room temperature. Remove and discard the thyme sprigs and set the béchamel aside.

Dice the onion and cook over medium heat in the remaining tablespoon of butter. When the onion becomes translucent, after about 5 minutes, add the sliced green garlic and 1 teaspoon salt and lower the heat. Add a little water to keep the vegetables from browning. Cook until the garlic is soft and the water nearly evaporated, about 10 minutes. Add more water during the cooking if necessary.

Cool the mixture and purée in a food processor or food mill. Stir the purée into the béchamel. Add the cayenne, Gruyère, and some freshly ground pepper, and mix well. Taste and adjust the seasoning—the sauce should be fairly highly seasoned. Add the egg yolks, lightly beaten, and mix well again.

Preheat the oven to 400°F. Generously butter six 8-ounce ramekins. Beat the egg whites until they form soft peaks and fold them into the soufflé base. Fill the ramekins and place them in a deep baking dish. Pour hot water halfway up the sides of the ramekins. Bake for 20 to 30 minutes, until the soufflés are puffed and golden brown on the top. Carefully remove the ramekins from the water bath. When the soufflés have cooled a bit, unmold them: run a paring knife around the edge of each ramekin, invert the pudding-soufflé into the palm of your hand, and place it in a shallow baking dish, top side up. The pudding-soufflés can now be held at room temperature for a few hours.

When ready to serve, preheat the oven to 425°F. Pour the cream over and around the soufflés. Bake until the cream is hot and bubbling and the soufflés are puffed up again, 6 to 8 minutes. Serve with the hot cream.

Variation: If green garlic is unavailable, you can make a similar purée using leeks, scallions, and a few cloves of garlic.

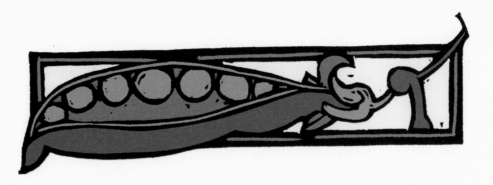

PIZZETTA WITH FARM EGG AND PROSCIUTTO

An individual pizza with a baked egg makes a great main course for an autumnal weekend lunch. Start with a simple salad and finish with Wood Oven–Baked Figs with Raspberries (page 238). If you can get a white truffle, it will be fantastic shaved over the pizzetta. If you can't, try drizzling the pizzetta with white truffle oil. Or add a layer of cooked broccoli raab, seasoned with garlic and hot pepper.

Makes 1 pizzetta; serves 1.

One 4-ounce portion Pizza Dough (page 51)
1 garlic clove, chopped fine
Extra-virgin olive oil
Salt and pepper
½ small onion, sliced thin
1½ tablespoons grated mozzarella
1½ tablespoons grated fontina
1 egg
2 slices prosciutto di Parma
1 teaspoon chopped parsley
Optional: 1 white truffle, or white truffle oil

PREHEAT the oven to 500°F. and set a pizza stone on the middle rack.

Roll out the dough into an 8- to 9-inch circle and place on a well-floured peel. In a small bowl, cover the garlic with olive oil. Brush oil and garlic over the dough with a soft-bristled pastry brush. Season with salt and pepper. Evenly distribute the onion slices over the surface, leaving a ½-inch border of dough uncovered. Evenly sprinkle the grated mozzarella and fontina over the onion.

Slide the pizzetta onto the stone in the oven and bake for about 5 minutes. Slide out the oven rack, crack the egg directly onto the pizzetta, as if you were frying it. Slide the pizzetta back in the oven and continue baking until the edges of the crust are golden brown and the egg yolk still a little runny.

Carefully remove the pizzetta from the oven. Drape the slices of prosciutto over the pizzetta, leaving the egg exposed. Drizzle a little olive oil over the egg, sprinkle the pizzetta with parsley, and shave the truffle, if you have one, over the pizzetta as generously as you wish. Alternately, drizzle on some white truffle oil.

PIZZA DOUGH

Makes enough dough for about 6 pizzas.

SPONGE
2 teaspoons dry yeast
¾ cup lukewarm water
⅔ cup bread flour

DRY INGREDIENTS
4 cups unbleached white flour
¼ cup rye flour
1 teaspoon salt

⅓ cup olive oil

To make the sponge, dissolve the yeast in ¾ cup lukewarm water and stir in the ⅔ cup bread flour. Allow this mixture to sit until quite bubbly, about 30 minutes.

Mix together the white flour, rye flour, and salt in another bowl. Stir 1 cup of cold water and 1 cup of these dry ingredients into the sponge. Mix thoroughly and let sit for another 30 minutes.

Add the remaining dry ingredients and the olive oil and knead, by hand or in an electric mixer fitted with the dough hook. Knead until the dough is soft and elastic, about 5 minutes. It may be necessary to add more flour if the dough is too wet, but add only enough flour to form a soft, slightly sticky dough. A very soft, moist dough makes the best crust.

Put the dough in a large bowl, cover, and let rise in a warm place until doubled in size, about 2 hours. For an even better-tasting, more supple dough, let the dough rise slowly overnight in the refrigerator.

Punch down the dough and divide into portions—4-ounce balls for pizzettas, 3-ounce balls for crostatas, or 7-ounce balls for standard pizzas. Form each portion into a nice smooth sphere. Allow the dough balls to rest at room temperature, wrapped in plastic, for an hour or so before shaping and baking. Individual dough balls may also be frozen, then thawed overnight.

CROSTATA DI PERRELLA

We served a pizza stuffed with goat cheese and prosciutto the first day
the Café opened for business. We called it a calzone in those days, and
we had no idea we would never take it off the menu. It is so impressive
when it comes to the table— puffed, golden, and aromatic—that some
die-hard old guard customers never order anything else, though we try
to wean them away from it and entice them to sample something new.

A few years ago, we rebuilt our pizza oven. To inaugurate the new
oven we changed the shape of our calzone a bit, started making it with
a thinner crust, and named it after Michele Perrella, who has been our
resident pizza chef for over fifteen years. Scores of Café diners and their
children know Michele by name and stop to chat with him on the way
to their tables. The kids sometimes stay behind to get a few pizza-
making tips.

> 4 ounces fresh goat cheese
> 7 ounces mozzarella
> 1 tablespoon chopped parsley
> 1 tablespoon thinly sliced chives
> 1 tablespoon chopped chervil
> 1 teaspoon chopped thyme
> 1 teaspoon chopped marjoram
> 2 small cloves garlic, chopped fine
> Black pepper
> Two 3-ounce balls proofed Pizza Dough (page 51)
> Extra-virgin olive oil
> 2 slices prosciutto di Parma

PUT a pizza stone in the oven. Preheat the oven to 500°F. for at least
half an hour.

In a bowl, crumble the goat cheese and grate the mozzarella. Add
the parsley, chives, chervil, thyme, marjoram, garlic, and some black
pepper. Lightly toss everything together, being careful not to overwork
the mixture.

With a rolling pin, stretch the balls of pizza dough into two 14-inch
circles, rolling them out as thin as possible.

Place one dough circle on a well-floured pizza peel (or improvise
one using the back of a baking sheet); brush the dough with olive oil
and top with the cheese mixture, leaving a 1-inch border of dough ex-

posed. Tear the prosciutto slices into rough ribbons and lay them over the cheese. Place the second round of dough over the prosciutto, and crimp the edges of the dough together to form a seal. With a paring knife, make a small incision in the top of the crostata to allow steam to escape.

Slide the crostata off the peel and onto the preheated pizza stone. Bake for 15 minutes, or until it is quite crisp and brown. Brush the top with a little olive oil and serve.

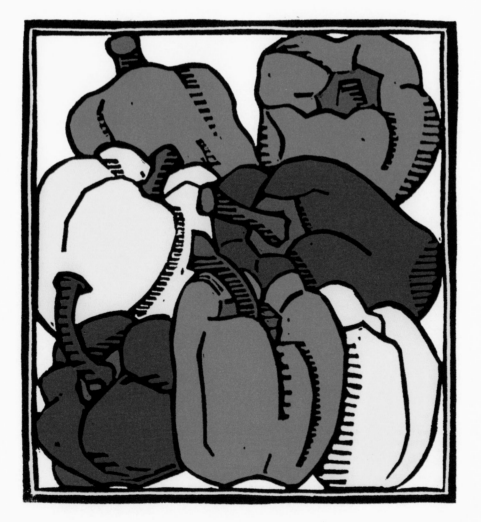

FRESH MOZZARELLA SALAD

As in all simple recipes, success here lies in the quality of the ingredients. You must begin with very fresh mozzarella, the kind still floating in its milky whey. For this reason, locally made cheese is preferable. When we make our own mozzarella in the Café, we serve it within hours, still soft and creamy. Many Italian specialty shops around the country make excellent mozzarella. (One especially good kind with a creamy center is known as *burrata*. It is a specialty of Puglia, but is now being made in Los Angeles.) When fresh mozzarella is unavailable, explore the possibilities at Middle Eastern or Latino groceries, substituting any fresh, mild white cheese you like—yogurt cheese is excellent. This is the classic Mediterranean breakfast, but it is good any time of day.

Serves 4.

8 ounces fresh mozzarella
Sea salt
Pepper
Extra-virgin olive oil
Basil, marjoram, parsley, mint, or thyme
Optional: vine-ripened cherry tomatoes, sliced prosciutto, olives

HAVE the mozzarella at room temperature. Cut it into ¼-inch slices and arrange on a platter. Season very lightly with sea salt and generously with freshly ground pepper. Drizzle with extra-virgin olive oil. Roughly chop the herbs (one herb or a combination), and scatter them over the cheese.

Serve the cheese salad very plain, or add an assortment of different-colored cherry tomatoes, sliced in half and salted; surround with prosciutto slices, and decorate with black olives.

BAKED GOAT CHEESE WITH GARDEN LETTUCES

We have kept this dish on the menu every day since we opened. We vary the accompaniment sometimes, according to what's available, adding slices of ripe pear and watercress in the fall, for instance, or rocket leaves and hazelnut oil. Delicious as a first course, it can also be served after a meal, as a combination salad-and-cheese course. Our goat cheese is made for us in Sonoma County. Investigate fresh local goat cheeses in your area, or use a French chèvre.

Serves 4.

½ pound fresh goat cheese (one 2 by 5-inch log)
1 cup extra-virgin olive oil
3 to 4 sprigs fresh thyme, chopped
1 small sprig rosemary, chopped
½ sour baguette, preferably a day old
1 tablespoon red wine vinegar
1 teaspoon sherry vinegar
Salt and pepper
¼ cup extra-virgin olive oil, walnut oil, or a combination
½ pound garden lettuces, washed and dried

CAREFULLY slice the goat cheese into 8 disks about ½ inch thick. Pour the olive oil over the disks and sprinkle with the chopped herbs. Cover and store in a cool place for several hours or up to a week.

Preheat the oven to 300°F. Cut the baguette in half lengthwise and dry out in the oven for 20 minutes or so, until dry and lightly colored. Grate into fine crumbs on a box grater or in a food processor. The crumbs can be made in advance and stored until needed.

Preheat the oven to 400°F. (A toaster oven works well.) Remove the cheese disks from the marinade and roll them in the bread crumbs, coating them thoroughly. Place the cheeses on a small baking sheet and bake for about 6 minutes, until the cheese is warm.

Measure the vinegars into a small bowl and add a big pinch of salt. Whisk in the oil and a little freshly ground pepper. Taste for seasoning and adjust. Toss the lettuces lightly with the vinaigrette and arrange on salad plates. With a metal spatula, carefully place 2 disks of the baked cheese on each plate and serve.

PAN-FRIED STUFFED SQUASH BLOSSOMS

As everyone knows, zucchini and other summer squash are among the most prolific garden vegetables. The first few tender squash are a joy to behold, but we get a bit jaded as summer progresses and the squash crop keeps pace. Squash blossoms, on the other hand, always seem like a good idea. You can gather them all summer long by choosing male blossoms (the ones with a long stem) and allowing the female blossoms to fruit. It's best to pick squash blossoms in the cool early morning. If you don't have a garden, ask your favorite vendor at the farmers' market. Once stuffed, the blossoms can be pan-fried, baked, or poached.

Serves 4 to 6.

12 squash blossoms, with stems
About 1 cup Ricotta Filling (from Green Cannelloni, page 58)
Olive or peanut oil for frying
Salt and pepper
Flour
Fine cornmeal
2 eggs, lightly beaten

TRIM the squash stems to 3 inches and brush the blossoms clean. Using a pastry bag or a teaspoon, stuff each flower with about 2½ teaspoons of the ricotta filling, twisting the petals closed after filling them.

Into a wide cast-iron pan, pour frying oil to a level of about 2 inches. Heat the oil to 375°F.

Roll each blossom in a seasoned mixture of flour and cornmeal; then dip into beaten egg, and again, briefly, in the flour mixture. Fry for 2 or 3 minutes per side, until golden. Drain on paper towels and sprinkle with salt and pepper.

Variation: Poach or steam the stuffed blossoms and serve them in a broth with summer vegetables, or with a butter sauce with fried sage and lemon. Baked and brushed with olive oil, the blossoms are delicious with a light tomato sauce or a vegetable ragout.

FRESH RICOTTA BAKED WITH
HERBS AND OLIVE OIL

Baked ricotta cheese is a great accompaniment to all things Mediterranean. We serve baked ricotta in antipasti—with prosciutto and figs, for example—or to garnish a salad, a dish of herb noodles, or a plate of grilled summer vegetables. We get our fresh ricotta weekly from Bellwether Farms, in Tomales Bay. They make both sheep's-milk and Jersey cow's–milk ricotta, and deliver it the day they make it, in two-pound loaves, handsomely ridged from the baskets in which they were drained. Ricotta that fresh doesn't really need to be baked; we just slice it thick and drizzle it with good, fruity olive oil. Throughout the week, we also use ricotta, unbaked, in ravioli and stuffings.

Every year there are more small cheesemakers starting up production. Look for farmhouse cheeses at farmers' markets, or ask about local cheeses at a specialty cheese shop. Using locally produced cheese is a pleasure; you get cheese that is impeccably fresh, while supporting local agriculture and artisan farmers.

Serves 4.

12 ounces ricotta cheese
Salt
Fresh marjoram, sage, and thyme sprigs, or dried *herbes de Provence*
Pepper
Extra-virgin olive oil

Mix the ricotta with salt to taste. Pack the cheese into a lightly oiled shallow earthenware baking dish small enough so that the cheese is about 2 inches thick. Strip the leaves from the herb sprigs and press them into the surface, or sprinkle with a good pinch of dried *herbes de Provence*. Grind pepper over the top and drizzle with olive oil. Bake in a preheated 425°F. oven for 25 to 30 minutes, until the cheese is puffed and nicely browned on top. Allow to rest 10 minutes before serving. Serve while still slightly warm or at room temperature.

Note: Commercially produced ricotta is much wetter and requires draining overnight. For this recipe, use a 15-ounce container of cheese. Wrap the ricotta in a double thickness of cheesecloth and drain in a colander in the refrigerator. Reserve the whey for another use.

GREEN CANNELLONI WITH RICOTTA, YELLOW TOMATOES, AND BASIL

Cannelloni are great for lunch, and easier to make than ravioli. The cannelloni can be prepared a few hours before the meal, but the yellow tomato sauce is best made at the last minute—it's barely cooked, so it requires only a few minutes. Perfectly ripe tomatoes are essential; get the best-tasting ones you can find, yellow or not.

Serves 4.

RICOTTA FILLING
½ pound ricotta
¼ cup grated Parmigiano-Reggiano cheese
Salt and pepper
A pinch cayenne
2 tablespoons chopped mixed herbs
    (basil, marjoram, thyme, and parsley)
1 egg, lightly beaten

PASTA
½ pound green pasta (Pasta Dough, page 30)
2 tablespoons melted butter
1 pound vine-ripened yellow tomatoes
¼ cup extra-virgin olive oil
2 or 3 cloves garlic, chopped fine
Green and purple basil
Salt and pepper

MIX the ricotta with the Parmesan, salt and pepper, cayenne, and herbs. Taste for seasoning. Add the egg, and mix again.

Roll out the pasta and cut it into 8 rectangles, each about 6 by 7 inches. Cook the pasta one piece at a time in salted boiling water, keeping it firmly al dente. Cool in a cold water bath and lay the rectangles on a clean cloth. (Don't stack them or they will stick together hopelessly.)

Put 1½ tablespoons of filling on each rectangle and roll loosely into a tube shape. In a buttered baking dish, arrange the cannelloni in one layer, and brush the tops with melted butter. Cover and store in a cool place until ready to serve, up to 4 hours.

Preheat the oven to 425°F. Peel, seed, and dice the tomatoes. Bake the cannelloni for about 15 minutes, until puffed and slightly crisped. While the cannelloni are baking, quickly make the tomato sauce. In a heavy-bottomed enameled or stainless steel pan, heat the olive oil over medium-high heat. Add the garlic; let it sizzle for a moment without browning, and add the diced tomatoes. Cook just until the tomatoes start to relax and become juicy, about 3 to 5 minutes. In the last minute of cooking, toss in a little chopped green and purple basil, and salt and pepper to taste. Serve with the tomato sauce and more chopped basil.

Variation: An additional garnish of sautéed chanterelle mushrooms makes the dish more festive.

Note: The same ricotta filling can be used for ravioli or lasagna, or for stuffing squash blossoms.

FISH & SHELLFISH

EVERY once in a while, for a grand occasion such as Bastille Day, we serve the same menu upstairs and down. One of our favorite festive dishes for these events is bouillabaisse, the famous provençal fish and shellfish stew. We make it the old-fashioned way, and cook the fish in a gargantuan cauldron in the downstairs fireplace, so that customers on their way to be seated in the Café often linger on the stairs, staring at the blazing fire and the bubbling pot and inhaling the powerful, alluring aromas of fresh fish and an open fire. We never make a bouillabaisse without thinking of our friends the Peyrauds, whose provençal vineyard, the Domaine Tempier, supplies us with marvelous red and rosé wines that are the perfect accompaniments to the dish, and especially of Lulu Peyraud, the family matriarch, whose incomparable bouillabaisse has inspired our own.

The Domaine Tempier is only a few miles from the small port city of Bandol on the Mediterranean, and when Lulu makes a bouillabaisse she meets the fishing boats in the morning as they return with the night's catch of a dozen or more varieties of fish and shellfish. We try to emulate Lulu and buy only fish caught that day. We never keep fish for more than twenty-four hours; if the customers don't order it we consume it ourselves, for staff dinner.

Fish and shellfish dishes are on the menu every day in the Café. The tuna, sardines, lobsters, oysters, and other sea creatures, although mostly of different, Pacific Ocean species, evoke the smells and flavors of the sea life of the Mediterranean. They also bring us a sense of the beauty and the sustaining qualities of nature, as they are the last foods regularly seen on the dinner table that are wild and hunted commercially.

Because they are wild, many fish and shellfish are caught in a specific

FISH & SHELLFISH   63

season, and vary in quality and availability within that season. Part of knowing how to buy and to cook fish depends on being aware of these differences.

Where we live in California there is a rich fishing history and heritage. Fishermen on this part of the coast still bring in catches of spot prawns, sardines, and squid from Monterey Bay, and salmon, rockfish, and Dungeness crab caught near the Golden Gate. All of these delicious fish are important to our cooking.

Pacific king salmon is one of the foods that defines summer for us. This brilliantly colored, flavorful fish is caught just off the coast, so it's extraordinarily fresh, and our fishmonger, Paul Johnson, buys them off the boats the same morning they come in to Fisherman's Wharf.

The first salmon in the late spring are fish that have come in close to shore after spending years at sea, in prime condition for their trip up coastal rivers to spawn. These fish have lean but tender flesh and an exquisite, delicate flavor. They are sensational simply steamed or poached. The only sauce they need is a very light beurre blanc, or their own poaching juices with a dot of herb butter. Later in the season, king salmon are oilier and their flavor is more intense, so they are best grilled, the wood smoke balancing their stronger flavor. They should be served with flavorful, slightly acid sauces like zinfandel wine butter or vinaigrette with shallots and lemon.

There was a time when we served salmon all year, supplementing the local catch with salmon from far away, but now we restrict ourselves to the Pacific salmon season, from May until October. This has spurred us to try other local fish that may be plentiful at other times of the year. Nevertheless, we are not complete local purists. There are fish and shellfish flown in from the East Coast that are either still alive or shipped so quickly after they're caught that in some cases they're fresher than some of the local fish. We're making an effort to use as little fish transported in this way as possible, but we can't quite yet imagine menus without the occasional Maine lobster or Chesapeake Bay soft-shell crab in season.

Fresh oysters are a wonderful treat. Perhaps they are best on the half shell, but they are also delicious barbecued, deep-fried, or in a ragout. We are lucky to have delectable varieties on both of our coasts. Here on the West Coast, from British Columbia down to California, the dominant species is *Crassostrea gigas*, sweet and tender, at least when small, in deep cupped shells. Some of our favorites are Hog Island sweet water, Skookum inlet oysters, Hamma Hamma, Dabob Bay, and Quilcene. At the Café, we always order "extra smalls" for the oysters we serve on the half shell. There are two more Pacific oysters that belong to their own distinct species: the crisp, tangy, and extra tiny Olympia from Puget Sound, and the tender and mild Kumamoto.

The European oyster, *Ostrea edulis*, grows on both coasts. In California, they are called "flats" because of their very flat, round, shallow shells. Their flavor is much brinier, with a crisper texture and a tangy mineral finish that is very refreshing. Pearl Bay and Discovery Bay flats are two popular types on the West Coast.

The Hog Island Oyster Company in Tomales Bay also grows an Atlantic oyster, *Crassostrea virginica*, the dominant species on the East Coast. It is a flat, thicker-shelled oyster with a briny, more vegetal taste, like a crisp piece of lettuce. The blue point oyster is a classic example of this oyster; the best ones are grown in Peconic Bay. Some other favorites are Wellfleet, Sakonnet Point, Diamond Point, Malpeque, and Cape Breton oysters.

Oysters vary in brininess from species to species but also according to location. The colder the water, the saltier the oyster; thus the oysters found farther north will be brinier and crisper in flavor. As they say, oysters are best eaten in the months with the letter *r* in their names. When the water warms up in the summer months the oysters spawn, which makes their proteins chalky, giving the oyster a creamy quality that is not very pleasant. The most important thing to remember about oysters is that they must be very fresh. Right out of the ocean, they are irresistible.

OYSTERS ON THE HALF SHELL
WITH MIGNONNETTE SAUCE

When I came back to California from my first visit to France, I wanted oysters. During my stay in Brittany I had discovered how delicious and satisfying a dozen or two fresh raw oysters could be for lunch. They slid down so easily—cool, sweet, salty, and restorative. But what a disappointing shock I had upon my return. Whenever I tried oysters, even at some of the best oyster bars in San Francisco, they just weren't right. Was it the variety? Was it where they were grown? It wasn't until I went up to Tomales Bay, just north of San Francisco, where oysters are grown, that I learned the complete answer.

There I discovered, probably for the first time, the difference between fresh and *fresh*. The oysters I had been eating were not fresh! They were alive, yes, but not just out of the water, dripping of the sea and smelling like heaven. You just won't find that perfect balance of sweet and salty flavors and firm texture from oysters that are several days old. If you can't get really fresh oysters where you live, complain to your fishmonger, or go to the source. Try them with this classic French mignonnette sauce, but first try them fresh and unadulterated!

Serves 4.

MIGNONNETTE SAUCE
½ cup Champagne vinegar
½ cup dry white wine
2 shallots, finely diced
Ground pepper

24 oysters

STIR together the vinegar, white wine, and shallots in a stainless or ceramic bowl. Let stand for 20 to 30 minutes. Add pepper.

Shuck the oysters and arrange on a platter of shaved ice. Spoon a little mignonnette sauce on each oyster and devour immediately.

OYSTER STEW WITH THYME AND FENNEL

A cool fall or winter day is a good time for oyster stew. This one is based on M. F. K. Fisher's version—American, but French in spirit. We sometimes bake this stew in the wood oven, but this stovetop version is equally delicious. Oyster stew shows up on the menu at lunchtime, although one year we served it on New Year's Eve, made with tiny Olympia oysters and a splash of Champagne. Generally, because this stew is so rich, we serve three oysters per person as a first course, or four as a light main course for lunch.

Serves 4.

½ yellow onion, diced fine
1 small carrot, diced fine
1 stalk celery, diced fine
1 small fennel bulb, diced fine
3 branches thyme
1 tablespoon butter
Salt
1 cup heavy cream or half-and-half
12 to 16 medium oysters, freshly shucked
Oyster liquor from shucking
Chervil, parsley, and fennel leaves, roughly chopped
Pepper

SAUTÉ the diced vegetables with the thyme branches in the butter over gentle heat until just cooked, about 5 or 6 minutes. Season lightly with salt. Add the cream and simmer for another 2 minutes, but don't let it boil. Add the oysters and oyster liquor. The oysters will cook very quickly—in 1 minute or less. Taste the broth and add salt, if necessary. Remove the thyme branches.

Ladle quickly into warmed bowls. Garnish with the chopped chervil, parsley, and fennel leaves, and a little freshly ground pepper.

Variation: A few drops of Pernod will intensify the fennel flavor, or try a splash of good Gewürztraminer. Grated Meyer lemon peel is also a nice touch, as are buttered croûtons.

SALMON CAVIAR

Steelhead salmon come into season in December and January—big beautiful fish with deep red meat and lovely large skeins of eggs. Most steelhead fished commercially are caught on Indian reservations in Washington state. Some come from the Columbia River, but the majority are from the rivers on the Olympic peninsula. Their eggs are tasty little jewels that add wonderful flavor as well as an elegant appearance. Some of our favorite ways to use salmon caviar are in an endive salad with crème fraîche, as a garnish for soup, scattered over a piece of sautéed fish, or on top of warm blinis with more crème fraîche and chives.

Preparing the roe is a very easy and quite enjoyable process. Make a brine with water and salt of about the same salinity as sea water (about 3½ percent salt, or roughly ¼ cup per half gallon water). Heat the brine to 110°F. in a large pot. Immediately take a skein of roe, put it in a coarse-meshed conical strainer, turn on hot tap water, and swirl the strainer vigorously under the running water. The egg sac will cook, becoming tough and breaking apart, freeing the eggs. Pluck out the chunks of egg sac as they swirl to the top. When the eggs are all free and most of the sac has been removed, pour them into the brine. Take a flat skimmer or strainer and swish it through the eggs, catching as much of the remaining egg sac as possible. Leave the eggs soaking in the brine for approximately 20 minutes, or until seasoned to taste. If they accidentally become too salty, just soak them in some fresh water. Drain the eggs well. Next run your dry, clean hands through the eggs to gather up the last remaining bits of egg sac. This is a wonderful sensory experience, running your hands through the shimmering, soft, and satiny eggs. Put the eggs in a clean glass container on ice to chill well. The eggs will stay reasonably fresh for a week but should really be eaten within a couple of days.

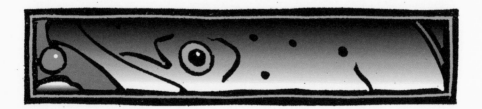

GRAVLAX AND CUCUMBER SALAD

Served ice-cold, this cured salmon hors d'oeuvre is a refreshing start to a late-summer meal. Look for just-picked, small-seeded cucumbers at the farmers' market—a good fresh firm cucumber can be a surprising revelation.

Serves 4 to 6.

GRAVLAX
1 pound king salmon fillet, skin on
2 juniper berries, sliced coarsely
⅓ cup salt
⅓ cup sugar
¼ teaspoon allspice, crushed
½ teaspoon black peppercorns, crushed
A few sprigs dill, stems removed
A few sprigs tarragon, stems removed

CUCUMBER SALAD
1 large or 2 small cucumbers
Extra-virgin olive oil
Lemon
Salt
Fresh mint, dill, chervil, or tarragon

THE fillet may contain little pin bones, which run from the head end about halfway back along a whole side of salmon. These bones will interfere with slicing later, so they should be removed. They can be easily located with your fingertips and pulled out with small needle-nosed pliers or tweezers. Place the fillet in a glass or stainless steel dish, skin side down. Sprinkle the sliced juniper berries over the fish, pressing lightly into the flesh. If you especially like juniper, use more, or a few drops of gin instead.

In a small bowl, combine the salt, sugar, allspice, and pepper. Spread this mixture evenly over both sides of the salmon. Scatter the dill and tarragon leaves evenly over both sides as well. Wrap the salmon tightly in cheesecloth, cover, and refrigerate for 36 hours.

To serve, scrape off the herbs and any undissolved salt mixture. Slice at an angle into wafer-thin slices with a sharp, thin-bladed knife.

To make the simple cucumber salad, slice the cucumber as thinly as possible (we use a Japanese mandolin) and dress to taste with olive oil, lemon, and salt. Chop the herb of your choice—or a combination—and toss with the cucumber.

Arrange the gravlax slices on individual plates, and spoon the cucumber salad over the fish.

Variations: Make tea sandwiches on buttered brown bread topped with sliced gravlax and cucumber salad. Or serve gravlax with pickled beets and a bit of crème fraîche flavored with mustard and horseradish.

Note: The gravlax will keep for a week in the refrigerator, tightly covered. Double the recipe for a larger piece of salmon.

JEAN-PIERRE'S CURED SALMON

Jean-Pierre Moullé, a passionate Frenchman, forager, and fisherman, has been the downstairs restaurant chef for many years. He devised this recipe as a first course for a special wine dinner a few years ago. It was so well loved that we now serve it upstairs as an appetizer.

Serves 8 to 10.

1 side salmon, skin on, 2 to 3 pounds
1 pound rock salt
½ bottle sauvignon blanc
½ cup extra-virgin olive oil
3 large shallots, diced fine
2 tablespoons thinly sliced chives
2 tablespoons chopped parsley
2 tablespoons chopped chervil
2 tablespoons white peppercorns, coarsely cracked
3 tablespoons whole coriander seeds
Additional herbs for garnish

THE side of salmon will contain little pin bones running from the head end about halfway back; they will interfere with slicing later unless removed. They can be easily located with your fingertips and pulled out with small needle-nosed pliers or tweezers. Place the fish in a shallow glass or stainless steel pan, skin side down. Cover the flesh side with rock salt. Refrigerate for at least 6 hours or, preferably, overnight. Rinse well, pat dry, and return to a shallow pan, this time with the skin side up.

Prepare the marinade: in a glass or stainless steel bowl, combine the wine, olive oil, shallots, chives, parsley, chervil, white pepper, and coriander. Pour the marinade over the fish, then cover and refrigerate for 8 hours or overnight.

Strain the marinade through a fine sieve, reserving a few coriander seeds. Taste and correct the seasoning.

Slice the salmon thinly on an angle and arrange a few slices per person on chilled plates. Spoon a little of the marinade over each serving and garnish with freshly chopped chives, parsley, chervil, and the reserved coriander seeds.

SLOW-COOKED KING SALMON

Of the various ways king salmon can be cooked, this one is shockingly simple and strikingly good. The salmon is baked in a very slow, humidified oven, which yields a moist, tender, velvet-textured fish. When it is served at room temperature with fennel and fava beans, or tomatoes and green beans, or beets and garden lettuces, we find it has versatility and appeal the entire season. And since it holds well for a few hours, it's also perfect for a picnic or buffet.

Serves 6 to 8.

1 king salmon fillet, about 3 pounds
Extra-virgin olive oil
Salt and pepper

PREHEAT the oven to 200°F. Place a pan of warm water on the lowest rack in the oven. This creates a humid environment that helps keep the salmon moist.

Lightly brush a baking pan with olive oil. Brush the salmon with olive oil and season generously with salt and freshly ground pepper. Place the salmon in the baking dish and put it in the oven. Allow about 1 hour for the salmon to cook through. If it seems to be cooking too fast, turn the oven down a bit. The salmon is cooked when it is just barely firm to the touch and juices are beginning to collect on top of the fillet. Let it rest at least 10 minutes, or up to 3 hours, at room temperature.

To serve, break into rough pieces, surround with summer vegetable salads, and accompany with Aïoli (page 85), Meyer Lemon Relish (page 89), or Sauce Gribiche (page 18).

Variation: Season the salmon with roughly chopped fresh herbs (such as basil or tarragon), grated citrus peel, and finely sliced shallots before baking.

KING SALMON IN FIG LEAVES

Cooking in fig leaves has become a Café tradition. Early king salmon is a perfect candidate for this treatment, because its fat content is low, and the fig leaves keep it moist. While the fig leaves impart a wonderful sweet coconut flavor to the fish, the leaves themselves are tough and not good to eat. Sauced with a little nasturtium butter, this dish is easy, beautiful, and wonderfully aromatic. It is equally good cooked over a wood fire, and wrapping fish in fig leaves is a great way to keep it from sticking to a grill.

Serves 6.

1 salmon fillet (about 2 pounds), boned and skinned
Olive oil
Salt and pepper
6 large fig leaves, washed
6 tablespoons (¾ stick) butter, softened
1 teaspoon lemon juice
½ teaspoon finely chopped lemon zest
1 medium shallot, diced fine
24 nasturtium blossoms

PREHEAT the oven to 400°F. Cut the salmon into 6 equal portions and coat lightly with olive oil. Season the fish with salt and freshly ground pepper. Wrap each portion of fish individually in a fig leaf, folding the edges of the leaf over the fish. (It is all right if the fish is not completely enclosed.)

Prepare the nasturtium butter: stir together the softened butter, lemon juice, lemon zest, and shallot. Remove the stems from the nasturtiums, chop the blossoms, and stir into the butter. Season with salt and pepper. Let the butter sit for a few minutes, taste, and adjust the seasoning. Leave the butter at room temperature while you bake the fish.

Place the salmon on a baking sheet and bake in the upper part of the oven until the fish is just cooked through, 6 to 8 minutes. Transfer the salmon packages to a serving platter or individual plates. Peel the fig leaves back to expose the salmon and spread some of the nasturtium butter on each portion.

Variation: Add some herb blossoms or a few chopped capers to the butter instead of nasturtiums.

SAFFRON PASTA WITH BOTTARGA DI TONNO

Bottarga di tonno, tuna roe that has been salted, pressed, and dried, is a wonderful ingredient imported from southern Italy, a region where nothing edible goes to waste. It is available in specialty shops, and it keeps forever. We love it shaved over giant white beans in an antipasto, and we especially like it in this simple first-course pasta. (The French make a similar product from the roe of gray Mediterranean mullet.)

Serves 4 to 6.

1 ounce bottarga di tonno
1 pound Pasta Dough (page 30)
¼ cup extra-virgin olive oil
1 scant teaspoon saffron threads, toasted and crumbled
1 lemon, cut in half
Salt and pepper
Chopped Italian parsley or chervil

BRING a large pot of water to the boil.

Peel the paper wrapping from the bottarga (it's packaged rather like a salami). Have ready a large sauté pan or pasta bowl and a Japanese mandolin or a sharp vegetable peeler—a truffle shaver also works well.

Roll out and cut the pasta into narrow ribbons, as for fettuccine. Salt the water and cook the pasta al dente. Drain the noodles and put them in the sauté pan along with a little of the cooking water. Add the olive oil, saffron, a generous squeeze of lemon, and a little salt and pepper. Shave about half the bottarga over the pasta, then toss.

Quickly divide the pasta among warm bowls, then shave the remaining bottarga over each portion and squeeze over a few more drops of lemon juice. Sprinkle with the parsley or chervil. Pass the pepper mill.

Variation: Add a little chopped orange zest when tossing the pasta. You can also substitute butter for half of the olive oil.

RARE YELLOWFIN TUNA
WITH CORIANDER AND FENNEL SEED

Since the ingredients are available almost all year, this dish has become a popular and versatile mainstay on the menu. However, it requires the freshest, most pristine tuna you can find. The tuna is seared very briefly, so the fish remains quite rare, almost like sashimi.

Serves 6 to 8.

2 pounds center-cut tuna
3 to 4 tablespoons olive oil
Salt
Cracked black pepper
2 tablespoons coriander seeds
1 tablespoon fennel seeds

VINAIGRETTE
3 small shallots, diced fine
Juice of ½ lemon
3 tablespoons Champagne vinegar
Salt
½ cup extra-virgin olive oil

1 medium fennel bulb, trimmed
1 small bunch radishes, trimmed
1 small bunch cilantro, tough stems removed

Ask your fishmonger for 2 pieces of tuna weighing 1 pound each, the pieces about 3 inches in diameter and 8 inches long. Rub the tuna fillets with olive oil and season generously with salt and cracked pepper. In a mortar, crush the coriander and fennel seeds coarsely, until their fragrance is released. Sprinkle the crushed seeds evenly over the tuna, pressing them into the flesh. This can be done several hours before cooking. Hold in the refrigerator.

Heat a large cast-iron skillet over medium-high heat until almost smoking. Carefully place the seasoned tuna in the skillet and sear for 30 seconds on each side. Remove the tuna to a platter and cool for an hour or so at room temperature.

Make the vinaigrette by macerating the shallots in the lemon juice and Champagne vinegar with a good pinch of salt for 10 minutes. Whisk in the olive oil, taste, and adjust the seasoning.

Use a very sharp knife to slice the tuna into even ⅛-inch slices. Place 2 slices side by side on each serving plate. Using a Japanese mandolin, shave the fennel bulb into thin ribbons and strew them over the fish. Shave over some radish slices in the same way. The result should be a playful mosaic effect. Splash the vinaigrette over the tuna, fennel, and radishes. Add a light sprinkling of salt. Roughly chop the cilantro, scatter it over each plate, and serve.

TUNA DUMPLINGS WITH
CURRANTS AND PINE NUTS

These unusual little dumplings sautéed in olive oil make a savory first course in the Sicilian spirit. We serve them for lunch with a little fresh tomato sauce as a main course, or with a salad of rocket leaves and shaved pecorino cheese for a first course. The belly meat and scraps of tuna, which would otherwise go to waste, are perfect for this dish.

Makes 24 dumplings; serves 4 to 6.

1 medium onion, diced fine
1½ tablespoons extra-virgin olive oil
1½ tablespoons chopped marjoram
1 small pinch saffron threads, toasted and crumbled
¼ teaspoon red pepper flakes
Salt
3 tablespoons pine nuts
3 tablespoons currants
Optional: 1 ounce pancetta, thinly sliced
½ cup fresh bread crumbs
¼ cup milk
1 pound fresh tuna, preferably belly meat
1 egg, slightly beaten
¼ teaspoon cayenne
Pepper
All-purpose flour
Olive oil for frying

SAUTÉ the onion gently in the 1½ tablespoons extra-virgin olive oil over medium-low heat for 5 minutes. Add the marjoram, saffron, pepper flakes, and a little salt, and continue cooking for about 5 minutes longer, until the onion is translucent and tender, but not colored.

Toast the pine nuts until lightly browned, and chop coarsely. Plump the currants in a little hot water and drain. If using pancetta, render it over medium-low heat. Moisten the bread crumbs with the milk and let them soften.

Cut the tuna into fine dice: cut thin slices, cut the slices into strips, and cut the strips into small cubes.

Combine the diced tuna with the onion, pine nuts, currants, bread crumbs, pancetta (if using), egg, and cayenne. Add 1 teaspoon salt and a little freshly ground pepper, and mix well. Fry a little of the mixture, taste, and adjust the seasoning. With wet hands, form the mixture into small balls the size of walnuts. Refrigerate the dumplings until ready to cook.

Roll the dumplings lightly in flour. Pour olive oil in a heavy-bottomed pan to a depth of ⅓ inch. Over medium-high heat, fry the dumplings for about 2 minutes per side, until nicely browned and crisp. Drain on absorbent paper and serve.

TUNA CONFIT WITH GREEN BEANS
AND SHELL BEANS

We make this "preserved" tuna in much the same way we would a duck confit, salting it ahead and stewing it slowly in flavorful oil. It is perfect for dishes like this simple provençal salad; it also makes a great pasta with the very same ingredients. We frequently embellish the salad with hard-cooked egg, a few cherry tomatoes, strips of roasted pepper, or rocket leaves, depending on what the season has to offer and the whims of the cooks.

Serves 6 as a first course.

Salt
1 pound tuna steak, cut 1½ inch thick
Thyme branches
Garlic cloves, crushed but not peeled
Fennel seeds
Dried chili pepper pods
Peppercorns
3 cups extra-virgin olive oil
1 pound (unshelled) fresh shell beans (preferably cranberry beans)
1 pound green beans
1 medium shallot, diced fine
2 tablespoons red wine vinegar
Pepper
1 cup Aïoli (page 85)

SALT the tuna generously and put it in a deep bowl with the thyme, garlic, fennel seeds, chili pods, and peppercorns. Use your own intuition for amounts of these ingredients. Cover with 3 cups of olive oil and refrigerate for several hours, or preferably overnight.

To cook, transfer everything to a heavy-bottomed nonreactive pot and heat slowly over medium heat. When the oil is warm, lower the heat and continue cooking for 12 to 15 minutes, turning the fish over occasionally for even heating. Probe the tuna with a paring knife to check for doneness—it should still be slightly pink at the center. Remove the tuna from the oil and cool, reserving the oil. It is now ready to eat, or it can be refrigerated in the oil and stored for up to 5 days.

Remove the shell beans from their pods and simmer the beans in enough water to cover by 1 inch. Add a little salt, a thyme branch, and a splash of olive oil, and cook until tender, about 30 minutes. Let the beans cool in their cooking liquid. The shell beans can be cooked several hours in advance and kept at room temperature.

Top and tail the green beans and parboil in rapidly boiling salted water for 2 minutes. Drain and spread on a baking sheet to cool.

Make a vinaigrette in a small bowl with the diced shallot, red wine vinegar, and ½ teaspoon salt. Whisk in ½ cup of the confit oil and add freshly ground black pepper. Taste and add more salt and vinegar, if necessary.

Drain the shell beans and toss with the green beans in the vinaigrette. Arrange on a platter with the tuna, broken into pieces, over the top. Serve with aïoli alongside, or thin the sauce with a little water and drizzle it over everything.

RUSTIC PIZZA WITH ANCHOVIES

Anchovies find their way into lots of the dishes we serve, and even people who say they can't eat anchovies end up eating and liking them. Sometimes we use anchovies for seasoning, or for adding depth to a lamb sauce, for instance, or in an herb butter for fish. An Italian cook we know adds anchovies and capers to chicken livers for crostini, and we nearly always use them in salsa verde and tapenade. Other times, as in this pizza, they are featured more prominently.

Mostly we use salt-packed anchovies from Italy, which we fillet under running water and bathe in olive oil. When fresh anchovies are available, we cure them for salads (a recipe is given in *Chez Panisse Vegetables*). Our importer friends Kermit Lynch and Darrell Corti offer anchovies from France and Spain in their shops. The French anchovies are slightly pickled and spicy; the Spanish anchovies, from Barcelona, are sweet and meaty—in Spain, especially in Catalonia, anchovies are considered to be a cultural necessity! Most Italian specialty stores carry salt-packed anchovies, and you can keep them indefinitely in the refrigerator packed in coarse salt in an airtight container.

We make several versions of anchovy pizza, and we have found that any one of them will sell better if the menu lists it as Alice's Anchovy Pizza. I don't mind lending my name to encourage people to try anchovies!

Serves 4.

    4 to 6 salt-packed anchovies
    Extra-virgin olive oil
    7-ounce portion Pizza Dough (page 51)
    2 garlic cloves, chopped fine
    Salt and pepper
    A pinch red pepper flakes
    3 tablespoons Simple Tomato Sauce (page 81)
    ½ small red onion, thinly sliced
    1 ounce mozzarella cheese, grated
    1 Hard-Cooked Egg (page 44), cut into 8 slices
    Italian parsley and fresh oregano, roughly chopped

PLACE a baking stone on the middle rack of the oven and preheat to 500°F. Rinse and fillet the anchovies. Cut each fillet into 4 long strips and cover with a little olive oil. Set aside.

Roll out the dough into a 10-inch circle and place on a well-floured peel. Using a pastry brush, paint the dough with olive oil and scatter the chopped garlic over. Season with a little salt, black pepper, and pepper flakes. Evenly distribute the tomato sauce, red onion, and mozzarella over the pizza, leaving a ½-inch border of dough uncovered.

Slide the pizza onto the hot baking stone and bake until the crust is well browned and the top is bubbling, about 10 minutes. Remove from the oven and cut into 8 slices. Garnish each with a slice of egg and a few strips of anchovy. Finish with a fine drizzle of olive oil and sprinkle with the chopped herbs.

SIMPLE TOMATO SAUCE

This tomato sauce, made quickly and almost without effort, is a good one to have on hand for general cooking, or for a fast pasta or pizza. It can be enlivened with chopped capers, olives, hot pepper, and anchovy, added at the end of cooking, or finished with a little good oil and snipped summer herbs. On a pizza, use the sauce cold, or the crust will be compromised.

Makes about 2 cups.

2 tablespoons extra-virgin olive oil
1 yellow onion, diced fine
3 garlic cloves, chopped fine
2 pounds sweet, ripe tomatoes, skinned, seeded, and chopped
1 teaspoon salt
Bouquet garni of parsley, thyme, and basil sprigs

WARM the olive oil in a heavy-bottomed nonreactive saucepan over medium heat. Cook the onion, stirring occasionally, until softened and slightly browned, about 5 minutes. Add the garlic and let it sizzle for half a minute. Stir in the chopped tomatoes and salt, and add the herb sprigs, bundled together with kitchen twine.

Bring the sauce to a boil, then reduce the flame to low. Simmer the sauce, uncovered, for 30 to 45 minutes; it will thicken as it cooks. Remove and discard the herb bundle. Taste for salt and adjust. The sauce will keep for 5 or 6 days refrigerated.

Note: For a more refined sauce, pass through a food mill or purée in a blender.

BAKED PASTA WITH SARDINES AND WILD FENNEL

We serve sardines whenever we can get big fresh ones from Monterey Bay. Over the years we must have done sardines at least fifteen different ways; this wonderful dish is one. (Our other favorite is much simpler: Fillet the sardines and leave them for an hour or so on a plate in a light marinade of olive oil, paper-thin slices of garlic, thyme, and maybe bay leaves. Slice a baguette in half lengthwise, and on good-sized, roomy pieces about a half-inch thick, place the fillets, slightly overlapping and with their beautiful silvery spotted skin up. Lightly salt and pepper them, drizzle the oil from the marinade over and around them, toast them for four or five minutes in a hot oven, and serve with a salad of wild rocket or very flavorful young mizuna greens.)

If beautiful fresh sardines are not available, you might substitute slices of mackerel, tuna belly, or fresh anchovies. In Palermo, bundles of wild fennel are sold at every market, as are all the other ingredients for this traditional dish. Here in Berkeley, we gather tender green wild fennel tops on the way to work, for this and other Sicilian-inspired dishes.

Serves 4 to 6.

6 large fresh sardines
Salt and pepper
Extra-virgin olive oil
1 pound dried pasta, such as penne rigate or ziti
⅓ cup golden raisins
1 cup tightly packed fennel tops, preferably wild
¼ cup pine nuts
1 large yellow onion, diced fine
1 fennel bulb, diced fine
1 scant teaspoon saffron threads, lightly toasted and crumbled
4 garlic cloves, chopped fine
4 anchovy fillets, rinsed and pounded
½ teaspoon red pepper flakes
1 lemon
2 tablespoons chopped parsley

SCALE, gut, and fillet the sardines, leaving the skin on. Season the flesh side with salt and pepper, drizzle with olive oil, and refrigerate.

Bring 8 quarts of water to the boil, add salt, and boil the pasta until it is just a little more al dente than you want it to be—it will cook a bit more later. Drain the pasta, toss lightly with oil, and spread on a baking sheet to cool.

Preheat the oven to 325°F.

In another pot bring 4 quarts of water to a boil. Put the raisins in a small bowl and ladle a little boiling water over them, then set aside to plump. Plunge the fennel tops into the boiling water and cook for 3 minutes. Drain, saving 2 cups of the cooking liquid. Allow the fennel tops and liquid to cool separately.

Toast the pine nuts on a small baking sheet until barely colored. Remove and cool. Raise the oven temperature to 450°F.

Gently sauté the onion and diced fennel in 2 tablespoons of olive oil over medium-low heat. Add the saffron and a pinch of salt and cook until tender, about 10 minutes. Add the garlic, anchovies, and red pepper, and cook a minute more.

While the diced fennel is cooking, purée the fennel tops in a blender with enough of their cooking liquid to achieve a pestolike consistency—or for a more rustic texture, use a mortar and pestle.

To assemble, put the cooled pasta in a large bowl and add the drained raisins, pine nuts, diced fennel and onion mixture, and fennel purée. Mix well and taste. The pasta should be quite juicy and well seasoned. Add more olive oil and fennel water as needed. Turn the pasta into a shallow gratin dish. Randomly tuck the sardine fillets into the pasta, and drape a few fillets decoratively over the top. Drizzle with a bit more olive oil and bake until the pasta is lightly browned, about 15 minutes. Cut the lemon into wedges to decorate the dish. Sprinkle with the chopped parsley and serve.

Note: Bake the pasta in individual baking dishes for easier service and a more elegant presentation. Toasted bread crumbs make a nice garnish, as does a little chopped mint or basil.

ROASTED SQUID WITH
BREAD CRUMBS AND OREGANO

Fresh squid from Monterey Bay are inexpensive but luxurious. We roast them in the pizza oven, which cooks them quickly and gives them an incredible flavor. If you don't have a wood-burning oven, this is still quite delicious cooked in a conventional oven. If tiny squid are available, simply clean them and roast them whole.

Serves 4.

1¼ pounds fresh squid
Salt and pepper
3 tablespoons extra-virgin olive oil
½ cup fresh bread crumbs
1 teaspoon chopped oregano
Aïoli (page 85)

CLEAN the squid: Separate the head from the body, and cut free the tentacles, trimming off and discarding the eyes and beaklike teeth. Starting at the tip of the body, with the back of a paring knife, push out and discard the insides and the transparent bone, or quill, within. Cut the body into ¼-inch rings. Season the rings and tentacles with salt, pepper, and 2 tablespoons of olive oil.

Toss the bread crumbs with the remaining tablespoon of olive oil and toast in a 400°F. oven until golden, stirring them after 5 minutes to help them brown evenly. Toss with the chopped oregano while still warm, and reserve.

Turn the oven up to 500°F., or have your wood-burning oven ready to go. Lay the seasoned squid on a flat baking sheet with sides (the squid give off liquid as they cook). Bake for 5 minutes, until the squid are nicely roasted and lightly browned. Pour off the liquid, arrange the squid on a serving platter, and sprinkle with the bread crumbs. Thin the aïoli a bit with water, drizzle over the top, and serve.

Aïoli (Garlic Mayonnaise)

We use a combination of pure and extra-virgin olive oil to make aïoli. The extra-virgin oil adds flavor, but can be overpowering by itself—a really strong oil gives an intensely olivaceous and sometimes very peppery flavor, which some aïoli eaters prefer, however. In the same way, depending on the size and strength of the garlic, three cloves may be too many—or not enough. Use your taste and preference to judge.

Makes about 1 cup.

3 cloves garlic, peeled
Salt
1 egg yolk, lightly beaten
¾ cup pure olive oil
¼ cup extra-virgin olive oil

Mash the garlic to a smooth paste in a mortar with a pinch of salt. Take out ⅓ of the paste and set aside. To the rest of the garlic add 1 teaspoon water, ¼ teaspoon salt, and the egg yolk, stirring well. Combine the two types of olive oil. Slowly whisk in the olive oil, a few drops at a time. As the mixture begins to thicken, begin adding the oil in a slow, steady stream. If the aïoli becomes too thick, thin it with a bit of water and continue. After all the oil has been mixed in, taste for salt and garlic and adjust accordingly. Refrigerate until needed. Aïoli should be used the day it is made, preferably within a few hours—the fresh garlic flavor dissipates and becomes unpleasant.

VENETIAN-STYLE PICKLED SAND DABS

Traditionally made with sardines, this dish is also delicious made with sole. Sand dabs, our local sole, are succulent and plentiful, so we've adapted the recipe to use them. This kind of soused or pickled fish was originally a way to preserve fish, but nowadays it is popular simply because it tastes good. The sweet-sour flavor is best a few hours after preparing the dish. We serve these sand dabs as a first course, but they also make an easy summer lunch, since all the cooking can be done ahead.

Serves 4 to 6.

2 tablespoons pine nuts
2 tablespoons sultana raisins
6 whole sand dabs, cleaned and trimmed
Salt and pepper
2 medium yellow onions
About 1¼ cups extra-virgin olive oil
1 bay leaf, fresh if possible
1 sprig thyme
A pinch red pepper flakes
Flour for dusting the fish
½ cup dry white wine
3 tablespoons sugar
1 tablespoon wine vinegar

PREHEAT the oven to 325°F. Toast the pine nuts on a baking sheet until lightly browned. Cover the sultanas with hot water in a small bowl to plump them.

Season the sand dabs with salt and pepper. Halve and peel the onions and cut into ¼-inch slices. Cook the onions in a sauté pan over medium-low heat in about ¼ cup of the olive oil. Add the bay leaf, thyme, red pepper, and a good pinch of salt. Cook slowly, covered, stirring occasionally until the onions are soft, about 10 minutes. Set aside.

Dust the sand dabs lightly on both sides with flour. Heat a cast-iron skillet big enough to hold all the sand dabs without crowding (or use two pans). Add olive oil to a depth of ½ inch. When the oil is wavy, slip in the sand dabs and fry over medium heat for 2 to 3 minutes per side. Adjust the heat as necessary to be sure the skin browns slowly and evenly. Check for doneness: the flesh should be opaque and separate into moist flakes when probed with a fork. Remove to absorbent paper and cool to room temperature.

Combine the wine, sugar, vinegar, and about ¼ cup of olive oil in a small saucepan. Bring to a boil, reduce the heat, and simmer for a few minutes. Cool.

Arrange the sand dabs in one layer in a deep-sided platter. Spread the onion mixture over the fish. Pour the wine mixture over everything. Sprinkle with the pine nuts and the drained sultanas. Cover loosely and let the sand dabs marinate at room temperature for at least an hour. Spoon a generous amount of onions and sauce over each portion when serving.

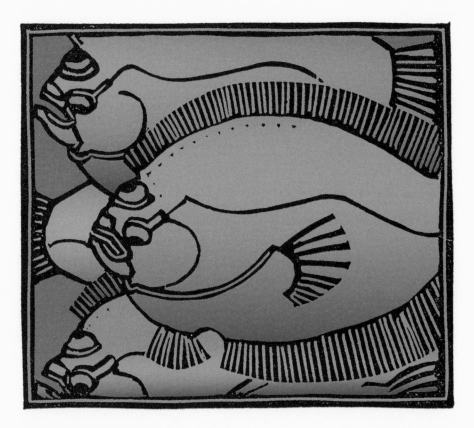

BAKED SCALLOPS WITH PROSCIUTTO

Firm, sweet, and briny day-boat sea scallops from Maine are a delicacy hard to resist. Serve just a few as a first course, or as a main course if the rest of the menu isn't too rich. We cook these scallops in the wood oven, but you can improvise at home with a cast-iron pan or a charcoal grill. A little wood smoke complements them nicely, and a little mildly salty prosciutto rounds out the dish. Sauces other than the Meyer lemon relish work well, too: depending on the season and our mood, we may serve these scallops with green olive and almond tapenade, salsa verde, or roasted pepper relish.

Serves 4 to 6.

    1 pound medium-size sea scallops
    Salt and pepper
    3 tablespoons extra-virgin olive oil
    6 to 8 slices Parma prosciutto
    Handful of young greens (lettuces, curly cress, rocket, or mâche)
    Few drops red wine vinegar
    ½ cup Meyer Lemon Relish (page 89)

PREHEAT the oven to 475°F.
    Pick over the scallops, removing the tough "foot" from each one and cutting any larger scallops in half. Season with salt and freshly ground black pepper.
    Heat a cast-iron or other heavy-bottomed ovenproof skillet over

medium-high heat. Pour in about 2 tablespoons of the olive oil, enough to coat the bottom of the pan. When the oil is nearly smoking, add the scallops in one layer. As soon as the scallops begin to sizzle, place the skillet, uncovered, on the top shelf of the oven.

Check the scallops after about 5 minutes. They should be nicely caramelized and firm to the touch, but juicy.

Arrange the warm scallops on individual plates and drape the prosciutto slices over and around them. Dress the lettuces with a little olive oil, vinegar, and salt, and garnish each plate with a few leaves. Spoon a tablespoon or so of the Meyer Lemon Relish over each serving.

Meyer Lemon Relish

Meyer lemons are sweet, thin-skinned, and famous for their ethereal perfume. Although common in California backyards, they are just beginning to be commercialized. Ask your friends or relatives in California to send you some.

This simple relish is good with most fish and shellfish. Unfortunately, it cannot be made with ordinary lemons. It is best made fresh and served within a few hours.

Makes about 1 cup.

1 large shallot, diced fine
1 tablespoon white wine vinegar or lemon juice
Salt
1 large Meyer lemon
½ cup extra-virgin olive oil
2 tablespoons chopped parsley
1 tablespoon chopped chervil or chives
Pepper

Put the diced shallot in a small bowl. Add the vinegar and a pinch of salt. Macerate for 10 or 15 minutes. Cut the lemon into 8 wedges. Remove the seeds and central core from each piece, then cut each wedge in half lengthwise. Slice the wedges crosswise into thin slivers. You will have about ½ cup. Combine the slivered lemon and shallot and add a little more salt. Stir in the olive oil, parsley, chervil, and some freshly milled pepper. Taste and adjust the seasoning.

FISH AND SHELLFISH CAKES

These crispy little cakes can be made in advance and fried at the last minute. We often serve them on New Year's Eve, with brightly colored pickled vegetables and peppery greens. The dish looks very festive, and the pickles are the perfect foil for the richness of the shellfish.

Serves 6 to 8.

Salt
1 live crab, 1½ pounds (or substitute lobster)
1 pound halibut or rockfish
½ pound sea scallops, muscle removed
Pepper
1½ loaves day-old French bread
1 medium onion, diced fine
1 small fennel bulb, diced fine
2 ribs celery, diced fine
2 tablespoons butter
A pinch cayenne
3 cups homemade mayonnaise
½ cup chopped parsley
¼ cup thinly sliced chives
½ cup chopped chervil
2 cups all-purpose flour
4 eggs
Juice of 1 lemon
Clarified butter for frying

BRING a large pot of salted water to the boil. Add the crab and boil, uncovered, for 10 minutes. Remove and allow to cool. Crack the crab, pick the meat from the shell, and refrigerate. (If substituting lobster, cook for 5 minutes, cool, then shell and dice the lobster meat.) Cut the fish and scallops into ¼-inch dice, season with salt and pepper, and refrigerate.

Cut the crusts from the French bread and discard. Cube the bread and pulse in a food processor to make fine soft bread crumbs.

Season the onion, fennel, and celery with salt and sauté gently in butter over medium-low heat until tender, about 10 minutes. Cool.

In a large bowl, mix together the crabmeat, fish, scallops, and onion mixture. Season with salt and a good pinch of cayenne. Add 1 cup of mayonnaise, 1 cup of bread crumbs, and half of the chopped parsley, chives, and chervil, and mix well. Fry a small amount of the mixture, taste for seasoning, and adjust. Form into balls the size of small tangerines. Spread the flour on a large plate. Beat the eggs and pour into a shallow dish. Spread the remaining bread crumbs into another shallow dish. Roll each ball lightly in the flour, then in the egg, and finally in the bread crumbs. Flatten the balls into disk- or oval-shaped cakes and smooth the edges. Place the cakes on a baking sheet, sprinkle with a few more crumbs, and refrigerate until ready to fry, up to 6 hours.

Stir the remaining chopped herbs into the remaining mayonnaise. Taste and adjust for lemon and salt. Thin with a tablespoon or two of water for a creamier consistency. Reserve.

Heat a cast-iron skillet over medium-high heat and pour in enough clarified butter to generously fill the bottom of the pan. When the butter is hot, slip the cakes into the pan, being careful not to crowd them. Fry until crisp and golden, about 2 minutes per side. Remove to absorbent paper and keep the cakes in a warm oven until all are fried.

Serve with the herb mayonnaise passed separately.

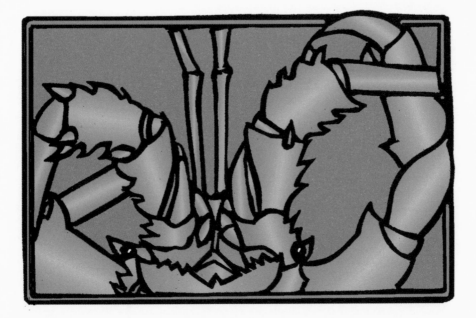

SALTED ATLANTIC COD BAKED WITH TOMATOES

Salted cod marries beautifully with the Mediterranean staple trilogy of garlic, olive oil, and tomato. Unfortunately, much of the salt cod available in this country is only suitable for shredded cod dishes like brandade. In some European fish markets, like the one at La Boquería in Barcelona, one can obtain salted cod prepared for specific dishes, with fillets of varying thicknesses, presoaked and ready for use (you can even specify a two-day soak), and the quality of the fish is generally much higher than the export grade. We've developed a recipe for a home-cured cod fillet that is succulent and not too salty. It's essential to use Atlantic cod in this dish for the best texture, although sea bass or halibut would also work. A combination of red and yellow tomatoes makes the most striking presentation. Fresh chopped herbs—parsley, chervil, basil, marjoram—are a welcome addition just before serving.

Serves 4 as a main course.

2½ tablespoons coarse salt
1½ pounds Atlantic cod fillet, skin removed
Thyme branches
Bay leaves
1 pound ripe tomatoes
Salt
2 medium sweet onions, diced
2 tablespoons extra-virgin olive oil, plus more for baking
4 garlic cloves, peeled and sliced
¼ cup white wine
Pepper
8 slices day-old baguette
1 cup Aïoli (page 85)

L IBERALLY sprinkle the salt over the skinned cod fillet. Scatter thyme branches and bay leaves over the fish, wrap in cheesecloth, and place on a rack over a rimmed baking sheet. Cover and refrigerate for two days.

Preheat the oven to 400°F. Core, halve, seed, and roughly dice the tomatoes. Lightly salt the diced onions and cook gently in 2 tablespoons of olive oil, without letting them color, until well cooked but not too soft, about 10 minutes. Add the sliced garlic and continue cooking for another minute or two.

Spread the tomatoes, onions, and garlic on the bottom of an earthenware baking dish. Add a few thyme branches and a bay leaf broken in pieces. Pour in the white wine and sprinkle with salt and pepper.

Cut the cod into 4 portions, lay them over the top, and press them into the juicy mixture. Drizzle a little olive oil over everything and bake uncovered for 20 to 30 minutes, until the fish is cooked through and a little crisp around the edges. When the cod is nearly done, brush the bread slices with a little oil and toast in the oven until golden. Serve each person a piece of cod with a spoonful of the warm tomato broth, 2 croutons, and a bit of aïoli.

Variation: Stew the onions with tender leeks and a little saffron and hot pepper.

SPICY BAKED CRAB

This is a delicious and very easy way to cook crab—a bit messy to eat, but that's part of the charm. In the winter, when local Dungeness crab is in season, we serve it nearly every day. Baked in the wood oven, it arrives at the table with a tantalizing aroma, making it the perfect appetizer. For a main course, simply serve with roasted potatoes and a good salad.

Serves 4 as an appetizer or 2 as a main dish.

Salt
1 live Dungeness crab
2 cloves garlic, peeled
1½ teaspoons sweet paprika
¼ teaspoon cayenne
Squeeze of lemon
3 tablespoons extra-virgin olive oil
3 tablespoons melted butter
Lemon wedges

BRING a large pot of salted water to a boil. Add the crab and cook for 13 minutes. Drain and cool to room temperature. To clean the crab, remove the top shell, carapace, and lungs, and rinse with cold water. Separate the legs and crack them with a mallet or nutcracker. This can be done several hours ahead of time—simply keep the crab well chilled until ready to use.

Meanwhile, prepare the sauce. In a mortar with pestle, pound the garlic into a smooth paste with a little salt. Stir together the garlic, paprika, cayenne, lemon juice, olive oil, and melted butter in a small bowl. Taste for salt and spiciness, and adjust to taste.

Preheat the oven to 425°F. Arrange the cracked crab legs in a baking dish and paint them with the sauce. Roast the crab for 12 minutes, until it is heated and sizzling all the way through. Serve with lemon wedges and the rest of the sauce in a ramekin, for dipping.

BASIC FISH STOCK

Tell your fishmonger you are making fish stock—you'll need fresh-smelling bones from mild-flavored white-fleshed fish such as sole, halibut, or bass. Heads, cheeks, and collars are good, too, but meaty bones make a mild, light, general-purpose stock. Like fresh fish, fish stock does not keep. For the best flavor, make and use fish stock the same day.

Makes about 3 quarts.

4 pounds meaty fish bones
½ carrot, peeled and sliced
½ leek, washed and sliced
1 small onion, peeled and sliced
1 stalk celery, sliced
2 sprigs Italian parsley
½ bay leaf
1½ cups white wine
½ teaspoon salt

RINSE the fish carcasses thoroughly in cold water. Put the bones, carrot, leek, onion, celery, parsley, and bay leaf in a large stainless steel pot and cover with 3 quarts water. Over medium-high heat, bring slowly to a boil, skimming any gray foam that rises to the surface. Reduce the heat to low, add the wine and salt, and cook at a bare simmer for 20 minutes.

With a wire skimmer, carefully lift the bones and vegetables from the stock and discard. Pour the stock through a fine-mesh sieve or a colander lined with cheesecloth, leaving behind and discarding the last inch or so of murky liquid and fish solids.

Variation: For a more full-bodied fish stock with a provençal flavor, first sauté the vegetables in a little olive oil, adding a little fennel (bulb, tops, or seeds); a few whole garlic cloves; a ripe tomato, roughly chopped; and a sprig of lemon thyme.

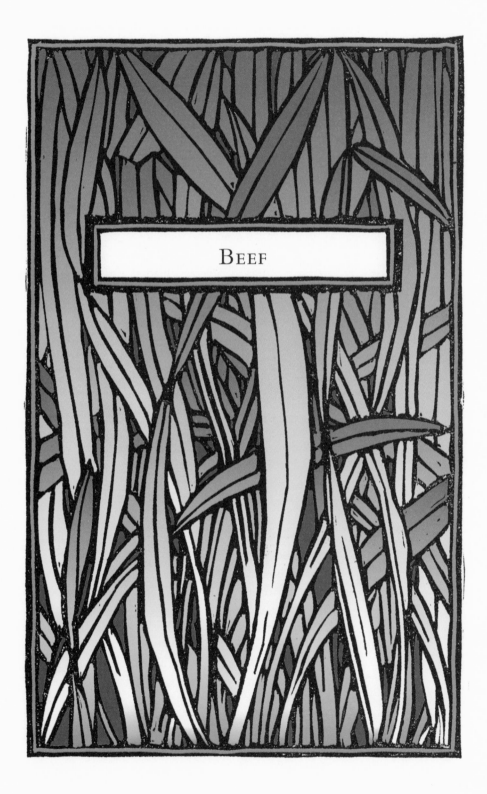

BEEF

Even before the Café opened on the second floor as a separate entity, we served café food at Chez Panisse late at night. Our friend Bob Waks would show up around eleven and start making steaks and french fries, ostensibly for the public, but in reality for the cooks and waiters and a few friends who would hang out long after the regular service was over in the dining room, talking, drinking wine, and playing cards or Scrabble. I can still taste those grilled sirloins slathered with lots of pepper, garlic, and lemon. I've always been an omnivore, and *steak frites* remains one of my favorite meals, although now I am much more mindful of where the steak comes from.

Our steak now comes from the Niman Ranch, a neighbor of Star Route Farm near the town of Bolinas in Marin County, no more than an hour's drive from Berkeley. Part of the thousand-acre ranch is located on the Point Reyes National Seashore, on land leased from the National Park Service, in an area of gently rolling hills within sight and sound of the Pacific Ocean. When I visit Bolinas and walk down to the beach, I always think how lucky those cows are.

We started using Niman Ranch beef early on in the history of the Café, and now we wouldn't use anything else. We began thinking about where our beef comes from after reading *Modern Meat*, by Orville Schell, Bill Niman's original partner in the ranch. In the book, Orville detailed the alarming consequences of the use of antibiotics and synthetic, growth-promoting hormones. Not only do these chemicals endanger the health of the animals, but there are increasing indications that as they work their way through the food chain, they affect the well-being of other animals and humans.

The slow, natural growth process that characterizes Niman Ranch beef must be one reason for its superior flavor. Bill continuously monitors his herd, and selects only the best young steers for fattening up. These steers are moved to roomy feedlots, where they are fed for three months on grain and hay. Barley, which grows abundantly in California on farmland that is not suited for much else, makes up most of their feed.

This finishing process gives the beef the perfect amount of internal fat marbling for juiciness and flavor. The result is meat with firm, very white fat, with a density and depth of flavor, a richness and intensity, that you don't find in factory-farmed beef.

The rib eye steaks we serve in the Café are from the same cut that the French call *entrecôte* and use for their traditional *steak frites*. Our Niman Ranch rib eyes are dry-aged for at least three weeks to enhance their flavor and tenderness. They are so good that we usually serve them very simply, cut thick and grilled over mesquite charcoal and vine branches, with a pile of *pommes frites* and a bunch of watercress. Or when chanterelle mushrooms are in season, we might serve the steaks with a mushroom sauce. We sometimes roast larger pieces of rib eye, browning them on the grill and finishing them in the oven. No matter which way it is cooked, this cut is always best when well browned on the outside and rare within.

Even though not as naturally tender as the rib eye, the top sirloin makes a flavorful roast. We eliminate the gristly areas running through the sirloins by separating the muscles along their natural seams, trimming carefully, to make several roasts out of one whole top sirloin. Roasted over a slow fire on the grill, and rested in a warm place for 15 minutes or so, the roasts, sliced thin across the grain, come out juicy and tender.

Short ribs are extraordinarily flavorful, but they do require long, slow braising to tenderize them and render out excess fat. In the summer, after a preliminary braising, they can be finished on the grill, and are excellent served with a sprinkling of gremolata or salsa verde. In the winter, they appear on the menu in a traditional French *daube*, with all the aromatic vegetables, or braised with green garlic, or given a provençal twist with anchovies and capers. They are great served on a bed of fresh noodles or next to a mound of mashed potatoes.

We also use short ribs in pot-au-feu and bollito misto, poached with pieces of brisket, tongue, and other meats. Any leftover pieces of tongue or brisket can be sliced the next day for a cold salad with pickled vegetables and salsa verde.

For beef carpaccio, we use either top round or, if we're feeling extravagant, tenderloin. In either case, the meat is trimmed of all exterior fat and then cut across the grain. Top round is usually sliced about ⅛ inch thick on the meat slicer, and pounded between sheets of parchment that have been brushed with good olive oil, until it is almost paper-thin. Tenderloin can be cut in thicker, ⅓-inch slices, and flattened in the same way. For either, we like to make the slices big enough to fill the serving plate completely. They can then be seasoned in various ways, with good olive oil, capers and anchovies, or mustard cream, for example.

All the beef we buy and prepare, from the meaty bones we use for stock to the standing rib roast we serve at Christmas time, is free of hormones and antibiotics. Our ultimate goal is to use cattle that are raised with organically grown feed. Ask your local butcher or supermarket to give you the same kind of choice.

BEEF CARPACCIO WITH ANCHOVIES, CAPERS, AND PARMESAN

Carpaccio is a satisfying first course when followed by a wild mushroom stew or a simple pasta. In this version, the beef is pounded thin rather than sliced. Like steak tartare, carpaccio requires fresh, naturally raised meat from a reputable butcher.

Serves 4.

10 ounces lean center-cut beef tenderloin
Extra-virgin olive oil
Salt and pepper
4 or 5 salt-packed anchovies, rinsed, filleted, and covered
    in a little olive oil
4 teaspoons capers, rinsed and coarsely chopped
1 tablespoon chopped Italian parsley
Wedge of Parmigiano-Reggiano cheese
1 lemon

THOROUGHLY trim the beef of any fat, connective tissue, and oxidized surfaces. With a sharp knife, slicing thinly across the grain, cut 8 equal slices, each about 1 ounce. Lightly oil two sheets of parchment or wax paper (we use the 9-inch parchment circles sold in pastry supply shops). Place 2 slices of beef side by side on one of the oiled sheets. Lay the second sheet, oiled side down, over the beef. With a heavy mallet, pound down and toward you, letting the weight of the mallet flatten the meat. Rotate the parchment and continue pounding gently. As the meat gets thinner, use lighter strokes to avoid tearing or pounding too thin. Flatten enough to form a 9-inch circle. Hold the package up to the light to make sure the meat is uniformly thin.

Repeat to make the remaining 3 portions. Cover and refrigerate while preparing the garnish ingredients.

To serve, remove the top sheets of paper from the pounded meat. Invert the carpaccio portions onto four chilled 9-inch plates, and carefully peel back the remaining paper sheets. Lightly season each portion with a pinch of salt and a few grinds of black pepper. Cut the anchovy fillets in half lengthwise and arrange 4 or 5 pieces randomly over the meat. Sprinkle with the capers and parsley. Use a vegetable peeler to shave large curls of Parmesan cheese over each serving. Finish with a good drizzle of extra-virgin olive oil. Serve with lemon wedges.

Other garnish options: Omit the Parmesan, and sauce with strong Dijon mustard, either plain or thinned with crème fraîche. A little finely diced shallot, macerated briefly in lemon juice or vinegar, adds a nice spark and refreshing crunch.

STEAK TARTARE CROÛTONS

Steak tartare calls to mind images of bustling Parisian bistros. In the Café we serve it the classic way, with the chopped beef in the center of the plate, topped with an egg yolk and surrounded by little piles of the garnish ingredients. While a large portion may be a little too rich, served in small portions as a stand-up hors d'oeuvre with drinks, or paired with a garden lettuce salad as an informal first course, steak tartare is just right. We make it with beef tenderloin for rich flavor and a silky, buttery texture, but lean sirloin can also be used. At the butcher shop, specify fresh-cut, naturally raised, hormone-free beef.

Serves 4 to 6.

1 baguette
Extra-virgin olive oil
10 ounces beef tenderloin
4 teaspoons finely diced shallots
4 teaspoons finely chopped cornichons
4 teaspoons chopped capers, rinsed
2 salt-packed anchovies, rinsed, cleaned, filleted, chopped,
     and smashed in a little olive oil
2 teaspoons chopped parsley
1 teaspoon Dijon mustard
Salt and pepper
4 small egg yolks

SLICE the baguette into ¼-inch slices; paint with a little olive oil and toast on a baking sheet in a 400°F. oven until golden, about 10 minutes.

Trim the beef carefully of any fat, connective tissue, or oxidized surfaces. Keep the beef chilled while preparing all the other ingredients. (For the best flavor, prepare the garnish ingredients—especially the shallots and parsley—as close to serving time as possible.)

Place the beef on a cutting board. With a very sharp knife, slice thinly across the grain; then cut the slices into julienne strips. Cut crosswise into very fine dice. Give the beef a brief finishing chop, working back over the pile 2 ounces at a time, until the meat holds together but still retains its texture.

Combine the beef with the shallots, cornichons, capers, anchovies, parsley, mustard, 1 teaspoon salt, several grinds of black pepper, and the egg yolks. Mix gently with a fork. Taste and adjust the seasoning. Add one or more tablespoons of extra-virgin olive oil for additional flavor and a silkier texture. Spread the mixture on the slightly warmed baguette croûtons.

COLD BEEF TONGUE SALAD WITH SALSA VERDE

This tongue salad is a sort of bonus dish, a reward for going to all the trouble of making bollito misto. It can be embellished with any number of things for a cold antipasto or with a few warm boiled new potatoes for a simple light lunch.

Serves 4 to 6.

1 pound leftover cooked beef tongue (see Bollito Misto, page 122)
Salt and pepper
1 recipe Salsa Verde (page 105)
2 bunches small radishes, washed and trimmed
2 bunches watercress or other spicy green, washed and stemmed
1 Hard-Cooked Egg (page 44)

Cut the tongue into thin slices and arrange on a platter. Season with a little salt and pepper. Spoon salsa verde liberally over all the slices and let rest for 10 minutes, or up to an hour. Decorate the plate with the radishes, whole or sliced, and sprigs of watercress. Roughly chop the egg and strew it over everything.

Variation: Dress the tongue with garlicky mustard vinaigrette, and serve with roasted beets and mâche. Lambs' tongues are also delectable and have a shorter cooking time.

Salsa Verde

Makes about 2 cups.

½ cup chopped Italian parsley or chervil
¼ cup thinly sliced scallions or chives
¼ cup chopped basil or mint
2 tablespoons capers, rinsed and roughly chopped
2 anchovy fillets, rinsed and chopped
1 large shallot, diced fine
Zest of ½ lemon
¾ cup extra-virgin olive oil
Salt and pepper
2 tablespoons wine vinegar or lemon juice

In a small bowl mix together the parsley, scallions, basil, capers, anchovies, shallot, and lemon zest. Stir in the olive oil and season with salt and freshly milled pepper. The sauce may be prepared several hours ahead up to this point. Just before serving, add the vinegar and adjust the seasoning.

RIB EYE STEAK WITH MARROW AND SHALLOTS

Rib eye is the same cut as prime rib, but without the bone. It's juicy, well marbled, and flavorful. We grill it over grapevine cuttings, a trick we learned from French friends years ago. Vine cuttings burn very hot and lend a marvelous sweet smoky character to just about anything—especially beef. Generously seasoned with lots of shallots, garlic, and black pepper, this is our favorite steak. We serve it simply, with a pile of fried potatoes and a spray of watercress or rocket.

Serves 4.

Three 2-inch marrow bone sections
Four 8-ounce rib eye steaks, about 1 inch thick, trimmed
Extra-virgin olive oil
3 cloves garlic, cut in slivers
Few sprigs thyme
4 bay leaves, coarsely broken
Salt and coarse-cracked black pepper
2 shallots, diced fine
2 tablespoons chopped parsley

About 15 foot-long pieces dry grapevine cuttings,
    each ½ inch in diameter

REMOVE the marrow from the bones by pushing it through carefully with your finger, avoiding the splintery interior of the bones. Soak the marrow overnight in ample water, refrigerated, to rid it of blood and whiten it. The next day, drain and mash the marrow through a sieve to make it smooth and remove any veins. Set aside at room temperature.

Marinate the steaks by rubbing with olive oil and the garlic, thyme, and bay leaves. Season generously with salt and cracked pepper. The steaks can stay in the marinade for several hours before grilling.

Prepare a hardwood or charcoal fire. When it has burned down to a small bed of hot coals, add the vine cuttings, which will produce a brief burst of flame. Be prepared to throw the steaks on the grill when the flames die and the embers are searing hot. Grill about 4 minutes on each side, until the juices start to rise.

Remove the steaks from the grill and arrange them on a platter. Spread each one with a spoonful of the softened marrow and sprinkle with the shallots and parsley. Spoon the juices that accumulate in the platter over the steaks.

Variation: Instead of beef marrow, spread the grilled steaks with 4 tablespoons (½ stick) softened butter mixed with the shallots and parsley. Ladle over each steak 1 ounce (2 tablespoons) Basic Beef Reduction (page 127).

Roast Beef Sirloin Sandwich

Sometimes the only thing for lunch is a great sandwich. We vary the presentation according to the season: thinly sliced raw spring onions, or summer garden tomatoes, or cooked greens in the winter (the Garlicky Kale on page 39 is a favorite). We use levain bread from the Acme Bread Company, but you could use focaccia for a less crusty texture.

Serves 4.

Mustard Mayonnaise
2 egg yolks
2 tablespoons Dijon mustard
1¼ cups peanut oil
1 clove garlic
Salt
1 teaspoon red wine vinegar
A pinch cayenne

2 pounds beef sirloin, 3 inches thick
Salt and pepper
Extra-virgin olive oil
2 medium red onions, peeled
Balsamic vinegar
8 large slices day-old levain bread, each ½ inch thick
¼ pound rocket or watercress

Prepare the mustard mayonnaise by whisking the egg yolks and mustard in a medium stainless steel or porcelain bowl and slowly adding peanut oil until the sauce begins to thicken. Gradually add the remaining oil; if the mayonnaise is too thick, add a few drops of water. In a mortar, mash the garlic and a pinch of salt into a smooth paste. Add the garlic paste, red wine vinegar, and cayenne to the mayonnaise. Chill.

Prepare a medium-hot charcoal fire. Trim excess fat from the sirloin, season liberally with salt and pepper, and rub with olive oil. Grill the beef for about 10 minutes on each side, until a meat thermometer registers 120°F. Remove from the grill and let rest 10 minutes.

Slice the onions crosswise ¼ inch thick. Brush with olive oil and season with salt and pepper. Place the onion slices side by side on the grill, turning every few minutes until evenly browned. Remove and sprinkle with a few drops of balsamic vinegar.

Paint the bread slices lightly on each side with olive oil. Grill carefully until golden, turning frequently. Thinly slice the sirloin against the grain. Spread 4 pieces of grilled bread with the mayonnaise. Arrange the beef over the bread, add the grilled onions, the rocket or watercress, and top with the remaining bread. Cut the sandwiches in half.

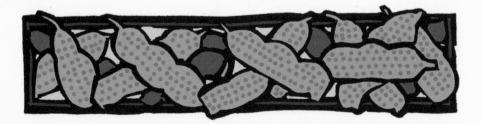

GRILLED SKIRT STEAK WITH
ANCHOVY AND GARLIC SAUCE

Skirt steak is an exceptionally flavorful cut of beef, and quite tender, too, if grilled quickly over a hot fire. Of the many possible accompaniments, we like baby artichoke salad, potato-cardoon gratin, or simple stewed cannellini beans, all of which pair beautifully with anchovy and garlic.

Serves 4 to 6.

10 salt-packed anchovies
6 garlic cloves, peeled and roughly chopped
1 cup extra-virgin olive oil
2 pounds skirt steak
Salt and pepper
2 tablespoons chopped parsley

FILLET the anchovies; soak in several changes of cold water and pat dry. In a mortar, pound the garlic and half of the anchovies into a paste. Coarsely chop the remaining anchovy fillets. Add the chopped anchovies to the anchovy-garlic paste, and whisk in the olive oil.

Prepare a very hot grill. Trim away any excess fat or sinew from the beef. Lay the skirt steak flat and cut into 6 even portions. Season with salt and pepper and let stand at room temperature for 20 to 30 minutes. Brush the steaks lightly with oil and grill for about 2 minutes per side, depending on their thickness, just until juices appear on the surface. Remove from the grill and let rest 3 to 4 minutes. Slice the steaks thin, against the grain, and arrange on a platter. Stir the parsley into the anchovy-garlic mixture and spoon over the meat.

Variation: Sauce the steaks with an anchovy, shallot, and garlic compound butter stirred into a little Basic Beef Reduction (page 127).

ALICE'S LOVAGE BURGERS

A delicious twist on the beloved hamburger. Lovage is a tall, beautiful herb with large leaves. It looks and tastes a bit like celery, with undertones of parsley and chervil, yet has some other elusive sweetness that is hard to describe. Lovage adds a crisp, bright flavor to beef. I made these burgers years ago for a staff picnic, and I've been trying to get them on the Café menu ever since!

Serves 4.

4 cloves garlic, roughly chopped
Salt
8 lovage leaves, coarsely chopped
1¾ pounds ground chuck
Pepper
Levain bread or focaccia
Grilled onions
Dijon mustard
Rocket or young lettuce leaves

IN a mortar, pound the garlic with a little salt. Add the chopped lovage leaves and pound briefly. Mix the garlic and lovage into the meat, and season generously with salt and pepper. Form into 4 patties. It is important to pack the meat well and make the edges of the patties smooth to ensure even cooking. Leave the center of the patty a bit concave; this corrects for the swelling that occurs in the center as the meat's circumference contracts during cooking.

For a medium-rare burger, grill the hamburgers for 4½ minutes on each side over medium-hot coals. Serve on bread toasted so it is lightly browned and slightly crisp on one side. Good choices for buns are levain bread or focaccia, both breads that are soft enough but still able to hold up to the juice of the burger without falling apart. The size of the bread is also important: it should just match the size of the hamburger. Garnish with grilled onions, Dijon mustard, and a few leaves of rocket or lettuce.

BOEUF À LA FICELLE WITH HORSERADISH CREAM

For this classic French dish, the beef filet is poached medium-rare in a
flavorful broth and sliced. It should be served simply, with a spicy
horseradish sauce and some of the poaching juices. Though it is prepared with European ingredients, there's something almost Japanese
about the final result—clean-tasting but rich. For a very traditional
French repast, start with Dandelion Salad (page 9), serve the beef with
grilled or boiled leeks, and finish with Apple and Brandied Currant
Tart (page 232).

Serves 4 to 6.

3 pounds beef tenderloin, top end
Salt and coarse-cracked black pepper
1 medium yellow onion, sliced
1 small carrot, peeled and sliced
Olive oil
2 quarts Basic Beef Stock (page 126)
2 quarts Basic Chicken Stock (page 206)
3 chicken legs
1 bay leaf
1 sprig thyme
2 cloves garlic, peeled
1 cup Horseradish Cream (page 113)

WITH a sharp knife, remove all of the exterior fat, "silver skin" or
connective tissue, and oxidized dark spots from the beef. Tie the tenderloin with butcher's twine around its circumference at 2-inch inter-
vals; then weave a piece of twine lengthwise around the filet to make a
secure, compact roast. A good butcher can do this for you.

Season liberally with salt and cracked black pepper. Refrigerate for
6 to 8 hours, or overnight. Bring the beef to room temperature before
cooking.

To make the broth, stew the onion and carrot gently in a little olive
oil until softened. Cover with the beef and chicken stocks, and add the
chicken legs, bay leaf, thyme, and garlic. Bring to a gentle boil, skimming occasionally. Reduce the heat and simmer for 20 to 30 minutes.
Strain the broth, skim the fat, and set aside until you are ready to poach
the beef. The broth may also be prepared the day before and refriger-

ated. Reserve the chicken legs for another dish—chicken ravioli, for example.

Place the beef in a heavy-bottomed pot large enough to accommodate the roast but small enough that it will be submerged in the broth. Pour in the broth and slowly bring to a boil. Season the broth with salt. Adjust the heat so the broth remains at a very gentle simmer to ensure that the filet will be tender and evenly cooked; simmer for 20 to 25 minutes. Check the internal temperature with a meat thermometer: the meat will be rare at 115°F. and a perfect medium-rare at 120°F. Remove the beef from the broth and place it on a warm platter. Cover loosely and allow to rest for 10 to 15 minutes. Slice the filet into ½-inch slices and serve in deep-sided plates with a spoonful of Horseradish Cream and a ladleful of the slightly reduced poaching juices on each serving.

HORSERADISH CREAM

Serves 6; makes about 2 cups.

6 to 8 ounces fresh horseradish, peeled
White wine vinegar
Salt and pepper
A pinch sugar
1 cup heavy cream or crème fraîche
Optional: cayenne pepper

GRATE the horseradish as finely as possible—a food processor or blender obtains better results than a box grater. Add to the grated horseradish a tablespoon or so white wine vinegar, salt and pepper, and a good pinch of sugar; let macerate for 15 to 30 minutes.

Whip the cream, but not too stiffly. Fold the horseradish mixture into the cream. Adjust the seasoning, adding salt, pepper, vinegar, and cayenne to taste (if you wish). Chill. The sauce may be prepared several hours in advance.

GRILLED TENDERLOIN WITH
CHANTERELLES, GARLIC, AND PARSLEY

Cooking and serving a whole beef filet, or tenderloin, is impressive and relatively easy, and the meat is equally good hot or cold. Much of your success depends on obtaining a well-aged piece of meat. Tenderloin is aptly named, for it is absolutely the tenderest cut. Seasoning aggressively is key. Grilling will add a wonderful smoky dimension, especially if fruit wood is used. We serve grilled tenderloin all year with, depending on the season, roasted shallots, sliced summer tomatoes, grilled porcini, ratatouille, or other garnishes.

Serves 8 to 10.

    1 whole beef tenderloin, about 7 pounds
    Salt and pepper
    Extra-virgin olive oil
    1 whole head garlic, peeled
    2 pounds chanterelle mushrooms
    1 small bunch parsley, stemmed
    1 small lemon

TRIM most of the fat from the beef. Leave the "silver skin" connective tissue intact, but trim away most of the "chain," the fatty strip attached to one side of the filet. Using butcher's twine, tie the beef into a compact, secure roast, doubling over the meat at the thin end of the filet. A good butcher can do this for you.

Six hours ahead, or the night before, season the filet generously with salt and coarsely ground pepper. Rub the meat with a few tablespoons of olive oil, thinly slice 6 to 8 peeled cloves of the garlic, and rub the garlic slices all over the tenderloin. Wrap and refrigerate; remove 2 hours before cooking.

Prepare a hardwood or charcoal fire. Let the coals burn down, and be ready to cook the filet when the fire is medium hot. Cook the beef slowly, turning frequently, for about 45 minutes, until it looks nicely roasted and the juices begin to rise. Keep a spray bottle of water handy, and douse the flames as they flare up, or the meat will acquire a disagreeable burnt flavor. Check the internal temperature with a meat thermometer. Remove the roast from the grill when the thermometer registers 118°F. Cover it loosely, keep warm, and allow to rest for 15 to 20 minutes. The roast will continue to cook while resting, and will be a perfect medium-rare when sliced.

Meanwhile, pick over the chanterelles and trim away discolored ends and soft spots. Rinse briefly in a bowl of warm water and blot dry. Slice the mushrooms ¼ inch thick. Heat 2 tablespoons of olive oil in a cast-iron skillet over medium heat. Add the mushrooms, season with salt and pepper, and sauté for 2 to 3 minutes, letting them color a bit. Turn off the heat.

Cut the tenderloin into ½-inch slices, arrange on a warm platter, and spoon some of the juices over the meat. Finely chop 3 or 4 garlic cloves. Coarsely chop the parsley. Reheat the mushrooms over a medium flame. Toss in the garlic and parsley when the mushrooms begin to sizzle. Cook for a minute or so, without letting the garlic color. Add a squeeze of lemon juice, scatter the mushroom mixture over the beef, and serve.

Variation: To roast the tenderloin in a conventional oven, preheat the oven to 450°F. Make sure that the meat is at room temperature before cooking. Remove the garlic slices and tuck a few rosemary and thyme branches under the butcher's twine. Heat a large heavy sauté pan or cast-iron skillet until quite hot, and brown the meat on all sides. Place it on a rack in a roasting pan, and roast for 25 to 30 minutes. Check the internal temperature with a meat thermometer and remove the roast when it reaches 118°F. Place the meat on a warmed platter, cover loosely, and allow to rest for 15 to 20 minutes before serving garnished with mushrooms, garlic, and parsley as in the master recipe.

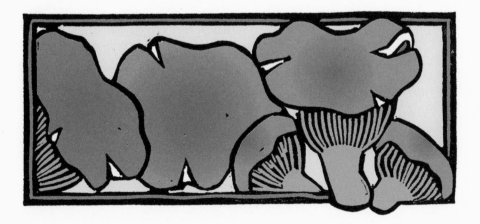

BRAISED BEEF CHEEKS IN RED MOLE

In this dish, a Mexican-style mole sauce adds interest to an old-fashioned French standard, braised beef cheeks. Patience is a virtue here. The braise takes anywhere from five to seven hours in a slow oven; as with all braises, cooking the day before improves flavor and simplifies life in the kitchen on the day of service. Beef cheeks are perfect for Sunday dinner or a hearty lunch, accompanied by pinto beans, pickled onions, a little spicy green salsa, and a pile of hot corn tortillas.

Serves 6.

MOLE
1 yellow onion, sliced
Olive oil
8 ounces dried guajillo or pasilla chili peppers
3 slices day-old French bread
¼ cup almonds
¼ cup peanuts
¼ cup raisins
3 tablespoons sesame seeds, toasted
¾ cup Basic Chicken Stock (page 206) or water
2 teaspoons chopped fresh thyme
2 teaspoons chopped fresh marjoram
1 teaspoon chopped fresh oregano
¼ teaspoon ground cinnamon
¼ teaspoon ground cloves
¼ teaspoon ground allspice
1 ounce Mexican chocolate, roughly chopped
2 tablespoons red wine vinegar
Salt

6 beef cheeks, about 3 pounds
1 tablespoon black peppercorns
3 tablespoons coriander seeds
3 bay leaves
Salt
8 yellow onions, sliced
A few cilantro stems
3 heads garlic, cloves separated but not peeled

Small bunch thyme, broken apart
2 cups red wine
3 quarts Basic Beef Stock (page 126)

To make the mole, first sauté the onion in olive oil over medium heat until softened, letting it color slightly. Set aside.

Split the chili peppers and remove and reserve the seeds. Place the chilies in a small bowl, cover with boiling water, and soak for 20 minutes. Toast the chili seeds over medium heat in a cast-iron pan (be careful of the fumes—they can burn your eyes and make you cough), and add them to the soaking chilies.

In the same cast-iron pan, fry the bread slices until golden in a few tablespoons of olive oil. Add to the onion.

Still using the same pan, lightly fry the almonds, peanuts, and raisins.

Drain the chilies and seeds, and place in a blender with the bread, onion, peanuts, almonds, raisins, and toasted sesame seeds. Add the chicken stock or water and blend to a rough paste. Add the thyme, marjoram, oregano, cinnamon, cloves, allspice, chocolate, and vinegar. Blend to a smooth purée, adding more water if necessary. Salt to taste. The mole may be made several days ahead and stored in the refrigerator.

With a sharp knife, trim the beef cheeks of all fat and "silver skin." In a mortar, crush the peppercorns, coriander, and bay leaves, and sprinkle over the beef. Season liberally with salt. Refrigerate 4 to 6 hours, or overnight.

Preheat the oven to 500°F. Spread the onion slices in the bottom of a large roasting pan with the cilantro stems, unpeeled garlic cloves, and thyme. Add the mole, red wine, and beef stock, and mix together. Place the seasoned beef cheeks on top. Roast, uncovered, for 30 minutes, until the meat has browned and the broth is simmering. Cover with foil; reduce the heat to 300°F. and bake, rotating the pan every hour or so to ensure even cooking. Check for doneness after about 5 hours: insert a wooden skewer into the meat. There should be no resistance and the meat should be quiveringly tender; otherwise, continue cooking. When the cheeks are done, remove the foil, turn the oven to 450°F., and bake 10 to 15 minutes longer, to glaze the meat. Remove the cheeks to a warm platter, strain and degrease the sauce, and pour it over the beef.

SAVORY HERB MEATBALLS WITH SPAGHETTI

These tender, delicate beef dumplings have no relation to the over-cooked, dry, flavorless meatballs that some of us remember from grade school cafeteria lunches. The bread crumbs and herbs give them their texture and flavor. The meatballs can be served with rice instead of pasta, or served by themselves as a first course with a little fresh tomato sauce. Sometimes we make tiny meatballs and poach them in a vegetable soup or broth.

Serves 6.

½ cup milk
¼ cup soft bread crumbs
1 small yellow onion, very finely diced
Extra-virgin olive oil
Salt
1 pound freshly ground beef sirloin
1 egg, beaten
3 tablespoons freshly grated Parmigiano-Reggiano cheese, plus more for garnish
2 tablespoons chopped Italian parsley, plus 2 tablespoons more for sauce
1 teaspoon finely chopped thyme
⅛ teaspoon cayenne
Black pepper

1 medium red onion, sliced thin
Olive oil
2 to 3 cloves garlic, very finely chopped
2 cups Simple Tomato Sauce (page 81)
¼ teaspoon hot pepper flakes
½ teaspoon finely chopped fresh oregano
Salt
1 pound spaghetti

PUT the milk and bread crumbs in a small bowl and mix with a fork. When the bread has softened, squeeze out most of the milk with your hands. Discard the milk.

Sauté the onion in a little olive oil without letting it color. Season with a light pinch of salt and set aside to cool.

Combine in a medium-size bowl the beef, bread crumbs, onion, egg, 3 tablespoons Parmesan, 2 tablespoons parsley, the thyme, cayenne, black pepper, and 1 teaspoon salt. Work the mixture gently and thoroughly with your hands until it has an even consistency. With wet hands, shape the mixture into walnut-size balls. This can be done a few hours ahead. Store the meatballs in the refrigerator in one layer, tightly wrapped, until you are ready to cook them. The meatballs can be cooked in the time it takes to boil the spaghetti.

Heat a skillet large enough to hold all the meatballs in one uncrowded layer. Add the red onion with enough olive oil to coat it lightly and cook over medium heat. When the onion begins to sizzle, add the meatballs, shaking the pan to keep them from sticking. Using tongs or a wooden spoon, gently turn and toss the onions and meatballs so they brown lightly. Add the garlic and cook for a few seconds, taking care that it doesn't color. Add the tomato sauce, hot pepper flakes, oregano, and the remaining 2 tablespoons parsley. Season with salt to taste. Simmer gently, uncovered, stirring the meatballs to coat them with sauce. Test for doneness by cutting one meatball in half with a paring knife. Keep warm.

A rule of thumb for gauging how much pasta to cook—one that actually uses the thumb—is to make a ring about the size of a dime with your thumb and forefinger. A dime-size bundle of pasta is one portion. Dry spaghetti will take 7 to 10 minutes to cook. Boil the pasta in a large quantity of salted water. Drain the spaghetti and turn into a deep warmed platter or pasta bowl. Pour the meatballs and sauce over the pasta. Serve with more Parmesan cheese.

BRAISED BEEF SHORT RIBS WITH GREMOLATA

Many of the cooks in the Café say that this is their favorite dish. Short ribs make the most succulent of all braises because they have extraordinary flavor and the perfect ratio of fat-to-lean marbling. In the fall and winter, we serve them with hand-cut herb noodles or soft polenta, and roasted root vegetables. The gremolata—the classic mixture of parsley, lemon zest, and garlic—plays the perfect counterpoint.

Serves 6.

6 to 7 pounds beef short ribs, cut 2 inches thick
Salt and pepper
3 large yellow onions, roughly chopped
Olive oil
2 leeks, white and pale green parts only,
    washed and roughly chopped
1 carrot, peeled and roughly chopped
2 plum tomatoes, roughly chopped
6 cloves garlic, smashed
6 sprigs thyme
8 sprigs parsley
3 bay leaves
1½ cups red wine
3 to 5 cups hot Basic Beef Stock (page 126)

GREMOLATA
¼ cup chopped parsley
Zest of ½ lemon, finely chopped
1 large clove garlic, finely chopped

CUT the short ribs into smaller pieces, roughly square, so that each piece includes a bone. Trim excess fat if necessary. Season generously with salt and pepper, and refrigerate for 4 to 6 hours, or overnight.

Preheat the oven to 475°F. Arrange the short ribs bone side down in a roasting pan, and roast until lightly browned, about 20 minutes. Meanwhile, sauté the onions in a little olive oil in a large skillet until lightly colored. Add the leeks and carrot, and cook until slightly softened. Add the tomatoes, garlic, thyme, parsley, and bay, and sauté a few minutes more.

Spread the vegetables in an earthenware baking dish large enough to hold the short ribs. Arrange the ribs on top of the vegetables, bone side up. Pour in the wine, and add enough hot stock to barely cover the ribs. Cover the dish tightly with foil and place in the hot oven. When the braise begins to simmer, after about 20 minutes, loosen the foil and lower the heat to 350°F.

Begin to test for doneness after 1½ hours. A skewer or paring knife inserted into the meat should encounter no resistance, and the meat should be nearly falling from the bone. When they are tender, uncover the short ribs and turn them again so that the bone side is down. Pour off and reserve the braising juices. Raise the heat to 450°F. and return the ribs to the oven for a final browning. When they are beautifully glazed, after about 10 minutes, remove from the oven. Strain the braising liquid into a bowl, pressing down on the solids to extract all the juices. Allow the liquid to settle, then degrease. Pour the liquid back over the short ribs and reheat if serving immediately, or cool, refrigerate, and serve the next day.

To make the gremolata, mix the parsley, lemon zest, and garlic (these ingredients should be chopped at the last minute) and scatter over the short ribs just before serving.

BOLLITO MISTO

Bollito misto (literally "boiled mixed [things]") is a close relative of pot-au-feu. With its deep, harmonious flavors, it is a cold-weather meal for hearty appetites and the kind of dish that makes winter worthwhile. And it provides delicious leftovers: tongue for a next-day salad (see page 104), and a superb broth for soups and for *risotto milanese*. It is, however, rather time-consuming to make. The tongue can take up to eight hours to become sufficiently tender, and the brisket needs at least three. Because the flavors develop well overnight, we find that this recipe works best prepared over a three-day period. In the end, it is a great meal for a dinner party, since everything is basically done in advance. Sometimes we serve bollito misto with carrots, turnips, cabbage, and little potatoes steamed over thyme branches. At the table, bowls of Salsa Verde (page 105) are passed, sometimes with a little grated horseradish added.

Serves 8 to 10.

3 pounds beef brisket
1 beef tongue, about 2 pounds
4 chicken legs, drumsticks and thighs separated
Salt and pepper
4 bay leaves
12 thyme sprigs
1 or 2 cloves
2 onions, peeled and halved
2 leeks, cut in 1-inch pieces and rinsed
2 carrots, peeled and sliced thick
2 ribs celery, sliced thick
8 sprigs parsley
½ bottle white wine
8 Fennel Sausages with Red Wine (page 141)

Two days before you plan to serve the bollito misto, season the meats. Generously salt and pepper the brisket and put it in a glass dish with 2 of the bay leaves and 6 of the thyme sprigs. Dissolve 4 tablespoons of salt in 2 quarts of ice water in a glass or stainless steel bowl and submerge the tongue in the brine. Season the chicken legs with salt and pepper and toss in another bowl with the rest of the bay leaves and thyme sprigs. Cover and refrigerate the meats.

The next day, remove the tongue from the brine and rinse it. Put the tongue and the brisket with its bay and thyme in a large stockpot. Add the cloves, onions, leeks, carrots, celery, parsley, and wine, and cover by an inch or so with water. Bring to a boil, then reduce the heat, skimming off the gray foam that rises to the surface. The bollito misto must simmer very gently for several hours.

Begin to test the brisket for doneness after 2½ hours by inserting a thin-bladed knife into the thickest part of the meat. It should pull out easily, with little or no resistance. When the brisket is tender, place it in a dish, ladle on some of the broth, and cover it loosely. Continue to cook the tongue until it, too, is tender—it will take 6 to 8 hours in all—then remove it from the broth and set it aside to cool. When the tongue is cool enough to handle, peel the skin and trim the fat and scraps from its base, and put it in the dish with the brisket. Strain the remaining broth over both the brisket and the tongue and refrigerate overnight.

The third day, remove and discard the congealed fat, and lift the brisket and tongue from the cold broth. Put the broth in a stockpot with the seasoned chicken legs and the fennel sausages. Bring the broth to a boil, cover, and turn off the heat. Leave the chicken and sausage in the covered pot—they will poach in the hot broth while you prepare the rest of the dish. Cut the brisket and some of the tongue into ¼-inch slices. After 20 minutes, carefully add the sliced meats to the chicken and sausage, and return to a simmer for another 10 minutes. Transfer the brisket, tongue, chicken, and sausage to a large, warmed tureen and pour the broth over. At the table, serve each person some of each meat and a large ladleful of broth.

BOLOGNESE SAUCE

This version of the classic rich meat sauce from Bologna was inspired by Lynne Rossetto Kasper's recipe in her 1992 cookbook *The Splendid Table*. We had been making this sauce for years, but always with beef chuck; however, skirt steak produces a more luxurious texture, and the meat remains moist. The sauce keeps well—in fact, it improves in flavor if made a day or two in advance. We serve Bolognese sauce over wide hand-cut herb noodles; with the rustic dried pasta called *strozzapreti*; in lasagna with fresh tomatoes, baked in the wood oven; or with polenta and Wood Oven-Baked Porcini Mushrooms (page 32).

Serves 8.

⅓ cup dried porcini mushrooms
Extra-virgin olive oil
4 ounces pancetta, diced fine
1 medium yellow onion, diced fine
4 ribs celery, diced fine
1 small carrot, diced fine
Salt
2 cloves garlic, chopped fine
1½ pounds skirt steak (or chuck), cut into ¼-inch cubes
4 ounces lean pork shoulder, coarsely ground
1 cup dry white wine
2 bay leaves
2 sprigs thyme
2 cups Basic Beef Stock (page 126)
   or Basic Chicken Stock (page 206)
1½ cups milk
3 tablespoons double-concentrated Italian tomato paste
¼ cup chopped parsley, for garnish
Freshly grated Parmigiano-Reggiano cheese
Pepper

COVER the dried porcini with boiling water and allow to sit for 15 minutes. Remove the porcini from the water, reserving the liquid, and chop the mushrooms fine. Heat a wide heavy-bottomed pan; pour in 2 tablespoons of olive oil and add the diced pancetta. After the pancetta has released some fat, add the onion, celery, carrot, and a little salt.

When the vegetables have softened somewhat, add the garlic and porcini, and cook until the vegetables are soft. Remove the vegetables from the pan and set aside.

Put the pan back on the heat (you don't need to wash it), pour in 2 more tablespoons of oil, and when it is hot, add the skirt steak, pork, and a little salt. Cook over medium-high heat until the meat begins to brown, about 15 minutes. Turn the heat to medium and add the cooked vegetables, wine, bay, and thyme. Adjust the heat to maintain a low simmer and let the sauce cook until the liquid evaporates and the contents begin to brown. Deglaze with 1 cup of the stock and a few tablespoons of the milk; add the tomato paste, making sure to scrape the brown bits off the bottom of the pan and stirring the sauce well to incorporate the milk. Continue to cook the sauce gently, adding a few tablespoons of milk and stock now and then. Reduce the sauce until the liquid evaporates and everything begins to brown again; this gives the sauce depth and color. Deglaze with the rest of the stock and milk, stirring and scraping well. Skim the fat that rises to the surface of the sauce. The sauce is done when its texture is velvety and the meat is completely tender, in about 1½ hours. Cool and refrigerate for up to 4 or 5 days.

Reheat and serve over pasta, garnished with the chopped parsley, and pass Parmesan cheese and the pepper mill.

Variation: This basic recipe can be used with other kinds of meat and even poultry—guinea hen is especially good. Another variation worth trying is to add sautéed fresh wild mushrooms at the end of the cooking.

BASIC BEEF STOCK

Good beef stock is essential for many sauces, soups, and braised dishes, and there is really no substitute. Your butcher should be able to provide meaty shanks if you request them a day in advance. Also request that the shank bones be cut into 2-inch pieces for easier handling.

Mushrooms and leeks are good additions to beef stock. For additional flavor and a deeper color, add a little fresh tomato (leftover tomato scraps, for example) in summer, or a couple of canned organic tomatoes in winter.

Makes 3 quarts.

6 pounds meaty beef shanks
3 large carrots, peeled and cut into 2-inch pieces
2 medium onions, peeled and quartered
3 stalks celery, cut into 2-inch pieces
3 tablespoons olive oil
4 parsley sprigs
2 thyme branches
½ bay leaf
½ teaspoon black peppercorns
Optional: 1 teaspoon salt

PREHEAT the oven to 425°F.

Roast the meaty shanks in a heavy-duty roasting pan for 20 to 25 minutes, until thoroughly browned, turning once. Over medium-high heat, sauté the carrots, onions, and celery in olive oil for 5 minutes to caramelize them lightly. Put the roasted bones and 5 quarts cold water in a large stainless steel stockpot and bring to a boil. Deglaze the roasting pan with a little water, vigorously scraping with a wooden spoon, and add these flavorful pan drippings to the stockpot. When the stock comes to a full boil, skim off the gray foam. Add the carrots, onions, celery, parsley, thyme, bay, peppercorns, and, if you wish, salt. Use salt sparingly if you intend to make a reduction later—the stock will become saltier as it reduces.

Turn the heat to low and simmer very slowly for 4 to 5 hours, until the broth tastes rich and is a light caramel color. Strain through a fine-mesh colander or sieve. Allow the stock to cool completely; remove fat from the surface and promptly refrigerate. The stock is ready to use as is, or it may be reduced further to create a glaze or sauce.

BASIC BEEF REDUCTION

We find that many cooks tend to overreduce sauces—the result can be somewhat sticky and a little too strong. This method produces a lighter, more natural-tasting sauce that won't mask the flavor of a good roast.

Makes about 2 cups.

5 cups Basic Beef Stock (page 126)
2 thyme branches
¼ teaspoon potato starch
Salt
A few drops red wine or balsamic vinegar

BRING the beef stock and thyme branches to a boil in a 2-quart stainless steel saucepan. Turn down the heat and continue cooking at a gentle simmer until the stock is reduced by nearly half (or more, depending on the concentration of flavor you desire).

Dissolve the potato starch in 1 tablespoon water and whisk into the reduced stock. Simmer for another minute or two. The sauce will thicken slightly. Taste for salt and correct. Strain out the thyme, and add a few drops of wine or vinegar.

Variation: For a richer, more intensely flavored sauce, sauté two diced shallots in olive oil to soften them slightly. Add ¾ cup dry red wine and 4 cups beef stock, and reduce by about half. Do not thicken with potato starch. Strain through a fine-mesh sieve, then whisk in 1 tablespoon butter. Add salt and cracked black pepper to taste.

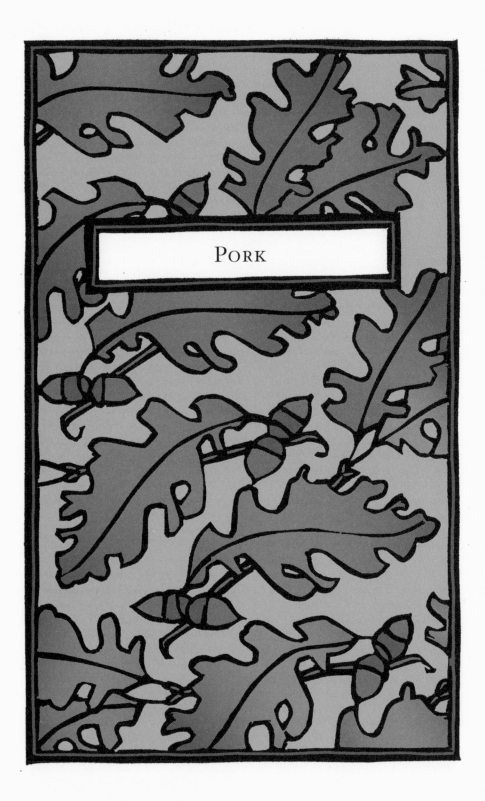

PORK

ONE of my happiest memories of the early days at Chez Panisse is of the preparations that led up to our second annual Bastille Day garlic festival, over twenty years ago. One of my partners had befriended a farm family in Amador County in the Sierra foothills who kept a few hogs and who had agreed to supply us with suckling pigs for the event. We got the notion that if we fed the sows with lots of garlic, the piglets were sure to suckle garlic-flavored milk, and in turn, they, too, would taste of garlic when they were roasted on the spit. I went to the farm to help feed the sows entire crates of new-crop garlic. They seemed to love it, and when the suckling pigs were roasted we all agreed that their meat was tender, succulent, and faintly alliaceous.

Unfortunately, most of the other pork routinely available to us in those days was problematically bland and very dry when cooked. To achieve the best possible flavor and texture, our only recourse in those days was to use the traditional French method of curing fresh pork for several days in brine. There were always a couple of huge earthenware brining crocks in the walk-in refrigerator for this purpose. This helped, but we still longed for pork like we remembered from Tuscan market stalls, where they sell delicious *panini* of roasted *porchetta*, from pigs raised the old-fashioned way.

Not long after that early garlic festival, at Il Vipore, a restaurant outside Lucca in Tuscany, I was served *lardo* for the first time—cured pure pork fat as white as snow, sliced as thin as could be, and served plain, with warm toast and rosemary. It immediately conjured up a whole raft of questions: How was it made? How was it cured? Was it really all right to eat plain fat like that? And after I tasted it, I asked myself why was it so incredibly good?

I've asked many of the same questions about other cured pork products I've eaten in Europe, especially the incomparable *prosciutto di Parma* and *jamón Serrano*. After a trip to Spain, I started carrying an image in the back of my mind of the Café with hundreds of hams hanging from the rafters, like a bar in Andalusia. But for pork, as for so many other ingredients, we have had to search to find the real thing. Now we procure pigs from a handful of farmers in the West who raise pigs in such a way that we don't have to worry about what harmful chemicals—and bad flavors—might be lurking in the fat. These are farmers who, like farmers generations ago, are committed to working with nature, not against it, and who are concerned about the well-being of their animals. Invariably they are small farmers, raising far fewer animals than the huge factory farms. With its sweet, clean flavor, the pork from these farms has been a revelation to us. Finally, we can serve the incomparable pork that can only come from a small farm.

At one time in America, almost every small farmer kept a few pigs. They were held in a fenced enclosure, and allowed access to pasture. They turned farm waste into meat for the family table. There was no attempt to make the animals conform to a precise, unvarying way of life, as there is on big hog farms today, where pigs are raised indoors, in harsh confinement, without access to fresh air and sunshine, and fed specifically formulated rations that may include antibiotics and hormones. And their waste creates environmental problems in its disposal.

Paul Atkinson, who raises pigs at Laughing Stock Farm, in the Willamette Valley of Oregon, is typical of the kind of farmer we prefer to work with. His pigs spend part of their time in roomy, cement-floored pens, but they most enjoy the time they have outdoors, in portable pens that Paul places around his pastures when the weather permits. These pens are moved about as the pigs forage through the pasture grasses.

To supplement their diet of green grass, the animals are fed a mixture of barley, corn, and soybeans. As the pigs mature they may also be fed fresh alfalfa, Sudan grass, and even winter squash grown on the farm. But what really makes these pigs special is the flavor they get from the fresh milk and hazelnuts they eat during their finishing period.

Our other pork suppliers also understand what makes good pork and good farming practice. Don Watson's pigs raised in the Napa Valley have a unique flavor from the acorns they forage every fall. The animals on Paul Willis's farm in Iowa play a part in his crop rotation system, spending the summer on pasture that then becomes naturally fertilized for a grain crop the following year.

This kind of carefully raised pork rivals veal and lamb for tenderness and delicacy of flavor, and it has an important place on the Chez Panisse table. We use pork every day, from whole suckling pigs to our own salt-cured prosciutto, not only in main course dishes, but as accents in salads and on antipasto plates. A few slices of pancetta improves a plate of sweet garden peas, and a little homemade fennel sausage enlivens a rustic pizza or pasta.

The most useful animals may be the roasting pigs, which typically weigh around sixty pounds dressed weight. These we can cut up in the kitchen; then we roast the loins and legs, grind the shoulders for sausage, and turn everything else into head cheese.

Larger, full-size hogs come to us already butchered as whole loins, shoulders, bellies, and legs. The loins are sometimes boned and roasted whole, or they may be cut into chops and grilled. The shoulders can be ground and made into sausage, or roasted on the spit. Bellies get turned into our own pancetta, and the legs become prosciutto.

It was our dissatisfaction with conventionally produced ham and pancetta that got us interested in doing more of our own curing, using the extraordinary pork we get from our suppliers. After years of study and trial and error, we have learned how to produce our own Parma-style prosciutto, as well as pancetta and salami.

About ten years ago we began experimenting with pork legs, trying to make a good prosciutto. Detailed information on prosciutto-curing was hard to find, even in Italy. Little by little we had to figure out the proper size for the pork legs, the amount of salt, the temperature and humidity, and the curing time. The process was very slow because the hams take twelve months or more to cure, so the outcome of each experiment was a long time coming.

Essentially, the curing is simple—a fine pork leg, salt, and time are the only ingredients—but there are several steps, each of which requires close attention. The steps are uncomplicated, but making prosciutto is not something lightly undertaken at home. It requires space and carefully controlled temperatures not found in home refrigerators or cellars.

The hams are rubbed with salt, pressed under a weight, and kept at a temperature of 35°F. for a month, during which time they lose a great deal of water and begin to absorb the salt. Then they spend several months in a slightly warmer room with good air circulation, where they continue the drying process.

At the end of this second curing period, we rub fat on the fleshy side of the ham to prevent it from hardening. The final curing stage is at an even warmer temperature. During the next nine to twelve months the hams develop their characteristic tang and flavor, as they slowly lose more water and undergo a mild fermentation.

Because we use the most deliciously flavored pork to start, and we control every step in its curing, the flavor and texture of our prosciutto surpasses any we have found in this country, domestically produced or imported. Only in Italy and Spain have we found any as good. And we serve it as they do there: draped over figs or slices of ripe melon, with spicy salad greens such as rocket, or with a few olives and a few shavings of Parmesan cheese.

HEADCHEESE

Headcheese, or *fromage de tête*, is a jellied meat dish that was invented to ensure that none of the edible parts of a pig would go to waste. It is one of those old-fashioned molded meat salads that are nothing short of exquisite when properly made. It is almost impossible to get a good one these days, even in France. The jelly must be just set and full of flavor. A small slice of headcheese served with a garlicky Dandelion Salad with Mustard Vinaigrette (page 9) makes a refreshing—and surprisingly light—start to a meal.

Serves 4 to 6.

1 small pig's head, about 5½ pounds
2 pig's feet
Salt
1 large onion, halved
3 cloves
1 leek, halved lengthwise and rinsed
3 carrots
½ head garlic, broken into cloves
2 bay leaves
8 allspice berries
4 sprigs thyme
4 sprigs parsley
1 cup dry white wine
Black pepper
Nutmeg, for grating
3 tablespoons chopped parsley
1 to 2 teaspoons Champagne vinegar

Ask your butcher to cut the pig's head in half and remove and discard the brain. Also have the pig's feet cut in half—they will supply the necessary natural gelatin. Salt the head and feet heavily, and refrigerate overnight. Rinse well and place in a stockpot along with the onion stuck with the cloves, the leek, carrots, garlic cloves, bay, allspice, thyme, parsley, and wine. Cover with cold water and bring to a simmer. Skim the foam that rises to the surface and cook slowly until the meat pulls away from the bones, about 2 to 3 hours. Be careful not to cook so much that the meat falls apart completely. Remove the head, feet, and carrots from the stock and set aside to cool.

Strain the stock and discard all the other vegetables, herbs, and spices. Return the stock to the pot and cook over high heat, skimming periodically, until it has reduced by half. Ladle a little reduced stock into a shallow bowl and refrigerate to see if it gels—it should be firm but not rubbery. A too-firm jelly may be diluted with a little water; if it is too loose reduce the stock further.

When the meat is cool enough to handle, tear the meat from the head and foot bones. Shred the meat, using a knife and your fingers. Include a little tender skin and fat. Thinly slice the ears and snout— you may encounter some cartilage that is too tough to eat, but it is nice to have a little crunch. Peel the tongue and cut into small cubes. Slice the carrot. In a large mixing bowl combine all these ingredients and season with black pepper, nutmeg, parsley, and Champagne vinegar. Taste and correct the seasoning; since the headcheese will be served cold, it must be highly seasoned. Put the mixture in a 5-cup terrine or loaf pan and ladle about 2 cups of reduced stock over it. Cover and refrigerate overnight. To serve, unmold carefully and cut into slices about ¾ inch thick.

COUNTRY TERRINE WITH PISTACHIOS

The words *pâté* and *terrine* are now used interchangeably, although a terrine was originally a savory meat loaf baked in an earthenware vessel of the same name, and a pâté was a meat pie encased in pastry. We prefer coarser, country-style terrines like this one to the rich mousselike pâtés on some buffet tables. A country terrine must be seasoned artfully and nursed along. After it is cooked, the flavors continue to develop, so it is best to wait a few days before serving. Although this recipe makes two terrines, they will keep for at least two weeks under refrigeration. A terrine is, after all, another delicious way to preserve meat, like a confit. It is also the centerpiece of a quintessential peasant lunch, along with a seasonal salad, good bread, and good red wine.

Makes 2 terrines, each serving 8 to 10.

3 pounds lean boneless pork shoulder
½ pound back fat
3 ounces pancetta
1½ tablespoons salt

2 bay leaves
1½ teaspoons black peppercorns
8 allspice berries
¼ teaspoon dried thyme
1 clove
A pinch cayenne

¼ cup chopped parsley
1 teaspoon chopped garlic
½ cup shelled whole pistachios
4 bay leaves
Optional: Caul fat (page 146)

Cut the pork shoulder, back fat, and pancetta into 1-inch-thick pieces. Toss the meat with 1½ tablespoons salt and refrigerate.

Pulverize the 2 bay leaves, the peppercorns, allspice, thyme, clove, and cayenne in a mortar or electric spice mill. Add ⅔ of this spice mixture to the meat, and mix together. Reserve the remainder.

Grind the seasoned meat using the ¼-inch plate of a meat grinder.

Grind ⅓ of the ground meat again. Combine the two meat mixtures, cover, and refrigerate overnight.

The next day, add the parsley, garlic, and pistachios, and mix lightly with your hands. Do not overhandle or the texture of the terrine will be too dense. To taste for seasoning, fry a bit of the mixture and chill it (it will taste different when cold); it may require more salt or spice mixture at this time. Don't fuss with it too much.

Preheat the oven to 325°F. Place 2 bay leaves on the bottom of each of two 5-cup earthenware terrines or glass loaf pans. Add half of the pork mixture to each terrine. Cover each with a lid or with foil. (If you wish, line the 2 pans with caul fat, leaving some hanging over the sides; add the bay leaves and pork mixture, wrap the caul over the top, and do not cover.) Tap the pans on a tabletop to settle everything. Put a kitchen towel in the bottom of a deep roasting pan and set the terrines on it (the towel will insulate the bottom of the pan). Fill the pan with enough hot water to come ⅔ up the sides of the terrines and bake until the internal temperature reaches 140°F., in about 1½ hours. Remove the terrines from the roasting pan and cool at room temperature for about 2 hours, then cover and refrigerate overnight.

The terrines can be eaten the next day, but will develop more flavor if left for 2 or 3 days. To unmold, dip the pans in hot water for a few minutes and invert. Cut into thick slices and serve with strong Dijon mustard and cornichons.

Variation: Use half the mixture to make a terrine and the other half to make rustic sausages wrapped in caul fat (see page 146) for a meal the same day. For a more complex terrine, add poultry livers and hearts, a little black truffle, and a splash of Cognac.

Prosciutto, Spring Onion,
and Artichoke Antipasto

Make this simple antipasto with excellent prosciutto and real spring
onions—the fresh, crisp, sweet sprouting onions that look like miniature bulbing onions and come to market only in the spring.

Serves 6 to 8.

4 large artichokes
1 lemon
1 bay leaf
3 sprigs thyme
A pinch red pepper flakes
4 cloves garlic, peeled and sliced
Salt
Extra-virgin olive oil
2 red or white spring onions
1 teaspoon Dijon mustard
1 tablespoon lemon juice
1 tablespoon red wine vinegar
Pepper
2 tablespoons chopped parsley
12 thin slices prosciutto di Parma
Optional: rocket leaves for garnish

PULL off the outer leaves of the artichokes until you reach the yellow
tender central leaves. With a paring knife pare the artichokes down to
their hearts. Remove all but 1 inch of the stems and trim off the tops
of the hearts. Cut the artichokes lengthwise into halves and scoop out
their chokes with a teaspoon. Cut the artichoke halves into sixths and
place them in water to cover, along with the juice of the lemon, to prevent discoloration.

Put about 1 quart water, the bay leaf, thyme, pepper flakes, garlic, 2
teaspoons salt, and ¼ cup olive oil into a stainless steel or other nonreactive pot and bring to a slow simmer. Add the artichoke pieces and simmer until just tender, about 10 minutes. Remove the pan from the heat
and let the artichokes cool in their cooking liquid.

Trim the roots and stems from the spring onions and peel away the outside layer, as it may be tough. Cut the onions in half, slice very thinly, and submerge in cold water until you are ready to assemble the salad.

To make the vinaigrette, whisk together the mustard, lemon juice, and red wine vinegar in a small bowl. Season with salt and pepper, and whisk in ⅓ cup extra-virgin olive oil. Taste for acidity and adjust if necessary.

Put the drained artichokes and spring onions in a bowl and season lightly with salt. Add the vinaigrette and the chopped parsley, and toss. To serve, pile the artichoke salad on a large platter or on individual plates, surrounded with thin slices of prosciutto di Parma and garnished with rocket leaves, if you wish.

PIZZA WITH BACON, ONIONS, AND GREENS

Good bacon improves a sandwich or a pizza. Look for sweet spring onions and vibrant-looking greens at the farmers' market and ask your
butcher for wholesome, naturally cured bacon. Try it as a late morning
snack, or for lunch, with the Heirloom and Cherry Tomato Salad on
page 14.

Serves 4.

   1 small onion, thinly sliced
   Extra-virgin olive oil
   Salt and pepper
   2 cups greens (preferably kale or mustard), washed and chopped
   2 garlic cloves, chopped fine
   A pinch red pepper flakes
   One 7-ounce portion Pizza Dough (page 51)
   1 ounce mozzarella cheese, grated
   4 slices lean smoked bacon, sliced paper-thin

PREHEAT the oven, fitted with a baking stone, to 500°F.
   Season the sliced onion with a little olive oil and salt and pepper, and
roast in a shallow baking dish for 15 minutes or so, stirring now and
then, until it is lightly caramelized, sweet, and tender. Set aside to cool.
   Heat 1 tablespoon of olive oil in a wide, deep pan over medium heat.
Add the greens and a little salt, and stir well to coat the greens with oil.
When the greens begin to wilt, add the garlic and pepper flakes, and
continue cooking until most of the liquid is gone and the greens are
soft. Drain and cool in a colander.
   Roll out the pizza dough and place it on a floured peel. Drizzle a
little olive oil over the dough and season with salt, pepper, and more
pepper flakes. Evenly distribute the roasted onions, the mozzarella, the
greens, and finally, the strips of bacon, leaving a ½-inch border of
dough uncovered.
   Slide the pizza onto the preheated baking stone and bake for 6 to 7
minutes, or until the crust is golden and the bacon is crisp. Remove
from the oven, cut into 8 slices, and serve.

Fennel Sausage with Red Wine

Sausage-making at home need not be complicated. A sharp knife is really all you need for a small batch of simple sausage. Special products and equipment—casings, caul fat, a large funnel, a grinder, a stuffer if you become serious—are all available from your butcher or by mail order (see Sources and Resources, page 245).

In these sausages, the combination of pork and fennel is both inspired and intoxicating—a traditional flavor pairing that really works. Serve with Creamy White Beans (page 36) and a salad of bitter greens.

Serves 4 to 6.

2 pounds boneless pork shoulder
4 ounces back fat
2 ounces pancetta
2 large garlic cloves
2½ teaspoons salt
2 teaspoons fennel seed, finely ground
2 teaspoons fennel seed, coarsely crushed
1 teaspoon finely ground black pepper
½ teaspoon sugar
½ teaspoon cayenne
¼ teaspoon coriander seeds, finely ground
½ cup dry red wine
1 tablespoon chopped parsley
Natural hog casings

Cut the pork shoulder, back fat, and pancetta into ½-inch cubes. In a mortar, pound the garlic to a paste with a little of the salt. In a large bowl, mix the cubed meat with the garlic paste, the remaining salt, fennel seed, black pepper, sugar, cayenne, coriander, red wine, and parsley. Spread the seasoned meat on a baking sheet and chill in the freezer for an hour.

Run the seasoned meat through the ½-inch plate of a meat grinder. Immediately grind the meat again while it is still quite cold. Fry a small piece of the mixture, taste, and correct the seasoning if necessary.

Stuff the mixture into hog casings and twist into ten 5-inch links. Refrigerate the sausages overnight. Grill over medium coals for about 7 minutes per side.

Smoky Garlic Sausage with Kale

This is a highly seasoned, full-flavored sausage. The smoky Spanish paprika is beguiling and the cooked greens inside the sausage are a pleasant surprise. Quatre épices is a traditional sausage seasoning mixture
made of black pepper, allspice, clove, and nutmeg or ginger. It should
never be an identifiable flavor in sausage, but should merely add a mysterious, enhancing undertone. Serve potatoes—pan-fried and finished
with lots of garlic and parsley—with these sausages.

Serves 4 to 6.

2 pounds boneless pork shoulder
4 ounces back fat
2 ounces bacon or pancetta
6 large garlic cloves
2½ teaspoons salt
1½ tablespoons smoked Spanish paprika (see Note)
1 teaspoon finely ground black pepper
¼ teaspoon coriander seeds, finely ground
½ teaspoon quatres épices
¼ teaspoon cayenne
1 tablespoon chopped thyme
¼ cup white wine
2 tablespoons Cognac or brandy
½ pound young kale or chard leaves, washed and trimmed
Natural hog casings

Cut the pork shoulder, back fat, and bacon into ½-inch-thick
pieces. In a mortar, pound the garlic to a paste with a little of the salt.
In a large bowl, mix the cubed meat with the garlic paste, the remaining salt, paprika, black pepper, coriander, quatres épices, cayenne,
thyme, white wine, and cognac. Spread the seasoned meat on a baking
sheet and chill in the freezer for an hour.

Parboil the kale leaves for 30 seconds in a large pot of boiling salted
water, drain, and cool. Squeeze the water from the kale and chop it
roughly.

Remove the meat from the freezer and run it through the ½-inch
plate of a meat grinder. Immediately grind the meat again while it is
still quite cold. Stir in the chopped kale by hand, mixing well.

Fry a small piece of the mixture, taste it, and correct the seasoning if necessary. Stuff the mixture into hog casings and twist into ten 5-inch links. The sausages will keep several days in the refrigerator. Grill them over medium coals for about 7 minutes per side.

Note: The smoky paprika we use is *pimentón de La Vera*, made from red peppers that are grown in the Spanish regions of Extremadura and Murcia, dried and smoked over oak wood fires, and ground into powder. See Sources and Resources, page 247.

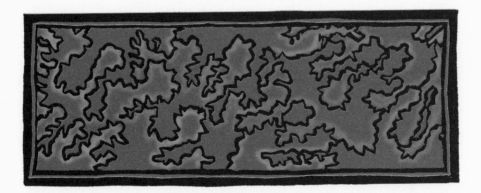

CATALAN-STYLE SAUSAGE AND CLAMS

This rather unusual combination of pork and shellfish in a stew is found not only in Catalonia, but in other cuisines as well. It makes a very special dish for a large group of friends. Serve some almonds and olives before, and a little sheep's-milk cheese with quince paste afterward.

Serves 6.

12 ounces dried chickpeas
1 small onion
1 carrot, peeled
1 rib celery
2 bay leaves
4 sprigs thyme
Salt
Extra-virgin olive oil
1 pound Fennel Sausage with Red Wine (page 141)
1 large onion, diced fine
5 cloves garlic, peeled and sliced
1 tablespoon paprika
¼ teaspoon red pepper flakes
2 medium tomatoes, peeled, seeded, and roughly chopped
    (about 1 cup), or 1 cup canned tomatoes
4 pounds clams, preferably Manila or littleneck
1 bunch chard, washed and cut into 1-inch ribbons
½ cup dry white wine
6 large slices rustic bread
1 clove garlic, peeled

COVER the chickpeas generously with cold water and soak overnight. They will swell to twice their size. The next day, drain the chickpeas and put them in a pot with fresh cold water to cover, the onion, carrot, celery, 1 bay leaf, 2 sprigs of thyme, and 2 tablespoons salt. Bring to a boil and skim the foam that rises to the surface. Turn down the heat and simmer until very tender, about 1½ hours. Let the chickpeas cool in their cooking liquid. Drain them and remove and discard the vegetables and herbs.

Heat 1 tablespoon olive oil in a large skillet or wide, heavy-bottomed pot. Add the sausage, crumbled or in slices, and cook over medium heat until browned and just cooked through, about 5 minutes. Remove the sausage from the pan, discarding the fat, and add 2 tablespoons olive oil. Over medium heat, sauté the diced onion until lightly browned, about 5 minutes. Add a little salt and the 5 cloves sliced garlic, and continue cooking for a few minutes longer. Add the paprika, pepper flakes, and the remaining bay leaf and 2 sprigs of thyme, and continue to cook for a minute or two. Add the tomatoes and continue cooking, stirring occasionally, until most of the liquid has evaporated.

Add the drained chickpeas, the clams, sausage, chard, and white wine. Turn the flame to high and cover the pan. Toast the bread. Rub each slice with the garlic clove, drizzle with olive oil, and season with a tiny bit of salt. When all the clams have opened, after 5 minutes or so, pour the stew into a deep platter and garnish with the garlic toasts. Serve in shallow soup bowls, spooning the stew over the toast. A final drizzle of oil is a welcome but optional flourish.

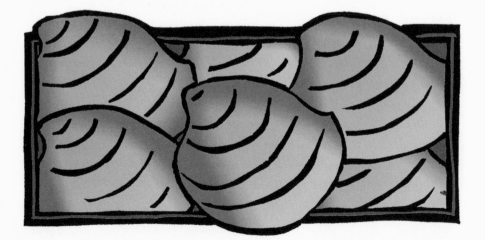

CRÉPINETTES WITH SWISS CHARD

Crépinettes take their name from *crépine*, the French word for caul fat. Caul is the beautiful veil-like lacy fat used to wrap simple homemade sausages like these, and is also used in terrines and other dishes when meat stuffing needs containing. Readily available in Europe, here it must be ordered ahead from the butcher and is usually sold frozen. To prepare it for use, rinse it briefly in cold water to which a few drops of vinegar have been added. The caul fat should look fresh and white and have a sweet smell. These crépinettes can be grilled and served as is, or as part of a mixed grill. They are also delicious eaten cold, on a picnic, like miniature pâtés.

Serves 4 to 6.

2 pounds boneless pork shoulder (about 20 percent fat)
Salt and pepper
Cayenne
1 small onion
2 tablespoons olive oil
¼ pound green chard or spinach, washed and trimmed
1 garlic clove, chopped fine
1 teaspoon chopped thyme
2 tablespoons chopped parsley
1 pound caul fat

Cut the pork shoulder into 1-inch-thick pieces and season with 1 tablespoon salt, a generous amount of freshly ground black pepper, and a pinch of cayenne. Grind the pork through the ¼-inch grinding plate of a meat grinder, or hand-chop with a sharp knife. Refrigerate.

Cut the onion into small dice and sauté in the olive oil with a little salt until lightly browned and cooked through. Refrigerate until cool. Meanwhile, blanch the chard for about 20 seconds in a large amount of boiling salted water. Drain and spread on a baking sheet to cool. Squeeze the water out of the chard and chop roughly.

Mix the onion, chard, garlic, thyme, and parsley into the ground pork with a wooden spoon. Fry a piece of the mixture and taste for seasoning. As with all sausages, if the pork is tasty and sweet, very little seasoning will suffice. If it is not, you may have to resort to trickery— a little more garlic and cayenne, perhaps, or more fresh herbs. When you are satisfied with the seasoning, spread the caul fat onto a work surface. Divide the sausage mixture into 12 little balls and space them on the caul fat about 3 inches apart, avoiding any thick, veiny parts of the caul. Flatten each ball so it resembles a small hamburger patty. With a sharp paring knife, cut the caul between the patties, forming squares. Wrap each patty in its square of caul fat, pressing lightly. The crépinettes may be formed and refrigerated a day in advance. To serve, grill over coals or pan-fry until well browned and cooked through, about 5 minutes per side.

BOUDIN BLANC

Boudin blanc, the traditional French white sausage of chicken and pork, is made almost every Monday in the Café. After much experimenting, Russell Moore, one of the chefs, developed a boudin with a complex yet delicate flavor. For a smooth, creamy texture, it is especially important that all ingredients be as cold as possible. Boudin blanc is served all year with various accompaniments. In the autumn, for instance, perhaps new-crop applesauce and fried potatoes, or a sauté of apples, cabbage, and onions. For special occasions, add a little chopped black truffle to the sausage mixture and serve with pickled beets, fried potatoes, and watercress.

Makes about 15 sausages; serves 6.

1¼ pounds boneless pork shoulder
1 pound chicken breasts, skin removed
½ pound pork fat
4 teaspoons salt

1 bay leaf
1½ teaspoons peppercorns
1 clove
3 allspice berries
¼ teaspoon dried thyme
¼ teaspoon coriander seeds
¼ teaspoon caraway seeds
A pinch cayenne
Nutmeg, for grating

½ cup fresh white bread crumbs
1½ cups heavy cream
1 medium onion, sliced thin
1 tablespoon butter
1½ teaspoons chopped fresh thyme
Natural hog casings
Optional: bay leaves, thyme, or other aromatics
Clarified butter or oil

Cut the pork shoulder, chicken breasts, and pork fat into 1-inch-thick pieces and season with 4 teaspoons of salt. With a mortar and pestle or an electric spice mill, grind the bay leaf, peppercorns, clove, allspice, thyme, coriander, and caraway into a powder. Add the cayenne and a little freshly grated nutmeg. Sprinkle 1 tablespoon of this spice mixture over the meat and refrigerate. (Refrigerate and save the rest of the spice mixture for adjusting the seasoning later.) This can be done a day ahead.

Soak the bread crumbs in the cream and refrigerate.

Sauté the onion in butter over medium heat until softened but not browned. Cool. Combine the cooked onion with the seasoned meat and grind through the medium holes of a meat grinder. Grind the chilled meat mixture a second time, through the smallest holes of the meat grinder. At this point the meat should be very finely ground, almost a purée. If it seems chunky, grind a third time, to ensure a smooth-textured sausage.

Put the meat mixture into the chilled bowl of an electric mixer. Add the chopped thyme, the soaked bread crumbs, and any remaining cream. Using the paddle attachment, beat the mixture at medium speed until it looks fluffy and mousselike, about 5 minutes. Bake or poach a small amount and taste for seasoning. This is the most critical step: the sausage should be juicy and highly seasoned; no herb or spice should dominate, but there should be an overall brightness. Adjust the seasonings for flavor and texture, adding salt, spice mixture, or cream as necessary.

Stuff the mixture into hog casings and twist into 5-inch links, taking care to avoid air pockets. Leave the links connected and tie the ends with butcher's twine. Prick each sausage link several times with a needle or skewer to prevent bursting.

Poach the sausages in a large kettle of barely simmering salted water, adding bay leaves, thyme, or other aromatics to the poaching liquid if desired. The sausages will be done in 7 to 10 minutes—check for doneness by cutting a sausage in half. Cool the sausages and separate into individual links. They may now be refrigerated until you are ready to serve them. They will keep for several days. To serve, heat the sausages in a cast-iron skillet in a little clarified butter or oil until nicely browned and warmed through, about 4 minutes per side.

ROAST SUCKLING PIG

Few things in the kitchen are more splendidly delicious than a young pig roasted on the spit. On market day in Tuscan villages, shoppers wait eagerly for a sandwich of salty, herby, crisp-skinned *porchetta*, served on a thick slice of country bread moistened with the cooking juices. Late at night, for a special event, we might offer a similar menu: crisp slices of suckling pig, grilled garlic toast, and bitter chicory salad.

You can cook a small pig in a conventional home oven, but with a little effort and ingenuity you can construct a workable outdoor spit from a few pieces of wood tied together to form tripods and a rod to hold the pig 18 or 20 inches above the coals. Or rent a motorized spit-roaster from a party supply company.

The ideal way to obtain a suckling pig is to befriend a small hog farmer, one who practices sustainable agriculture and takes good care of his stock. Otherwise, a good butcher or ethnic market may be able to procure a milk-fed pig for you. Ask for one whose dressed weight is 15 to 20 pounds, as fresh as possible, with head, tail, and feet left attached. Pick it up the day before you plan to cook it.

When you have your pig, make a paste of salt, pepper, garlic, and wild fennel seeds, flowers, and fronds, pounding everything together in a mortar. Moisten the paste with a little olive oil and massage it into the flesh inside the body cavity. Rub the outer skin with olive oil and more of the fennel paste. Make small slits in the legs, loins, and shoulders, and press some of the paste into the slits. Wrap up the pig and refrigerate overnight.

The next day, remove the pig from the refrigerator and begin to build a fire. Use oak, grape, almond, apple, or fig wood—or any combination. When the fire has burned down to low flames and you have a good bed of coals, start the pig on the spit. Insert an apple or potato into its mouth to allow the air inside to escape. Adjust the fire to obtain a slow, even browning of the skin, adding wood to keep a small flame going, especially at either end underneath the shoulders and hind legs. Be sure the bed of coals always extends slightly beyond the length of the pig.

Baste the pig from time to time with a mixture of olive oil, a little dry white wine, wild fennel, and salt. Do not use sweet wine—it will burn. Roasting will take about 4 hours. If the ears and tail begin to brown too much, cover them with pieces of foil. Test for doneness by piercing the leg and shoulder at the thickest part with a skewer. The juices will run clear when the pig is fully cooked. Remove the pig from the spit and allow it to rest at least 15 minutes before carving. It will serve about 15 to 20 guests, depending on the rest of the menu.

ROAST PORK LOIN WITH ROSEMARY AND FENNEL

Cooking over a bed of hardwood coals always adds flavor, especially to roasts. For those unable to roast over an open fire, here is a method that approximates the result. Overnight seasoning cures the meat lightly, and the fennel and herb branches perfume the meat as it roasts. Serve with roasted root vegetables.

Serves 4 to 6.

2½ pounds boneless pork loin
3 garlic cloves, peeled and sliced
Salt and pepper
1 tablespoon fennel seed
4 branches rosemary
4 branches sage
Optional: extra-virgin olive oil

ONE day in advance, lard the pork loin with garlic, making incisions into the underside of the roast with a small sharp knife and inserting the garlic slices. Season the roast generously with salt and pepper. Crush the fennel seeds coarsely in a mortar and sprinkle over the meat. Press the rosemary and sage branches into the meat, and, using butcher's twine, tie up the roast, using a simple slipknot finished with a half hitch every 3 inches. Refrigerate.

The following day, bring the pork loin to room temperature. Preheat the oven to 425°F. Roast the pork loin on a rack, uncovered, until the internal temperature registers 130°F on a meat thermometer, about 1 hour. Remove the roast from the oven, cover loosely with foil, and let rest in a warm place for at least 15 minutes. This allows the juices to stabilize and the roast to continue cooking slowly without drying out. The meat will be moist, with the barest tinge of pink. Slice the pork and arrange on a warm platter with the herb branches. If you wish, drizzle with fruity Tuscan olive oil.

LONG-COOKED PORK SHOULDER

The long cooking renders most of the fat from the roast, and leaves the meat meltingly tender on the inside while crispy on the outside, perfect for impromptu tacos or a warm pork sandwich. This might be served with fresh fava beans and greens in spring, or with polenta and braised fennel in the fall, or with a mixture of roasted root vegetables—turnips, carrots, parsnips, celery root—in the winter.

Serves 4 to 6.

1 pork shoulder roast, about 4 pounds
Salt and pepper
Red pepper flakes
Fresh sage leaves

HAVE your butcher trim the excess fat and tie the pork shoulder, leaving the bone in; it makes for a more flavorful roast.

The night before, season the meat generously with salt and pepper, red pepper flakes, and coarsely chopped sage to taste and refrigerate.

The next day, bring the pork to room temperature and roast in a heavy earthenware baking dish at 400°F. for about 2 hours and 20 minutes. Half an hour before the roast is done, baste it with the rendered fat. Allow to rest 20 minutes before carving. The meat will be very tender and will separate easily from the bones. If you prefer, you can roast the shoulder in advance and warm the sliced meat on the grill.

RED WINE–BRAISED BACON

We became enamored of braised bacon when Bruce Cost organized an amazing Chinese New Year's dinner a few years ago. Bruce's bacon is flavored with ginger, soy, garlic, and Asian spices. Our version is a delicious addition to traditional French stews like coq au vin or boeuf bourguignonne. We also like it as an element in winter salads with curly endive, beets, and egg, for example.

Serves 4 to 6.

2 bay leaves
½ yellow onion, sliced thick
½ pound smoked bacon, sliced ½ inch thick
2 cups Basic Chicken Stock (page 206)
2 cups red wine

Preheat the oven to 375°F.

Choose a shallow baking dish deep enough to accommodate the long bacon slices and cooking liquid. (A rectangular glass Pyrex dish works well.) Put the bay leaves and onion slices in the dish. Arrange the bacon slices on top and pour in enough of the broth and wine, in equal parts, to just cover the bacon. Cover tightly with aluminum foil and bake for 45 minutes to 1 hour, or until the bacon is tender when probed with a fork. Cool the bacon in its cooking liquor and refrigerate until you are ready to use it. Be sure to save the liquid to add to soups or sauces.

To serve, pat the bacon slices dry and brown them lightly over medium heat in a cast-iron skillet or nonstick pan. The bacon can now be cut into ½-inch lardons and added to a braise or salad.

Variation: For a richer flavor that goes well with roasted game birds, substitute a sweet white wine for the red and add some whole spices such as star anise, allspice, and juniper.

Simple Cured Pork Chops

To add flavor, season the pork chops the night before. This simple curing technique allows the salt to penetrate the meat, tenderizing and flavoring it. You will also find that the meat cooks more evenly. Cooking meat on the bone and with a bit of a fat cap makes it tastiest. The fat bastes the meat naturally, the bone helps distribute the heat, and both fat and bone add succulence and flavor as the meat cooks. Always allow grilled meats and roasts to rest about 10 minutes in a warm place before serving, even small cuts like these chops, so the juices redistribute and stabilize.

Serves 4.

4 center-cut pork loin chops, 1½ inches thick, bone in
Salt and pepper
Optional: allspice, bay leaf

Generously season the pork chops with salt and pepper. (For more flavor, add some pulverized allspice and crushed bay leaf to the salt and pepper.) Cover and refrigerate overnight. Half an hour before cooking, remove the chops from the refrigerator. Grill over medium-hot coals about 7 minutes per side. If neither weather nor space permits grilling, pan-frying is a fine alternative. Allow the pork chops to rest 10 minutes before serving. Pork chops are delicious with stewed lentils and grilled escarole.

BRINE-CURED PORK

The classic French way to cure pork is to brine it. Typically, brine for curing contains salt, sugar, herbs, and spices. It acts as a marinade and a cure at the same time, producing pork a bit like a mild ham. (The most delicious turkey I ever tasted was cured in brine in just the same way.) A pork loin or shoulder will need to sit in brine, completely submerged, for about 5 days; large chops will be ready in 2 or 3.

Serves 6 to 8.

1 cup salt
¾ cup sugar
2 bay leaves
A few peppercorns
1 clove
6 allspice berries
2 small dried chili peppers
3 garlic cloves, peeled
1 tablespoon dried thyme
3 pounds boneless pork loin or shoulder
Optional: chopped parsley and garlic

Put 2½ gallons cold water in a large nonreactive container that will hold the meat and brine. Stir in the salt and sugar. Slightly crush and add the bay, peppercorns, clove, allspice, and chili peppers. Add the garlic and thyme. Add the pork and put a plate on top to keep the meat submerged. Refrigerate for 5 days or more.

Remove the pork from the brine and pat dry. Roast pork loin for about 1 hour, grill over a medium fire, or slice into very thin chops and brown them in a cast-iron pan. They will cook very quickly, about 1 minute per side. Finish with a good fistful of chopped parsley and garlic if you wish. A brined shoulder is good boiled or braised, and is delicious to add to cooked beans.

HOME-CURED PANCETTA

Pancetta is the delicious salt-cured pork belly used in so many Italian dishes. Pancetta adds flavor to any number of things—warm asparagus salad, baked sea scallops, grilled quail, and many other dishes, including pasta. Some Italian pancetta is smoked, but we generally prefer the simpler salt-cured version. Commercially produced domestic pancetta varies in quality. Some Italian butcher shops still make their own, flavored with pepper, allspice, and bay. We've had good success making our own pancetta over the last several years, and the method works well at home. Ask your butcher for the thickest belly available, evenly streaked with lean and fat. The powdered dextrose counteracts the saltiness. It is used instead of table sugar because it tastes less sweet. Note that this procedure takes nearly two months.

> 2 ounces coarse, additive-free salt
> 1 ounce powdered dextrose
> 1 teaspoon curing salt (for cooked meats)
> 2½ pounds fresh pork belly

Mix together the salt, dextrose, and curing salt, and rub the mixture into the meat until all sides are well coated. It is important to use all of the salt mixture. Place the seasoned pork belly in a shallow glass pan just large enough to contain the meat. Cover the meat with a piece of parchment paper, place a weight on top, and refrigerate for 24 hours, during which time a brine will form.

After 24 hours, check the level of the brine. If it has not covered the pancetta, make an additional brine with 1½ ounces salt, ¾ ounce dextrose, and ¾ teaspoon curing salt dissolved in 2 cups water, and pour it over the pancetta to cover completely. Refrigerate, covered, for 15 days.

Remove the pancetta from the brine; rinse quickly under cold water and blot dry with paper towels. Lay the pancetta on a rack and refrigerate uncovered for 10 to 12 days, turning it once a day, until the surface is completely dry. Wrap the pancetta loosely in parchment paper or cheesecloth, to allow air circulation, and continue to refrigerate for another 45 days. The pancetta is now ready to use and may be sliced as needed.

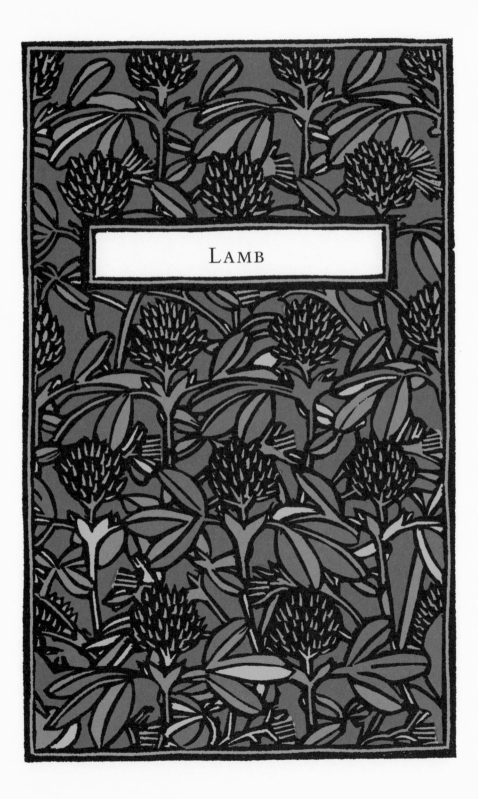

LAMB

ONE of the most cherished traditions at Chez Panisse is serving spring lambs from the Dal Porto Ranch. We have been getting lamb from the Dal Portos every year since we opened. Usually the first lambs are ready around mid- to late March, depending on the winter rains.

The Dal Porto Ranch is located in Amador County, in the foothills of the Sierra not far from the mother lode that was a magnet for gold seekers in 1849. Frank Dal Porto's grandparents moved here from Tuscany as part of the first wave of Europeans settling in the area. They saved their money while running a boarding house, and bought the land for the ranch in 1910. The landscape is one of rolling, grassy hills with clusters of oaks and a few pine trees and patches of wild lilacs and elderberries. Zinfandel grapes were planted here shortly after the gold rush, and today many wineries have located in the area. There are still areas of vineyards with hundred-year-old vines, and for a time grapes from the Dal Porto Ranch made our house red wine.

Frank Dal Porto says that they "rely on Mother Nature for everything." The sheep and young lambs graze on about 100 acres of pasture, where they fatten on the abundant grasses and herbs brought by the winter rains. By April, the grasses have started to mature and dry as the rains become infrequent and meager. Typically, the rain will not return until mid- to late autumn. The end of the rains determines how long we will have Dal Porto lamb, since the lambs destined for the table eat only what they can forage from the hills. Normally there are fat lambs until the end of May. Dry feed grown on the farm is used only to keep the breeding herd over the summer. No pesticides or chemical fertilizers are used on the pasture, and the lambs are never given drugs, so they are certainly certifiably organic.

The region surrounding the Bay Area is perfectly suited to raising sheep in an ecologically sound and sustainable way. The land affords plenty of feed and water for the lambs in winter and spring, and dry feed for later in the year. Besides Dal Porto lambs, we serve lambs from other Gold Country ranches in Amador and Nevada counties and from sheep farmers in the hilly, grassy areas of coastal Mendocino, Sonoma, and Marin counties, and the wine country of the Napa Valley.

In California, spring lambs are born in late fall and early winter, and reach marketable age in four months or so. In cold winter areas, spring lambs are usually born in February or March, and brought to market from the first of April through the summer. Early in the year, the dressed weight of a true spring lamb is about thirty to thirty-five pounds. Later in the season, we may see lambs weighing up to fifty or sixty pounds.

These lambs grow first on mothers' milk, and later on the abundant forage and grasses in late winter and early spring. Some of the later lambs may be finished on grain, as the flocks need supplemental feed in the dry summer and fall months.

True spring lamb is the best, but it is available for only a short time. The flavor is very mild, and the meat is juicier and more tender, and at the same time less fat, than the meat of lambs later in the year. The bones of spring lambs are pink, rather than the red of older lambs, and the spinal cord is very white, not yellow. Above all, spring lamb has a lovely fresh smell and no strong muttonlike aroma.

The lamb we get from the Dal Portos and our other suppliers comes to us as whole carcasses, which we break down into the cuts we cook. Usually the legs are boned and butterflied, so that they will cook evenly on the grill. The necks and shoulders are often braised, bone in, for better flavor, or boned and cut into chunks for lamb stew. Racks and saddles are cut into chops or roasts. All the trimmings and scraps go into the stock pot.

SPICY LAMB SAUSAGE

This is a versatile sausage similar to the North African merguez, which
the French have long admired. Serve it for lunch, surrounded by
Moroccan-spiced carrot, tomato, and eggplant salads; crumbled on a
sweet pepper pizza; or tucked into a crusty baguette. For dinner, add
steamed couscous, grilled vegetables, and a dab of harissa; or add these
sausages to a mixed grill. We like them long—about eight inches—and
skinny (lamb casings have a much smaller diameter than other sausage
casings) so that they curve around the plate. They also look wonderful
grilled in a large coil and served family-style, with each guest cutting
off a portion. Or omit the sausage casings, make patties, and grill them
like little burgers.

Makes about 15 sausages; serves 6.

2 ounces dried ancho chili peppers (about 3 chilies)
1½ teaspoons cumin seed
1½ teaspoons anise seed
1½ teaspoons caraway seed
4 or 5 garlic cloves, peeled
1 tablespoon salt
1 teaspoon freshly milled black pepper
1 tablespoon paprika
2 tablespoons olive oil
2½ pounds boneless lean lamb shoulder
Optional: ¾ pound pork fat
Lamb casings

TOAST the ancho chilies slowly in a very low oven, or leave them
overnight in a turned-off gas oven, warmed only by the pilot light. The
chili peppers must be brittle enough to grind to a powder, but not at all
burnt—burnt chilies have an unpleasant, bitter flavor. When they are
completely dry, break the stems off the chilies, and shake out and discard the seeds. Grind the flesh in a spice mill to yield about 3 tablespoons ancho chili powder.

In a dry skillet over medium heat, toast the cumin, anise, and caraway seeds for 3 or 4 minutes, until they are aromatic, lightly colored,
and beginning to pop. Grind coarsely in a spice mill or mortar and add
to the ancho chili powder. In a mortar, pound the garlic to a paste with

a little salt. Mix together the garlic, ground chilies and spices, black pepper, paprika, olive oil, and additional salt.

Cut the lamb shoulder and optional pork fat into 1-inch-thick pieces. Add the spice mixture to the meat and mix well. Cover and refrigerate overnight.

Grind the seasoned meat through the medium plate of a meat grinder, then run half the ground meat through the grinder a second time. Mix the meat well with your hands. To test for seasoning, make a small patty and fry it. Taste and adjust—for a spicier sausage, add cayenne pepper to taste.

Stuff the mixture into well-rinsed lamb casings and twist into long, slender links. Grill over hot coals for 2 or 3 minutes per side, until juicy and still slightly pink in the middle.

Variation: For a leaner sausage, omit the pork fat, but if you do, reduce the amount of seasoning slightly and take great care when grilling. The sausages must be cooked medium-rare or they will be dry.

LAMB BRAISED WITH TOMATOES AND GARLIC

We were all honored and excited when the Dalai Lama came for lunch in the Café—especially the Tibetan members of our staff. We didn't know what to serve him, and were a little surprised to learn he was not a strict vegetarian—the landscape in most of Tibet is not suitable for farming, and the traditional diet is meat-based. We had heard he was fond of spaghetti and meatballs, but we wanted to do something a bit more special, and finally settled on a provençal lamb stew, which we served with hand-cut noodles. We were happy when he cleaned his plate.

Serves 4 to 6.

4 pounds boneless lean lamb shoulder, cut in 1½-inch cubes
Salt and pepper
Olive oil
1½ cups dry white wine
2 onions, thinly sliced
2 leeks, thinly sliced
1 celery rib, chopped
1 carrot, peeled and chopped
3 ripe medium tomatoes, halved, plus 6 more, peeled,
    seeded, and chopped (about 3 cups)
A few thyme sprigs
2 bay leaves
6 cups Basic Chicken Stock (page 206)
3 small heads garlic, peeled (about 36 cloves),
    plus 2 medium cloves, peeled and finely chopped
1 pound Pasta Dough (page 30)
Butter
¼ cup chopped Italian parsley
2 teaspoons grated lemon zest

SEASON the lamb cubes generously with salt and pepper, and refriger-ate for several hours or overnight.

Preheat the oven to 475°F. Brown the lamb in a few tablespoons of olive oil in a wide, heavy-bottomed saucepan. Working in small batches, taking care not to crowd the pan, remove the browned lamb to a deep enamelware casserole or Dutch oven, draining off the oil.

Turn up the heat and add the white wine to the saucepan, scraping the bottom of the pan with a wooden spoon. Add these deglazed juices to the lamb.

Wipe out the pan and return it to a medium flame. In 3 tablespoons olive oil, slowly cook the onions, leeks, celery, and carrot, stirring occasionally, until softened. Add these to the lamb, along with the halved tomatoes, thyme, bay, and chicken stock. Bring to a boil, cover, and place the casserole in the oven. Reduce the heat to 350°F. and cook until the lamb is quite tender, about 2 hours.

When the lamb is done, carefully remove it from the broth with a slotted spoon. Strain the broth, discarding the vegetables, and let it settle for a few minutes. Skim any fat that rises to the surface and bring the broth back to a boil. Add the small whole garlic cloves, reduce the heat, and gently simmer for 20 minutes. Heat 2 tablespoons olive oil in a stainless steel pan and gently stew the chopped tomatoes for a few minutes. Season the tomatoes with salt and pepper. Add the tomatoes and the cooked lamb to the simmering broth. Cook for another 5 minutes. Taste the sauce and adjust the seasoning. The dish may be prepared up to this point several hours ahead, or the day before.

Roll out the pasta dough and make hand-cut noodles (see page 30). Cook the noodles in boiling, salted water. Put them in a warmed platter with a lump of butter. Spoon the lamb and sauce over the noodles. Mix together the parsley, the 2 medium cloves finely chopped garlic, and the lemon zest (these ingredients should be chopped at the last moment) and sprinkle the mixture over everything.

GRILLED BONELESS LAMB LEG WITH OLIVE SAUCE

In a family setting, nothing is more festive, or more French, than a roasted gigot, a whole leg of lamb, fragrant with garlic and herbs. A whole leg of lamb is, however, rather expensive, and a bit of a challenge to carve. A boneless roast, taken from the meatiest part of the leg, is more economical, more manageable, and takes less time to cook. What's more, the boneless meat is easier to grill. In the Café we butcher the leg into several small roasts, dividing the individual muscles along their natural seams. For the home cook, boning a leg of lamb may seem daunting, but can be learned with a little practice. A whole leg will yield four roasts of varying sizes, the bones and shank for broth, as well as meaty trim for sauce-making or sausage. At the butcher shop, ask for top round of lamb. (Double loin chops or boneless loin can be substituted.) The traditional French accompaniment of pale green flageolet beans—fresh or dried—is still our favorite. Other choices could be braised peppers and onions, wilted bitter greens and grilled polenta, or steamed baby turnips and green beans.

Serves 4 to 6.

3 pounds boneless leg of lamb, well trimmed
Salt and pepper
Olive oil
3 garlic cloves, sliced
Some thyme and rosemary sprigs
3 bay leaves, crumbled
1 pound lean lamb trimmings or meaty bones
1 small carrot, peeled and chopped
1 small celery rib, chopped
1 medium onion, chopped
½ cup white wine
2 quarts Basic Chicken Stock (page 206)
1 head garlic, separated into cloves, unpeeled
Bouquet garni: thyme, bay, and parsley
¼ cup rinsed, pitted, and roughly chopped oil-cured black olives
1 tablespoon capers, roughly chopped
3 or 4 salt-packed anchovy fillets, cleaned and chopped fine
Optional: lemon juice or vinegar

Season the lamb with salt and pepper, rub it with a good drizzle of olive oil, and press the garlic, thyme, rosemary, and bay into the flesh. Cover and refrigerate for several hours or overnight.

To make the sauce, heat 2 tablespoons of olive oil in a large heavy-bottomed saucepan over medium heat. Add the lamb trimmings and cook them slowly until well browned. Remove the browned lamb and cook the carrot, celery, and onion in the same pan, adding a little more olive oil if necessary. Cook the vegetables for about 10 minutes, stirring frequently with a wooden spoon to loosen the browned bits at the bottom of the pan. Return the browned lamb to the pan and add the white wine, stock, garlic cloves, and bouquet garni. Bring to a boil, then reduce to a bare simmer, skimming away the gray foam and fat that rises to the surface. Simmer, uncovered, for about 2 hours. Strain the sauce through a fine-mesh sieve into another saucepan and reduce over medium heat until 1½ to 2 cups remain.

Grill the lamb over medium-hot coals, turning frequently. Depending upon the size of the roast, cooking time will range from 15 to 25 minutes. The internal temperature should register between 125°F. and 128°F. for lamb that is quite rosy but not too rare. Let the meat rest at least 10 minutes, loosely covered, before carving. Slice across the grain. Just before serving, stir the olives, capers, and anchovies into the sauce. Taste and adjust the seasoning. (A few drops of lemon juice or vinegar may be a pleasant addition.) Spoon the warm olive sauce over the meat.

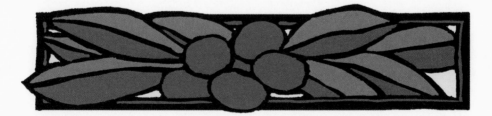

LAMB COUSCOUS WITH TURNIPS, CARROTS, AND HARISSA

Though not completely authentic, this lamb braise has a definite North African feel. We serve it with steamed couscous on the side, but for a family meal, serve a large platter of couscous with the stew in the center and the spicy harissa passed separately.

Serves 6 to 8.

One 8-pound lamb shoulder, bone in, well trimmed
Salt and pepper
2 teaspoons cumin seeds, toasted and ground
1 teaspoon caraway seeds, toasted and ground
¼ teaspoon turmeric
⅛ teaspoon cayenne
Olive oil
3 yellow onions, sliced
1 carrot, peeled and roughly chopped
2 celery stalks, roughly chopped
1 large ripe tomato, quartered
1 teaspoon whole cumin seeds
A pinch Spanish saffron (about 15 threads)
1 head garlic, halved crosswise
6 sprigs parsley
12 sprigs cilantro
1 cup white wine
2 quarts Basic Chicken Stock (page 206)
1 pound baby turnips, with tops
1 pound baby carrots, peeled
Optional: 4 cups cooked chickpeas

SEASON the lamb shoulder liberally with salt and freshly milled black pepper. Sprinkle on the ground cumin, caraway, turmeric, and cayenne, and rub into the flesh. Cover and refrigerate overnight.

The next day, bring the lamb to room temperature and preheat the oven to 475°F. Prepare the aromatics for the braise: warm a little olive oil in a deep, heavy-bottomed enamelware casserole or Dutch oven and sauté the onions, carrot, and celery until lightly colored, about 5 minutes. Add the tomato, whole cumin seeds, saffron, garlic, parsley, and cilantro, and cook a few minutes more.

Put the lamb shoulder on top of the aromatics. Add the wine, stock, and 1 quart water, and bring to a simmer. Put the casserole in the oven and lower the heat to 350°F. Braise the shoulder uncovered, turning it over in the broth every 20 minutes or so, until it is very tender, about 2½ hours. Draw off enough liquid to keep the top 2 inches of meat exposed, so it will brown at each turn. Add liquid occasionally as the juices concentrate.

While the lamb is cooking, bring a large pot of salted water to the boil. Cut the turnips in halves or quarters, leaving the tops attached (for larger turnips, peel and cut into wedges). Peel the carrots and halve lengthwise. Cook the turnips and carrots, in separate batches, until tender, about 5 minutes. Spread them on a baking sheet to cool at room temperature.

When the lamb is done, a paring knife will penetrate the meat easily. Remove it from the oven and let it rest in the broth for 30 minutes, adding any reserved cooking liquid. Remove the lamb to a platter and strain and degrease the broth. Discard the aromatics. Taste the broth and correct the seasoning. Tear the meat from the bones into rough 1 × 3-inch strips. Warm the meat in the broth, adding the turnips, carrots, and chickpeas (if using) 5 minutes before serving.

Serve with Buttered Couscous (page 168). At the table, pass a bowl of Harissa (page 169).

Variation: Add 2 cups of unpitted green olives, such as picholines, at the beginning of the braise. Remove and reserve the olives when you strain the broth. Return the olives to the dish when you add the carrots and turnips. Garnish with chopped preserved lemon.

BUTTERED COUSCOUS

Though couscous can be steamed over plain boiling water, it gains more flavor if a meat or vegetable stew or some other aromatic broth is bubbling beneath it. One of the many couscous lessons we have learned from Paula Wolfert, the author of the invaluable *Couscous and Other Good Food from Morocco*, is the importance of steaming it sufficiently. We now steam couscous three times, which makes it lighter, fluffier, and more digestible.

Serves 4 to 6.

3 cups couscous
Salt
1 tablespoon cumin seeds
1 tablespoon coriander seeds
1 tablespoon anise seeds
1 teaspoon turmeric
1 tablespoon coarsely chopped fresh ginger
A few cilantro sprigs
2 tablespoons melted butter

RINSE the couscous with cold water in a colander, then transfer to a large, wide bowl. With your fingers, crumble the couscous, separating the grains and breaking up the lumps. Season lightly with salt. Let the couscous swell for 10 minutes, and work the grains with your fingers again. Transfer the couscous to the top of a couscous cooker (essentially a steamer consisting of a large-holed sieve that sits over a large round pot; you can approximate one with a metal sieve or colander that fits tightly over a large pan).

While the couscous is swelling, bring 2 quarts of water to a boil in the bottom of the couscous cooker. Add the cumin, coriander, anise, turmeric, ginger, and cilantro. Reduce the heat to maintain a steady, brisk simmer.

Steam the couscous over the simmering broth, uncovered, for 20 minutes. Transfer the couscous from the steamer to a wide bowl and moisten with about ⅓ cup cold water. Fluff the grains with your fingers or a wooden spoon and let the couscous rest for 10 minutes at room temperature. Steam for another 20 minutes, then fluff, moisten, and allow to rest once more. Taste for salt and adjust if necessary. (These first two steamings may be completed several hours in advance.) Drizzle with melted butter and steam a third time, again for 20 minutes. The couscous should now be light, fluffy, and lump-free. Keep it warm in the steamer.

HARISSA

This is our version of the North African red pepper condiment. It is a delicious accompaniment to all kinds of dishes—stirred into a soup, with roast lamb, with sausages and grilled vegetables, or spread on a sandwich. It keeps several weeks in the refrigerator.

Makes about 1 cup

5 dried (about 2 ounces) ancho chili peppers
1 large sweet red pepper
4 garlic cloves, peeled
Salt
¾ cup olive oil
1 teaspoon red wine vinegar
Optional: cayenne pepper

TOAST the chilies on a hot griddle or in a hot oven until they are fragrant and puffed, taking care not to burn them. Remove and discard the stems and seeds. Put the chili peppers in a small bowl, cover them with boiling water, and let them soak for about 20 minutes.

Roast the red pepper over an open flame until the skin is thoroughly blackened and blistered, then set it aside, covered with a towel. After about 5 minutes, when the skin has loosened, peel the pepper and discard the skin, stem, and seeds.

In a food processor, blender, or mortar, grind the drained chili peppers, roasted pepper, garlic, salt, olive oil, and vinegar to a smooth, thick paste. (The sauce may be thinned with a little water or broth if you wish.) For a spicier sauce, add cayenne pepper to taste. Store the harissa in the refrigerator, covered with a little olive oil.

Variation: Add ½ teaspoon each of cumin, coriander, and caraway seeds, toasted and ground.

SOUPE AU PISTOU WITH LAMB SHANKS

This version of the classic provençal garlic- and basil-infused vegetable soup is quite substantial, more suitable for a main-course dish than the one we published in *Chez Panisse Vegetables*.

Serves 6 as a main course.

6 small lamb shanks
Salt and pepper
Olive oil
2 medium onions, sliced
1 large carrot, peeled and sliced
1 celery rib, sliced
14 garlic cloves, peeled and crushed
2 medium tomatoes, quartered
10 cups Basic Chicken Stock (page 206)
Bouquet garni: thyme, parsley, and bay

2 pounds fresh shell beans, shelled
1 pound romano beans, cut in ½-inch pieces
1 pound green beans, cut in ½-inch pieces
1 large bulb fennel, diced
2 carrots, diced
2 medium potatoes, diced
Extra-virgin olive oil
3 large onions, diced
2 small zucchini, diced
4 medium tomatoes, peeled, seeded, and chopped
2 tablespoons chopped parsley
2 teaspoons chopped thyme
Optional: 1 cup cooked pasta, such as orzo, mezzi tubetti,
    conchiglie, or orecchiette

2 tablespoons toasted pine nuts
3 garlic cloves
Salt
2 cups basil leaves
½ cup extra-virgin olive oil
Pepper

Season the lamb shanks generously with salt and pepper, and refrigerate for several hours or overnight. Heat 3 tablespoons olive oil in a large, deep skillet over medium heat and brown the shanks. In a large enamelware Dutch oven, heat 2 tablespoons olive oil over medium heat and lightly sauté the onions, carrot, celery, and garlic. Add the tomatoes, chicken stock, and bouquet garni. Season to taste and bring to a boil. Add the lamb shanks in a single layer, cover, and reduce to a gentle simmer. Cook on the stovetop or in a 350°F. oven for 2 hours, or until quite tender.

While the lamb is braising, bring about 2 quarts of salted water to the boil. Add the shell beans and cook until just tender, about 30 minutes. Remove the beans and let them cool at room temperature. In the same boiling water, replenishing as necessary, one vegetable at a time, parboil the romano beans, green beans, fennel, carrots, and potatoes until just done, and spread them out to cool.

When the shanks are done, remove them from the broth and set aside. Strain the broth, discarding the braising vegetables. Let the broth settle, and skim any fat from the surface. Measure the broth, and add chicken stock, vegetable cooking liquid, or water to bring the quantity to 10 cups. Return the shanks and broth to the Dutch oven. Set aside.

Heat 3 tablespoons extra-virgin olive oil in a large sauté pan over medium heat and sauté the diced onion until soft and translucent, about 5 minutes. Add the zucchini and continue cooking for 3 or 4 minutes. Add the parboiled romano beans, green beans, fennel, carrot, and potato, stirring well to coat with the oil. Add the tomatoes, shell beans, and chopped parsley and thyme. Season everything with salt and pepper, and cook for 2 minutes more.

Bring the broth and lamb shanks to a simmer. Stir in the sautéed vegetables and cook gently for a few minutes. Taste the broth, adjust the seasoning, and stir in the pasta if using. (The soup can be cooled to room temperature at this point, refrigerated, and reheated the next day.)

To make the pistou, pound the pine nuts and garlic with a pinch of salt in a mortar. Add a few basil leaves and continue to pound. Alternating basil and olive oil, continue pounding until a smooth paste is achieved. Stir in any remaining oil and season with salt and pepper. You will have about 1 cup of pistou.

To serve, heat the soup and ladle it into deep, wide soup plates, with a lamb shank in each. Swirl a heaping tablespoon of pistou into each serving.

Braised and Grilled Spring Lamb

There is a rural European tradition of eating milk-fed baby animals—
the milk lambs of Spain's La Mancha, for instance, and the suckling pigs
of Sardinia—roasted crisp in a wood-burning oven and served with
nothing more than a good green salad fragrant with olive oil, a few
roasted potatoes, rustic country bread, and local wine. Although some
may think this practice is cruel, the meat is extraordinarily lean, tender,
and succulent. Our spring lamb is slightly larger than true milk lamb,
but it has the same appeal, and each year we look forward to its brief
appearance. We grill the chops and legs (a little past medium-rare is best
for spring lamb), but braise the shoulders, warming them on the grill
after they are cooked to add smoky flavor and crisp the skin.

Serves 4.

1 spring lamb shoulder roast, bone in, about 3 pounds
Salt and pepper
3 medium tomatoes
1 medium onion, peeled
1 carrot, peeled
1 stalk celery
1½ cups Basic Chicken Stock (page 206)
½ cup white wine
5 garlic cloves, peeled
3 sprigs thyme or marjoram
5 peppercorns
1 small dried red chili pepper
8 spring lamb chops, about 1½ pounds

Season the shoulder roast with salt and pepper and refrigerate for
several hours or overnight.

Preheat the oven to 400°F. Coarsely chop the tomatoes, onion, carrot, and celery, and put them in an earthenware baking dish or roasting
pan just large enough to hold the meat. Add the chicken stock, white
wine, garlic, thyme, peppercorns, and chili pepper. Add the seasoned
lamb shoulder and roast for 1 hour, checking the level of liquid every
once in a while and adding more stock or water if it gets too low. Turn
the roast and cook for 30 minutes more. Turn again and roast for 20
more minutes, until golden and crisp. The meat should be soft and

tender, and almost falling off the bones. Carefully remove the meat and cool at room temperature. When the shoulder is cool, gently remove the bones and cut the meat into thick slices.

To make a simple sauce, pass the braising liquid and vegetables through the coarsest disk of a food mill. Allow the sauce to settle and thoroughly skim the fat. Taste for seasoning. Thin with a little stock, if necessary, or reduce over medium heat to thicken. You may roast the shoulder and prepare the sauce several hours before serving.

Season the chops with salt and pepper and grill over medium coals just past medium-rare, about 3 minutes per side. At the same time, grill the pieces of shoulder until warm and crisp. Arrange the meat on a platter, and spoon some of the warmed sauce over it. Serve with Garden Lettuce Salad (page 6) and Crispy Pan-Fried Potatoes (page 38).

WARM LAMB SALAD WITH
POMEGRANATES AND WALNUTS

Make this colorful main-course salad when new-crop pomegranates and walnuts coincide in the fall farmers' markets.

Serves 4.

  1 rack of lamb, about 2 pounds
  Salt and pepper
  4 garlic cloves, peeled
  2 tablespoons pomegranate molasses (Cortas brand;
      see Sources and Resources, page 245)
  2 tablespoons olive oil
  A pinch cayenne
  A few thyme branches
  1 shallot, diced fine
  1 tablespoon sherry vinegar
  1 tablespoon red wine vinegar
  2 tablespoons walnut oil
  2 tablespoons extra-virgin olive oil
  4 large handfuls curly endive, dandelion, or rocket, washed
  Optional: 4 kumquats, thinly sliced, or a little orange zest
  ½ cup walnuts, toasted
  ½ cup pomegranate seeds

TRIM the lamb rack of excess fat and season liberally with salt and pepper. Cut the garlic into fine slices and insert them into the flesh along the bone. Combine the pomegranate molasses, olive oil, and cayenne, and rub this mixture over the surface of the meat. Scatter the thyme branches over, then cover and refrigerate the roast for several hours or overnight. Bring the roast to room temperature before cooking.

Preheat the oven to 400°F. Roast the rack of lamb for about 30 minutes, or until the internal temperature is 125°F. Allow the roast to rest on a warm platter, lightly covered, for 10 minutes or so. If you prefer to grill the meat, do so carefully over medium coals, turning it frequently—the pomegranate molasses in the marinade will burn if the heat source is too close.

To make the vinaigrette, macerate the shallot in the sherry and red wine vinegars with a pinch of salt for 15 minutes. Whisk in the walnut oil and the extra-virgin olive oil. Taste and adjust the seasoning.

In a large bowl, sprinkle the greens lightly with salt and freshly milled pepper. Add the vinaigrette and the optional kumquat slices and toss gently. Pile the dressed greens in the center of a large platter. Slice the lamb rack into chops and surround the salad with them. Sprinkle the salad with the walnuts and pomegranate seeds, spoon some of the roasting juices over the meat, and serve.

LAMB INNARDS

The offal parts of the lamb are some of the most delicious and most economical. Because they are more perishable, and because the choice cuts can command a higher price, butchers often offer offal cheaply for quick sale. These lesser cuts rarely appear on the Café menu, because we purchase whole lambs in small quantities and each animal has only its own organs. The day the lambs arrive, only the adventurous staff, and not the customers, get to dine royally on "variety cuts." However, when our suppliers offer us lamb tongues in quantity, we always put them on the menu, usually sliced and served at room temperature as a first course.

Lamb tongues are no challenge to cook. Simply simmer them in a salty, highly seasoned court bouillon for about two hours, until they are tender and can be peeled easily. Cool them in their broth (they will keep for several days), then slice them thinly lengthwise and dress them with a good salsa verde. Or serve them warm with boiled carrots, potatoes, and leeks—and Dijon mustard, or horseradish—as a simple pot-au-feu. You will need one tongue per person.

Lamb hearts are best grilled. Trim them well of exterior fat, and cut them into 2-inch slices about ¼ inch thick, discarding any tough membranes and veins. Thread the slices loosely on skewers and marinate with olive oil, garlic, and herbs. Grill medium-rare over hot coals, about 2 minutes per side. Lamb livers can be prepared in the same manner. Both are good with a spoonful of Harissa (page 169) or garnished with freshly milled pepper, chopped shallots, parsley, and a drizzle of extra-virgin olive oil. For a mixed grill, add Spicy Lamb Sausage (page 160).

Kidneys are also good grilled, but gain more flavor when sautéed quickly in olive oil and finished with garlic, parsley, rosemary, and lemon juice. For an offal experience that rivals the best sweetbreads, try the testicles, euphemistically sold as "lamb fry" in most butcher shops. Richard Olney gives his peerless advice on the matter in *Simple French Food*.

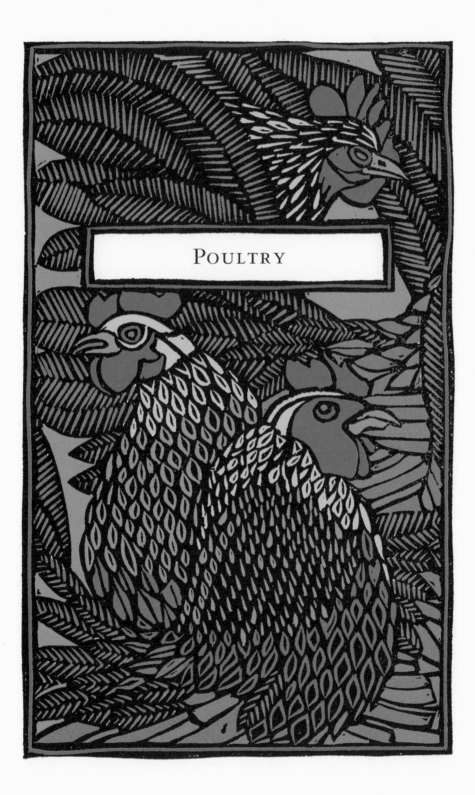

POULTRY

In the earliest days of Chez Panisse, when we were experimenting and cooking out of the classic cookbooks of French cuisine, we quickly learned that there weren't any commercially available chickens in California that inspired anything like the rapturous descriptions that the legendary chickens of Bresse regularly receive in French culinary literature. I got a clue why a few years later, when friends of mine in France invited me to come along on the trial run of a gastronomic tour they were going to guide. The tour included a visit to a poultry farm outside Bresse, in rural Burgundy, in the springtime, and I will never forget those white chickens with their red combs in the green field. I concluded that the Bresse chickens were so wonderfully good to eat because of the quality of their feed and the care with which they were raised, undoubtedly, but perhaps also because of the uncanny beauty of that scene.

We are still looking for extraordinary chickens. Our goal has always been to serve only healthy animals raised under humane conditions and fed organic grain. And, of course, they have to taste good, too. Our ideal chicken—like the *poulet de Bresse* and many another bird from rural France or Italy—is full of flavor and tender, but with a satisfyingly firm texture: completely different from ninety-nine percent of the chickens available in this country.

Most chickens today are grown on large factory farms, where tens of thousands of birds may share space in one building. A typical operation allots one square foot per chicken, and the birds must walk on wire mesh, never allowed to touch the ground. The growers maintain a specific lighting schedule so that these birds eat constantly. They reach a dressed weight of three and a half to four pounds in only five to seven weeks. Because so many animals are crowded into a small space, the chickens are routinely given antibiotics in their feed to prevent infections from wiping out the flock. This nonspecific use of antibiotics has encouraged the development of antibiotic-resistant strains of salmonella and other bacteria. But worst of all, these chickens, trucked from one part of the country to another just don't taste good.

The chickens we seek are those raised nearby in small flocks. They are allowed to forage outdoors during the day, where they feast on grasses and weeds, worms, grubs, and other insects. They have shelter at night from predators. They are fed organic feed—corn and soybeans. And they taste good, a fact confirmed by scientists who have discovered a chemical in free-range chickens that is associated with increased flavor.

One grower we have come to depend on for our chickens is Bud Hoffman. Bud tends his flock in the Central Valley of California, just over the coastal mountains from the Bay Area. The 700 or so chickens Bud sells each week are fed an organic formula that he developed himself. It includes corn and soybeans, as well as vegetable matter. He feeds no animal fat or bone meal, as other producers do. The chickens take about eight to ten weeks to reach the four-and-a-half-pound range we like. During this time they get no antibiotics or hormones.

The chickens roost in their pens at night, but during the day they forage for fresh greens and insects in a two-acre field. Here they also ingest the grit and small stones which help them digest their food. Bud sells his chickens to a few other restaurants in the Bay Area, and to his faithful customers at the Ferry Plaza Farmers' Market in San Francisco, who tell him that no other chickens are as good. We agree.

Start with a whole bird. Few dishes are better than a whole roast chicken. Or a whole bird can be cut up into enough parts for several meals, and the scraps and bones can go into the stockpot. Chicken stock is easy to make from the bones and scraps of a really good bird.

Chicken breasts can be cooked quickly on the grill or pan-fried with bread crumbs. The legs are better slow-cooked with moist heat, so we often braise them. Use them in coq au vin or in a ballotine stuffed with greens or mushrooms.

Bud Hoffman also raises poussin and guinea fowl for us. Poussin are very young chickens, weighing slightly more than a pound. They are good split and grilled "under a brick" (we use a heavy cast-iron skillet). They come out crisp and juicy.

Guinea fowl have a deliciously gamy flavor, more intense than that of chicken. They are usually smaller and leaner than chickens, weighing in at around two and three quarters to three pounds dressed, and require special treatment. The breasts can be grilled or pan roasted like chicken, but because the legs are tough and dry, even when braised, they are best made into confit. One of the best dishes we have ever served in the Café is ravioli stuffed with guinea fowl confit, with tiny sweet green peas and a little olive oil and parsley.

Guinea fowl are native to the west coast of Africa, and have never been completely domesticated. Rather difficult to raise, they love to roam in the fields and forage for their meals, so growers keep them in very large enclosures. Guinea fowl are not quiet neighbors. They emit a high-pitched, harsh cry—sounding to some like "Buckwheat, buckwheat!"—whenever they are startled, which seems to be often.

Most of the ducks we use are from Jim Reichardt's Liberty Farm near Santa Rosa, about an hour's drive north of San Francisco. Jim's family has been raising ducks in the Bay Area since his great-grandfather started farming in San Francisco nearly a century ago. Jim grew up on the family farm, which has evolved into a big operation that supplies most of San Francisco's Chinatown with ducks. Eventually he set out on his own, wanting to raise ducks the old-fashioned way.

The Liberty ducks we buy from Jim spend much of their time outdoors, with access to green pasture and the water that collects in ponds and puddles on the farm. They are fed a mixture of grains, primarily corn. These Peking ducks, from the same breeding stock as "Long Island" ducklings, are a pound or so heavier than those generally available, weighing around five to five and a half pounds. Ducks of this size have meatier breasts and legs, and a lower percentage of fat. The fat that we do trim from the meat and the carcasses is rendered for making confit, or used for frying potatoes, braising cabbage, and flavoring beans for cassoulet.

Cured Duck Breast "Prosciutto"

Easier and quicker to make than real prosciutto, this cured duck breast can be used thinly sliced in all kinds of salads and antipasti. It has the appeal and versatility of prosciutto, but with a deep duck flavor.

Each single breast serves 3 to 5 as an appetizer.

2 large whole boneless duck breasts, skin on
2½ tablespoons salt
2 teaspoons dried thyme
1 bay leaf, crumbled
1 teaspoon freshly ground black pepper

LAY the duck breasts skin side down on a cutting board. Pull off the tiny tenderloins and save them for another purpose. With a sharp knife divide each heart-shaped breast into 2 pieces along the natural division in the center. Trim any extra skin protruding from the edges.

Combine the salt, thyme, bay, and black pepper in a small bowl. Evenly sprinkle both sides of each of the 4 half-breasts with the mixture. Arrange the breasts in a single layer on a platter, cover, and refrigerate for 48 hours, turning them 2 or 3 times over the course of the 2 days.

Drain any accumulated juices and pat the breasts dry. Wrap each piece in cheesecloth and tie a knot on each end with butcher's twine, leaving a 12-inch length of twine on each end from which to hang them.

Hang the breasts for 10 days in a dry, cool place (we use the wine cellar), making sure they hang free and are not touching each other. Now turn them and hang them from the other end for another 8 to 10 days or until they are quite firm to the touch. Remove the cheesecloth, wrap the breasts in parchment paper or plastic film, and refrigerate for up to two weeks.

To serve, slice as thinly as possible on the diagonal with a very sharp knife.

SHAVED FOIE GRAS AND ROCKET SALAD

Fall is a time when we make delicious composed salads with bits of duck and gizzard confit, pigeon liver toasts, little grilled quails, or duck skin cracklings paired with new-crop nuts and autumn fruits. This is the luxurious extreme of such salads. A fresh duck foie gras is expensive, but a little goes a long way. The recipe makes enough cured foie gras for several meals.

Serves 6.

1 fresh duck foie gras, about 1 pound
Salt
⅓ cup hazelnuts
1 clove garlic
1½ teaspoons sherry vinegar
1½ tablespoons red wine vinegar
Pepper
6 tablespoons extra-virgin olive oil
6 large handfuls rocket

Prepare the foie gras several days in advance. Let it soften at room temperature for about an hour. When it is pliable, pull the two lobes apart, grasp the veins and gently pull to remove them. Don't worry about disfiguring the foie gras; it will be pressed later. When all the veins have been removed, lightly season the two lobes with salt and re-shape them into their original form. Cut a 2-foot length of cheese-cloth, place the foie gras at one end, and roll up the foie gras in the cloth. After 2½ turns, trim off any remaining cheesecloth and tie the ends firmly, making a tight sausage shape. In an earthenware or glass vessel that is 4 inches taller than the rolled foie gras and at least 2 inches wider, make a 1½-inch layer of salt. Add the foie gras and cover completely with a layer of salt at least 1 inch deep. Place a weight on top (a full wine bottle works well), and refrigerate for 3 to 4 days.

In a preheated 400°F. oven, toast the hazelnuts for about 15 minutes or until golden and aromatic. Meanwhile, make the vinaigrette. In a mortar, mash the garlic to a paste with a little salt. Add the sherry vinegar, red wine vinegar, ½ teaspoon salt, and freshly milled pepper. Whisk in the olive oil, taste for acid and salt, and adjust. While the nuts are still warm, rub them in a clean kitchen towel to remove their skins. Chop the nuts coarsely. Wash and dry the rocket.

Retrieve the foie gras from the salt and remove the cheesecloth. Wrap the foie gras in plastic and keep it very cold while preparing the salad, either in a bowl of ice in the refrigerator, or, briefly, in the freezer. Dress the rocket lightly with the vinaigrette, divide among 6 chilled plates, and sprinkle with the hazelnuts. Use a sharp vegetable peeler to make shavings of the cured foie gras over each salad. Be generous. Finish with a flourish of the pepper mill. The foie gras left over will keep a week in the refrigerator, well wrapped.

Variation: Serve the cured foie gras with a salad of thinly sliced sweet garden fennel, raw cèpes, and tender parsley leaves. Instead of shaving the foie gras, cut it into ¼-inch-thick slices, and drizzle the salad with a little aged balsamic *condimento* and fruity extra-virgin olive oil.

PIGEON SALAD WITH WHITE BEAN TOASTS

Enhanced by a little smoke from the grill, pigeon is so rich and succulent that it needs nothing more to accompany it than a simple salad with a shallot vinaigrette. Fresh, farm-raised pigeons are available in some Asian poultry shops and at some farmers' markets. If you can procure extra pigeon livers—the most flavorful liver we know—thread them on rosemary skewers, grill them, and chop them coarsely to make liver toasts. Pigeon bones make a delicious stock.

Serves 4 as a first course or a light lunch.

2 whole fresh squabs
Salt and pepper
2 tablespoons vin santo or grappa
1 small shallot, diced fine
2 tablespoons balsamic vinegar
1 teaspoon red wine vinegar
Extra-virgin olive oil
4 slices levain bread, ½ inch thick
1 garlic clove, peeled
1 cup white bean purée (see Creamy White Beans, page 36)
2 handfuls mâche, watercress, or rocket, washed

R INSE the birds under cold water and pat thoroughly dry, inside and out. Cut each squab in half from the breastbone down, removing the entire backbone. Flatten each side by pressing down with the palm of your hand. Season liberally with salt and pepper, and sprinkle with vin santo or grappa; cover and refrigerate for a day or two, turning occasionally.

Bring the pigeon to room temperature an hour or so before grilling and prepare a wood or charcoal fire. To make the vinaigrette, macerate the shallot for 15 to 20 minutes with the balsamic and red wine vinegars and a little salt. Whisk in ½ cup olive oil and a little freshly milled pepper. (Taste for salt and acidity.)

Rub the pigeon lightly with olive oil and grill over medium coals, skin side down, for about 8 minutes. Turn and cook for another 5 minutes, until the breast meat is medium rare. Detach the legs and return them to the grill to cook a bit more while the breasts rest. Brush the levain bread with a little olive oil and toast over coals until golden. Rub the toasts lightly with the peeled garlic clove. Warm the white bean purée.

With a sharp boning knife, remove the breast meat from the bone and slice on the diagonal. Save the bones to add to a sauce or stock.

Spread the toasts thickly with white bean purée and cut into triangles or finger shapes. Pour any juices from the pigeon into the vinaigrette, salt and pepper the greens, and dress lightly with the vinaigrette. Divide the dressed greens among four large plates. Arrange the breast meat over the greens, and top each salad with a leg, warm from the grill. Spoon a little more vinaigrette over the meat, and garnish with the white bean toasts.

Variation: Omit the bean toasts, add some mashed ripe fig to the dressing, and garnish the salads with fig slices; or serve the pigeon with fresh warm cranberry beans and slivered fennel bulb, and add a little pounded black truffle to the vinaigrette.

WARM DUCK BREAST SALAD
WITH GREEN OLIVE RELISH

Grilling a duck breast is no more challenging than cooking a steak. Look for large Peking or Muscovy breasts for this dish. The Peking duck breasts we get from Liberty Farm are quite large; one double breast is enough for three people. For a simple midday meal, garlic-rubbed toasts are the only accompaniment needed.

Serves 4 to 6.

2 large whole boneless duck breasts, skin on
Salt and pepper
1 large shallot, finely diced
1 tablespoon Champagne vinegar
¾ cup green olives (picholines or Lucques)
½ teaspoon finely chopped lemon zest
½ teaspoon chopped thyme
1 tablespoon chopped parsley
Extra-virgin olive oil
1 clove garlic
1 tablespoon red wine vinegar
1 tablespoon balsamic vinegar
6 small handfuls mixed young greens
     (rocket, cress, spinach, and mustard)

LAY the duck breasts skin side down on a cutting board. Pull off the tenderloins and save for another purpose. With a sharp knife divide each heart-shaped breast into 2 pieces along the natural division in the center. Trim any extra skin protruding from the edges, then turn the breasts skin side up. Score the skin, making ⅛-inch-deep slices in long diagonal lines, first in one direction and then at an opposing 45-degree angle, to create a checkerboard crosshatch. This helps the fat to render and the skin to brown nicely on the grill. Generously season the breasts on both sides with salt and freshly milled pepper. Cover and refrigerate for several hours or overnight.

To make the olive relish, macerate the diced shallot in the Champagne vinegar with a pinch of salt and freshly milled pepper. Rinse the olives, pit them, and chop medium-fine. In a small bowl, combine the chopped olives, lemon zest, thyme, and parsley with ¼ cup olive oil. Add the macerated shallot to the olives no more than 15 minutes before serving.

Make a vinaigrette by pounding the garlic to a paste with a little salt. Add the red wine and balsamic vinegars, black pepper to taste, and 6 tablespoons olive oil. Taste and correct for salt and acid.

Wash and dry the greens.

Prepare a wood or charcoal fire and let the coals burn down to medium heat—the duck breasts must cook slowly to render the fat. Fit the grill over the coals at a slant, and put a shallow pan at the lower end of the grill to catch the fat as it drips away from the fire. Put the breasts skin side down on the grill and let them cook for about 10 minutes. You will need to stand guard to watch for flare-ups. If the coals are too hot, or too much fat is dripping in one place, the coals will flame and the dish will be ruined; on the other hand, if the fire is not hot enough, the skin will not brown properly. If flaming does occur, remove the breasts immediately, douse the flames with a few drops of water, and return the duck to the grill. When the skin is nicely browned, turn the breasts and cook for 3 or 4 minutes more. The breasts should now be medium rare. Remove them from the grill and let them rest on a platter, covered loosely, for at least 10 minutes before slicing.

While the duck is resting, finish the olive relish, taste for acidity, and adjust the seasoning as necessary. Dress the greens with the vinaigrette in a stainless steel bowl. Slice the duck breast in thin diagonal slices, pouring any juices from the carving board into the bowl with the greens. Warm the bowl on the grill (or over a gas flame), tossing the greens until barely wilted. Divide the dressed greens among warmed plates and arrange the sliced duck breast over them. Spoon a little olive relish over each salad and serve.

DUCK CONFIT WITH BAKED FIGS

Traditional French farmhouse methods of preserving duck, geese, and even sausages and joints of pork, result in delicious, flavorful products that modern preserving methods cannot begin to match. We try to follow the old-fashioned French housewife's example and always keep a supply of duck confit on hand. Duck confit makes an easy meal year-round, and not just when figs are in season. It is a tasty addition to salads (try it with a warm salad of green beans and chanterelle mushrooms, seasoned with chopped toasted hazelnuts and pumpkinseed oil), or it can be used for making duck rillettes (see page 190). The leftover duck fat is useful for frying potatoes, or for flavoring bean dishes. The confit process takes two days, but once prepared, the duck will keep for two or three weeks, ready for an impromptu dinner.

Serves 6 to 8.

8 duck legs (drumsticks and thighs, attached)
6 tablespoons salt
6 bay leaves, crumbled
4 juniper berries, crushed
1 tablespoon dried thyme
1 teaspoon cracked black pepper
3 quarts rendered duck fat or homemade lard
16 ripe figs
A few thyme branches
Optional: a few drops balsamic vinegar

TRIM the duck legs of excess fat, but leave the skin intact. Make a small incision at the base of each leg, severing the tendon and cutting through the skin all around the bone. Combine the salt, bay, juniper, thyme, and pepper, and season each leg generously with the mixture. Cover and refrigerate overnight.

The next day, melt the duck fat over medium heat in a large, wide, heavy-bottomed pot. Gently slip the duck legs into the fat (they must be completely submerged) and raise the heat slightly. Stir with a wooden spoon as the fat comes up to temperature. Adjust the flame to maintain the barest simmer—the fat should never boil, but should swirl lightly, sending up the occasional small bubble.

Cook the duck legs, uncovered, for about 1½ hours. Test a leg for doneness by inserting a skewer into the thickest part of the drumstick; there should be little resistance. Carefully transfer the duck legs to a glazed earthenware or glass dish. Ladle the duck fat over the legs, making certain they are covered by an inch of fat. Cool the legs in the fat, then cover and refrigerate for up to 3 weeks.

Preheat the oven to 400°F. Cut the figs in half and arrange them side by side in a shallow baking dish. Tuck a few thyme branches here and there. Drizzle with a very little good balsamic vinegar—omit this step if the figs are truly ripe and sweet—and bake, uncovered, for 30 minutes. Cool to room temperature.

Meanwhile, bring the duck legs to room temperature and remove them from the fat, allowing a little fat to cling to each leg. Reserve the remaining fat for other cooking purposes, or save it for the next batch of confit—it will keep several months, refrigerated. Heat 2 cast-iron skillets. Add the duck legs in one layer, skin side down, and cook over medium heat until crisp and brown, about 5 minutes. Turn the legs and cook for an additional 4 to 5 minutes. Blot on absorbent kitchen paper.

Serve the crisp, warm duck legs with the baked figs and their juices, a simple rocket salad, and Crispy Pan-Fried Potatoes (page 38).

DUCK RILLETTES CROÛTONS
WITH CHICORY SALAD

Although common in France, rillettes—the savory spreads made from pork, duck, rabbit, or salmon—are relatively unavailable here. The French can buy them in any neighborhood charcuterie, but most Americans must make them at home, a not unpleasant chore. If you have duck confit on hand, it's a simple matter to make rillettes for a quick and lovely appetizer or first course. Rillettes make a great sandwich on a crusty baguette, and they are delicious spread on croûtons for garnishing salads, as in this recipe.

Serves 6 to 8 as a first course.

4 legs of Duck Confit (page 188)
¼ cup duck fat
2 garlic cloves
Salt
2 teaspoons chopped thyme or savory
Pepper
½ cup walnuts (preferably new-crop nuts)
3 tablespoons walnut oil
3 tablespoons extra-virgin olive oil
1 shallot, diced fine
2 tablespoons sherry vinegar
2 ripe pears
4 slices rustic bread
6 handfuls mixed chicories (radicchio,
    curly endive, escarole), washed

REMOVE and discard the skin from the duck legs and tear the meat into shreds. There should be about 2½ cups meat. In a sauté pan, warm the meat in the duck fat over medium heat for a few minutes, but do not let it brown. When the meat has softened, transfer the contents of the pan to a mixing bowl. Pound the garlic to a paste in a mortar with a little salt. Add the garlic, thyme, and a generous amount of freshly milled pepper to the meat. Work the meat into a rough paste with a wooden spoon or a potato masher. You may use an electric mixer or food processor instead, but take great care not to overwork the mixture, or it will get stringy. Taste and correct the seasoning. Wrap tightly and refrigerate overnight—the flavors will meld, and the texture will become more like a pâté. Rillettes will keep up to a week in the refrigerator. Remove the duck rillettes from the refrigerator an hour before serving.

To make the chicory salad, toast the walnuts for 10 minutes or so in a 350°F. oven. While they are still warm, season them with a few drops of olive oil or walnut oil and a little salt. (If the walnuts are new, just use them straight from the shell without toasting or seasoning.)

In a small bowl, macerate the shallot in the sherry vinegar with a pinch of salt. Whisk in the walnut oil, olive oil, and some freshly milled pepper. Peel, core, and slice the pears.

Toast the bread and spread it thickly with the duck rillettes. Cut each slice into triangles. Put the sliced pears into a salad bowl and dress with half the vinaigrette. Add the chicories and a little salt and pepper and toss carefully. Taste and correct the seasoning, adding more vinaigrette (or a few drops more vinegar) if necessary—chicories can take a bit more vinaigrette than tender young lettuces can.

Divide the chicories among 6 or 8 plates, lifting the pear slices to the surface of the salad. Scatter some walnut pieces over each salad and garnish each plate with 2 or 3 duck rillettes croûtons.

DUCK LEGS BRAISED IN ZINFANDEL

Each autumn for our annual Zinfandel Festival, we offer a week's worth of wine-inspired menus that feature deep-flavored, long-simmered stews like this one. For a classic bistro meal, start with leeks vinaigrette, serve a good potato gratin with the duck, and finish with the Apple and Brandied Currant Tart on page 232.

Serves 4 to 6.

6 duck legs (drumsticks and thighs, attached)
Salt and pepper
1 tablespoon rendered duck fat or olive oil
1 medium yellow onion, cut into ½-inch dice
2 medium carrots, peeled and cut into ½-inch dice
1 bay leaf
2 thyme branches
2 garlic cloves, sliced
Zest of ½ small orange
1 cup zinfandel or good-quality dry red wine
1½ cups hot Basic Chicken Stock (page 206)
Optional: ½ teaspoon potato starch

TRIM the duck legs of excess fat and season with salt and pepper. Cover and refrigerate for several hours or overnight.

Preheat the oven to 450°F. Put 1 tablespoon of duck fat in a cast-iron skillet over medium heat. Add the diced onion and carrots and sauté for 5 minutes, until lightly browned. Spread the cooked vegetables in the bottom of a deep earthenware baking dish and add the bay, thyme, garlic, orange zest, and red wine. Arrange the duck legs on top in one layer, skin side down. Add hot chicken stock to nearly cover them.

Seal tightly with foil and bake for 15 to 20 minutes, until the stock begins to simmer gently. Turn the oven down to 350°F. and continue to cook, covered, 45 minutes longer. Remove the foil, turn the legs skin side up, and cook uncovered for 15 minutes, until the skin is crisp and golden. To check the meat for doneness, probe with a small knife. If it offers no resistance and separates easily from the bone, it is done. Carefully remove the legs from the baking dish. Pour the braising juices and vegetables into a saucepan and skim off the fat. Over medium heat reduce the sauce to taste, thickening it slightly, if you wish, with ½ teaspoon potato starch dissolved in 1 tablespoon water. Just before serving, reheat the duck legs in the sauce for 5 to 6 minutes.

Variation: For a simple coq au vin, substitute chicken legs, and garnish the finished dish with glazed pearl onions, stewed chanterelles, and Red Wine–Braised Bacon (page 153). During the warmer months, braise the duck legs in white wine, substitute lemon zest for orange, and add whole Lucques green olives to the onion-carrot mixture. Serve with hand-cut noodles or roasted potatoes and wilted greens.

POLENTA WITH DUCK SAUCE

This comforting, all-purpose sauce, or *sugo*, makes a satisfying, easy lunch or a hearty first course. The ingredients and quantities can be altered to taste—depending on what is available at the market, you might make the sauce with duck, pigeon, guinea fowl, or from leftover Duck Legs Braised in Zinfandel (page 192). We like it with soft polenta, but it is equally good over pasta.

Makes about 6 cups; serves 4 to 6.

1 tablespoon olive oil
8 ounces pancetta, diced
4 duck legs, boned and coarsely chopped (to yield about
    2 cups duck meat)
2 carrots, peeled and diced
2 yellow onions, diced
1 bulb fennel or 2 celery ribs, diced
8 ounces chanterelles or cèpes (or cultivated mushrooms)
Salt and pepper
1 cup Simple Tomato Sauce (page 81)
3 cups dry red wine
1 cup Basic Chicken Stock (page 206)
4 to 6 garlic cloves, finely chopped
½ teaspoon red pepper flakes
2 tablespoons grappa or brandy

2 quarts stock or water
2 cups coarse yellow cornmeal
4 tablespoons (½ stick) butter
Optional: Parmigiano-Reggiano cheese for grating

İn a heavy-bottomed 4-quart saucepan, heat the olive oil over medium heat. Add the pancetta and duck meat, and let them sizzle for a minute or two. Add the carrots, onions, fennel, and mushrooms to the meat, and stir thoroughly. Continue to cook, stirring occasionally, until the vegetables and meat are lightly browned. Season with a little salt and pepper.

Add the tomato sauce, red wine, chicken stock, garlic, pepper flakes, and grappa, and bring to a boil. Reduce the heat and simmer very gently for 1½ hours, or until the liquid has reduced by about half. Skim off the surface fat. If the sauce is too thick, thin with a little water or chicken stock. Taste for salt and hot pepper, and correct the seasoning, if necessary. (The sauce may be cooled and refrigerated for up to 3 days. The flavor improves overnight.)

About 45 minutes before serving, salt the stock and bring to the boil. Add the cornmeal in a fine stream, whisking continuously. When the polenta begins to thicken, turn the heat to low, and cook, uncovered, stirring every few minutes, adding a little water if the polenta becomes too thick. It should be fully cooked after 40 minutes or so. Stir in the butter and season with salt and pepper. If you wish, stir in some grated Parmesan cheese.

Meanwhile, reheat the duck sauce.

To serve, pour the polenta into a deep platter and spoon the hot duck sauce over it, or serve on individual warmed plates.

Variation: Build lasagna-like polenta cakes, or *tortas*, in individual ramekins. Fill each ramekin with layers of warm polenta and duck sauce topped with Parmesan and Taleggio cheese, and bake them in a hot oven until brown and bubbling. If prepared a day in advance, the tortas can be unmolded and reheated.

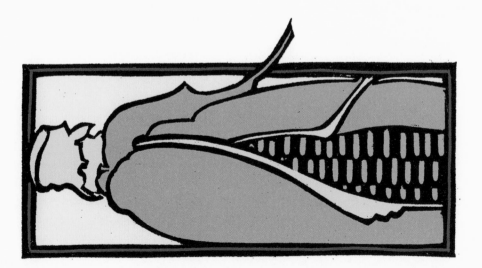

GRILLED QUAIL WITH BREAD CRUMB SALSA

Grilling little birds brings Tuscany to mind, especially if the birds are served with polenta, braised fennel, and Creamy White Beans (page 36). To brown their skins completely, quail must be roasted over a good hot fire. They are better almost overcooked than cooked too rare.

Serves 4 to 6.

8 quail
4 slices prosciutto di Parma
40 sage leaves
4 garlic cloves, peeled and sliced thin
¼ cup extra-virgin olive oil
Salt and pepper
2 cups Bread Crumb Salsa (page 197)

RINSE the quail and pat dry. Trim the wing tips and any excess skin. Tear the prosciutto into pieces and stuff them into the cavities of the birds. Put 2 or 3 sage leaves in each cavity as well. Put the quail in a shallow dish in a single layer. Add the remaining sage leaves, the sliced garlic, and olive oil. Turn each bird to coat thoroughly with the marinade. Cover and refrigerate for several hours or overnight.

Bring the quail to room temperature an hour before cooking. Remove from the marinade, wipe off the excess oil and garlic, and season liberally with salt and pepper. Prepare a charcoal or wood fire. Grill over medium-hot coals for 8 to 10 minutes, turning frequently, so the birds brown evenly. The quail are done when the breasts feel firm and clear juices run from the thighs when gently pierced with a skewer. Arrange them on a platter and spoon some Bread Crumb Salsa over each bird.

BREAD CRUMB SALSA

A variation on salsa verde, the Italian herb sauce, this version gains texture from coarse toasted bread crumbs. Abundant parsley is the other essential element. Thyme or sage works well with most grilled meats and fowl, but other herbs may be substituted—chives, chervil, and basil are all good with fish. To maintain texture and color, finish mixing the sauce at the last minute.

Makes about 2 cups.

2 shallots, diced fine
3 tablespoons red wine vinegar
Salt
1 cup chopped parsley
2 tablespoons chopped thyme or sage
2 tablespoons capers, rinsed and chopped
1 cup coarse toasted bread crumbs (see page 205)
Optional: 2 salt-packed anchovies, cleaned and chopped
1 cup extra-virgin olive oil
Pepper

MACERATE the shallots in the red wine vinegar with a pinch of salt for at least 15 minutes.

Mix together the parsley, thyme, capers, anchovy, bread crumbs, and olive oil. No more than 5 minutes before serving, add the macerated shallots. Taste and adjust for salt and acid. Add freshly ground pepper to taste.

ROAST CHICKEN

A good roast chicken is the best dinner of all. We used to agonize over how to make factory chickens taste good. Now, thankfully, a few local farmers raise grain-fed chickens to have flavor, the old-fashioned way. One trick for great roast chicken at home is to salt and pepper the bird a day in advance, to cure it very lightly. This produces a bird thoroughly seasoned down to the bone.

Serves 4.

1 roasting chicken, weighing about 3½ pounds
1 tablespoon salt
½ teaspoon fresh cracked black pepper
A few sprigs thyme or marjoram

REMOVE any organs from the cavity and reserve for another use. Rinse the bird with cold water and pat dry. Liberally salt and pepper the entire bird, inside the cavity and all over the surface, including the back, wings, and inner and outer thighs. Carefully loosen the skin from the breast meat with your index finger. Stuff tender sprigs of thyme or marjoram under the skin. Tie the legs together with butcher's twine. Cover and refrigerate for several hours or overnight.

Remove the chicken from the refrigerator at least 1 hour before roasting. Preheat the oven to 450°F. Place the chicken, breast up, in a roasting pan or earthenware baking dish, and roast for 10 minutes. Reduce the oven temperature to 350°F. and cook for another 45 minutes, turning the bird twice during the cooking, so each wing side is up in turn. This will circulate the juices and fat and keep the meat moist. Let the chicken rest for 10 minutes before carving.

Note: Do not ignore the delicious caramelized drippings in the pan. After the fat is poured off, the pan can be deglazed with white wine and the juices added to a sauce or vinaigrette.

Variation: Flavor the chicken with lemon, garlic, and rosemary, both under the skin and in the cavity.

PAN-FRIED TRUFFLED CHICKEN BREASTS

These chicken breasts are a very elegant, festive dish with great truffle flavor. We serve them often in January, February, and March, the months when the truffle season in France is at its peak. Sprigs of watercress, Pickled Beets (page 40), and Celery Root Rémoulade (page 37) are good accompaniments.

Serves 6.

1 small black truffle, about ½ ounce
5 tablespoons butter, softened
Salt and pepper
6 large boneless chicken breast halves, skin removed
½ cup flour
2 eggs, beaten
3 cups fresh white bread crumbs
Clarified butter or olive oil for frying

WIPE the truffle with a damp cloth to remove any dirt, then pound to a coarse paste in a mortar. Mix the pounded truffle with the softened butter and season with a little salt and pepper. Form the truffle butter into a flattened log shape, wrap, and chill until firm. This may be done a day or two in advance.

Lay the chicken breasts flat on a clean work surface. With a sharp paring knife, cut a pocket ½ inch wide and 2 inches deep in the thicker end of each breast. Cut the chilled truffle butter into 6 equal pieces and insert a piece into the pocket in each breast. Season the chicken breasts on both sides with salt and pepper.

Season the flour with salt and pepper. Dredge each breast in the flour, shaking off any excess, dip into the beaten eggs, and roll in the bread crumbs. Put the breasts on a baking sheet in one layer, and sprinkle both sides of the breasts with more crumbs, making sure they are evenly coated. Refrigerate, uncovered, for up to 4 hours before frying.

Heat ½ inch of clarified butter or olive oil in each of 2 cast-iron skillets over medium heat. Add the chicken breasts and fry gently for about 3 minutes or until nicely browned. Turn the breasts and cook for another 3 minutes or so. Drain on absorbent kitchen paper, and serve immediately.

GRILLED CHICKEN BREASTS AU POIVRE

Based on the old bistro favorite, steak au poivre, these simple chicken breasts are intensely flavorful. The explosive black pepper contrasts nicely with the mild sweetness of the chicken. Accompany with pommes frites or Artichoke Mashed Potatoes (page 35).

Serves 6.

6 large boneless chicken breast halves, skin on
2 chicken legs
Extra-virgin olive oil
½ cup white wine
2 quarts Basic Chicken Stock (page 206)
2 sprigs parsley
2 thyme branches
2 garlic cloves
3 tablespoons peppercorns
Salt
Optional: red wine vinegar

FIRST prepare the sauce: Remove the fillets from the chicken breasts. With a cleaver, chop each leg into 4 pieces. In a large, deep saucepan, brown the chicken leg pieces and the fillets in a little olive oil. When they are well browned, deglaze with the white wine and cover with the chicken stock. Bring to a boil, reduce to a simmer, and add the parsley, thyme, garlic, and 1 teaspoon of the peppercorns. Simmer 1 hour, then strain, reserving the cooked meat for another purpose, like ravioli stuffing. Skim off the fat. Reduce this broth until rich and slightly thickened; only about 1½ cups should remain. The sauce can be prepared several hours ahead, or the day before.

Prepare a moderately hot grill. Carefully pound the chicken breasts to flatten them slightly. Crack the rest of the peppercorns in a mortar or crush them on a cutting board with the bottom of a heavy pan. Coat the breasts lightly with olive oil and season with salt and the cracked peppercorns. Gently grill the chicken breasts skin side down, rotating them frequently for even browning, and when cooked two-thirds through, turn the breasts to finish cooking, about 8 minutes in all. Let the breasts stand for a few minutes. Warm the sauce, check for seasoning, and add a few drops of red wine vinegar, if you wish. Serve the breasts whole or slice each one diagonally into 4 thick slices. Spoon on the sauce and serve.

Variation: The same seasoning, and the same sauce, works wonderfully with rare-grilled tuna steaks and also with guinea fowl breasts. When grilling guinea fowl breasts, add a little allspice and bay to the cracked pepper, to augment the mildly gamy flavor, and add green peppercorns to the sauce.

POLLO AL MATTONE WITH LEMON AND GARLIC

This Italian stovetop method for cooking chicken under a brick traditionally uses a whole young chicken, split down the back and flattened.
The result is a deliciously crisp, well-cooked bird. In the Café, we have
adapted the technique for boned chicken legs. We like to serve Pollo al
Mattone with garlicky mashed potatoes and Spicy Broccoli Raab
(page 34).

Serves 4.

4 chicken legs (drumsticks and thighs, attached)
Salt and pepper
Extra-virgin olive oil
1 branch thyme
16 garlic cloves, peeled
1 teaspoon chopped lemon zest
1 or 2 garlic cloves, chopped fine
2 tablespoons chopped parsley
Optional: ½ cup warm chicken sauce (page 200)
Lemon wedges

Bone the chicken legs, opening them out into large flat pieces with
the skin intact. Trim excess fat from the edges. Season both sides of
each piece with salt and pepper, and refrigerate.

Warm ⅓ cup olive oil in a small saucepan over medium heat. Add
the thyme branch and garlic cloves, and bring the oil to a simmer; reduce the heat to low and stew the thyme and garlic very slowly until
softened, about 15 minutes. Carefully remove the garlic with a slotted
spoon and set aside. Reserve the garlic-flavored oil (discard the thyme
branch) for cooking the chicken.

Heat a large cast-iron skillet over medium heat. When the pan is
hot, pour in the reserved oil and add the chicken legs, skin side down,
in one layer. Lay a piece of parchment paper or foil over the chicken,
then weight the chicken with another cast-iron pan or a brick. Cook
for about 15 minutes, checking the chicken occasionally to make sure
the skin is browning evenly, and adjusting the heat so the legs are not
cooking too quickly. Turn the legs over and cook for 5 minutes more,
uncovered. The skin should be golden and crisp, and the flesh should
be tender when probed with a paring knife. Blot the chicken legs on

absorbent paper and arrange on a warmed platter. Put a few of the reserved cooked garlic cloves on top of each leg.

Mix together the lemon zest, chopped garlic, and parsley (these
should be chopped at the last minute), and sprinkle over the chicken.
Spoon on a little warm chicken sauce, if desired. Garnish with lemon
wedges.

Variation: Pound the legs to flatten them slightly and grill slowly over
medium coals, turning frequently, until good and crispy. Smear the
skin side with tapenade and serve with grilled radicchio.

CHICKEN BALLOTINE WITH CHANTERELLES

Ballotines are traditionally made from game birds too tough to roast, the whole birds boned and stuffed with a savory forcemeat, then braised slowly, to tenderize them. We use chicken legs, an inexpensive, flavorful part of the chicken too often ignored. Though a bit fussy to prepare, these ballotines can be made hours ahead, or even the day before serving. As for accompaniments, keep them simple—buttered herb noodles, mashed potatoes with celery root, or a ragout of romano and cranberry beans. A ballotine is also delicious served cold, sliced, like a pâté, with a good salad of leafy greens.

Serves 6 as a main course.

6 chicken legs (drumsticks and thighs, attached)
Salt and pepper
6 cups day-old bread, cut into 2-inch cubes
Extra-virgin olive oil
2 large onions
2 tablespoons butter
12 ounces chanterelles, sliced
2 teaspoons chopped thyme
2 tablespoons finely chopped Italian parsley
1 rib celery
1 small carrot
2 garlic cloves, finely sliced
A few thyme branches
1 bay leaf
¼ cup dry white wine
5 cups Basic Chicken Stock (page 206)

Bone the chicken legs, leaving them each in one large, flat piece with the skin intact. Season both sides of each leg and refrigerate.

Preheat the oven to 350°F. Pulse the bread in a food processor to make medium-size, rough-textured crumbs. Toss these with 1 tablespoon olive oil and a little salt, and spread evenly on a baking sheet. Bake for 20 minutes or so, until dry and golden, turning them with a spatula every few minutes for even browning. Set aside to cool.

Finely dice one onion and sauté in 1 tablespoon olive oil over medium heat until lightly colored, 5 to 7 minutes. Turn the heat to high. Add the butter and the sliced chanterelles, and continue cooking until the mushrooms are done, 3 to 4 minutes. Season with salt and the chopped thyme. Combine the onion-mushroom mixture and any mushroom juices with the toasted bread crumbs and chopped parsley. Taste for salt, adjust if necessary, and reserve.

Cut the remaining onion and the celery and carrot into large dice, and sauté over medium heat in 2 tablespoons olive oil until they are cooked through, about 5 minutes. Add the garlic slices and spread the vegetables on the bottom of a deep roasting pan. Increase the oven heat to 450°F.

Lay the seasoned chicken legs skin side down on a cutting board or baking sheet, and evenly distribute the mushroom stuffing among them. Fold each leg around some of the stuffing and tie with butcher's twine to form 6 sausage-shaped rolls. Put the stuffed chicken legs into the roasting pan in one layer. Add a few sprigs of thyme, 1 bay leaf, and the white wine. Pour the hot stock over to cover the chicken by two-thirds. Cover the pan tightly with foil and bake for 15 minutes, or until the stock starts to simmer. Remove the foil and turn the oven temperature down to 350°F. Braise the chicken, uncovered, for 1 hour, turning the legs every 15 minutes to brown the skin evenly. Remove the chicken legs from the braise and cool at room temperature. Cut off and discard the twine. Pour the braising liquid and vegetables into a saucepan and thoroughly skim the fat. All this can be accomplished several hours ahead, or even the day before serving.

To serve, warm the ballotines in the braising liquid over medium heat until heated through, about 10 minutes. Remove the ballotines to a cutting board, leaving the braising juices simmering to reduce slightly. Slice the ballotines in thick diagonal slices and arrange in a deep platter. Spoon the braising juices over and serve.

BASIC CHICKEN STOCK

Aside from being extremely easy to make, homemade chicken stock is better than anything you can buy. And while chicken stock can be stored in the refrigerator for a few days, or frozen, the aroma and purity of a freshly made broth is fleeting, best savored the same day it is made. Ideally, use the meatiest bones available—an assortment of backs, necks, and carcasses works well, and is inexpensive. These meaty parts make the best chicken stock, as opposed to using only bones, which do not impart much flavor, or yield a bony flavor at best. (We use whole chickens for stock.) The home cook might also consider removing the breasts from two chickens, reserving them for a meal, and using the remaining legs, wings, and meaty bones for a rich, flavorful stock.

Makes 3 quarts.

5 pounds meaty chicken parts
1 medium yellow onion, peeled
1 medium carrot, peeled
1 celery stalk
2 sprigs parsley
1 thyme branch
½ bay leaf
1 teaspoon salt

Cover the chicken parts with 3½ quarts cold water in a large stainless steel stockpot and bring to a boil. When the stock comes to a full boil, reduce the heat to a low simmer and skim off the gray foam that rises to the surface. Add the onion, carrot, celery, parsley, thyme, bay, and salt. (If you plan to make a reduction, salt the stock more sparingly—it will become saltier as it reduces.) Cook gently for 3 hours, until the broth tastes rich and is a light golden color. Strain through a fine-mesh sieve or a colander lined with cheesecloth. Allow the stock to cool completely; skim the fat and promptly refrigerate. The stock is ready to use as is, or may be reduced to create a glaze or sauce.

Variation: For a brown stock, roast the chicken parts and vegetables in a 450°F. oven until nicely caramelized, about 30 minutes. Deglaze the roasting pan with a little red wine, and add a little crushed tomato to the pot.

SWEETS

In a restaurant setting, one is almost always tempted to splurge and have a dessert. Though our desserts tend to be more like homemade ones—less rich, less sweet, and less decorated than those offered at most restaurants and fancy bakeries—often the most satisfying end to a meal is a simple plate of seasonal fruit, and for that reason we always have fruit on the menu.

In another departure from the restaurant norm, unless the customer asks for it, we don't automatically serve coffee with dessert. This gives diners a chance to enjoy dessert as a course in itself, and pair it with a dessert wine, perhaps. In any case, our favorite after-dinner beverage is not necessarily coffee or tea, although we are very proud of our organically grown coffee and our rare and expertly chosen teas. Instead, whenever I bring guests to the Café, at the end of the meal I always insist that they join me in a little *tisane*, which is nothing more than an herb infusion: a handful of fresh leafy branches of lemon thyme, lemon verbena, or mint, steeped for a few minutes in nearly boiling water. A tisane is aromatic, warm, and stimulating, but contains no caffeine—a clean and purifying way to end a meal. Many meals require no more perfect closure than some lemon verbena tisane and a plate of tangerines, for example—especially meals at home.

I decided we had to serve tisane in the Café after I took a trip to Morocco about ten years ago. Everywhere I went, I was served mint tea, poured with ceremony into little glass cups. I returned with 200 beautiful Moroccan tisane glasses and insisted that we put a fresh herb tea on the menu every day. The glasses disappeared quickly, all broken or pocketed, but tisanes remain on the menu, brewed in glass teapots and poured into little glass teacups that are slightly more restaurant-friendly. And now many of our regular customers order a tisane every time they come in for a meal.

We let our fascination with fruit drive the dessert menu at the Café. For example, every day in late summer figs are on the Café dessert menu, sometimes with late-season raspberries in sweet pastry galettes, sometimes roasted in the wood oven to accompany anise ice cream. And always the most beautiful and perfectly ripe figs will be offered unadorned, as an after-dinner plate of fruit—the best dessert of all.

More than other fruits, the fig evokes its native region, the lands surrounding the Mediterranean. Because fig trees are happiest growing in such hot, dry climates, they have thrived in California, where they were first planted in 1769 at the mission in San Diego. One of our favorite fig varieties, the Black Mission, is descended from those early trees. Like many other fig varieties, Mission figs have two crops. The first, in early summer, yields large, juicy figs that are not especially sweet or flavorful. Figs from the second crop, which peaks in September, are much better. Ripened on the tree and harvested just before they fall from the branches, these small figs have a concentrated sweet, honeylike flavor. They are fragile, and they must be eaten soon after harvest.

Fig trees produce more than just fruit. Look around the Café and you may notice that the shrimp emerging from the wood oven are loosely wrapped in fig leaves, absorbing the lovely perfume that seems one part roasted fig and one part toasted coconut. Watch the grill cook and you will see that the fire is being fed with fig branches. Note that the raspberries are presented on fresh, dark green fig leaves.

By using all of a plant, we not only learn about the variety and subtleties of what nature provides, we also learn to practice conservation and natural frugality. The wood of grape vines, apple, or almond prunings, for example, each gives its own particular flavor to foods cooked on the grill. Nor should leaves be discarded. The first tender grape leaves in spring can be chopped and made into a tangy sauce for fish, and the larger grape leaves of midsummer are wrapped around little rounds of goat cheese bound for the grill.

We save the skins of citrus fruits after juicing them for sherbet or ice cream, and candy the peels for soufflés and cakes or for an after-dinner treat, dipped in chocolate. We never throw away apple peels and cores without using them first to flavor a sugar syrup for an apple tart glaze, or to infuse in alcohol as a base for an apéritif.

A favorite activity of our many summer helpers is cracking open the pits of apricots, peaches, and nectarines, and extracting the kernels inside—the *noyaux*. In Italy these kernels provide the flavoring for amaretti cookies. We like to steep them in cream to flavor ice cream and custards. A few peach or nectarine kernels can be tossed in while cooking those fruits for ice cream or sherbet.

We try to be sensitive to the exact times when fruits are at the peak of their harvest in order to take full advantage of them. There's always a desire to jump the season and get something too soon, but if you just wait and tune in to the rhythms of the seasons, you will be able to make truly tasty fruit desserts.

Spring is always the most difficult time of year. The season for citrus fruit is ending, apples and pears kept over the winter have lost their appeal, and we impatiently await the first Chino Ranch strawberries, which always seem to come just in time for the Café birthday celebration on April 1. For a while the pastry kitchen is a vision of brilliant red, a flurry of strawberry sherbet, tarts, and shortcakes.

By the time Bing cherries ripen in May, the first apricots are coming in, too, for apricot and cherry tarts. May also brings the first raspberries, the first Springcrest peaches, and a few early nectarines. By early summer, stone fruits and berries of all kinds are crowding the kitchen. In August, the Gravenstein and Pink Pearl apples coming from Sebastopol remind us that fall is just around the corner. Late summer also brings the first French Butter pears from the Pettigrew orchards in the Sacramento River delta. These meltingly delicious pears are perfect sliced and baked in a puff pastry shell, sprinkled with the first sweet, crisp almonds from the late summer harvest.

Apples for cooking need to have a balance between sweet and sour. A sweet apple may be fine for eating, but it will be a boring cooked apple if it doesn't have enough acidity. Each area of the country has its favorite cooking apples, but for us nothing beats the flavor and texture of the Sierra Beauty, an old variety developed in California that is still grown in the Anderson Valley of Mendocino County.

Search out the best apples and pears in your area. According to the Seed Savers Exchange, as recently as 1992 there were over 1100 varieties of apple trees available from nurseries. Some of the old varieties are still favorites: the Rhode Island Greening and the Newtown Pippin in the northeast, the McIntosh and the Rome Beauty in the midwest. Of the pear varieties, good Bosc pears have the right texture and body for poaching and for using in tarts.

Fortunately, all the nuts are at their freshest and best in midautumn, in time to accompany apples and pears. By late fall we start to see the first citrus fruits: mandarins, clementines from Guru Ram Das Orchards in Esparto, and then the Fairchild and Dancy tangerines. Later come the Page and Pixie mandarins from Jim Churchill in Ventura County and the incomparable Satsuma tangerines from Fairview Gardens in Goleta, California—best served with their leaves still attached in a basket offered at the end of the meal.

Fresh dates begin to come to market in September, but the season peaks in November. We are particularly fond of a soft, luscious date variety called Khadrawy, which comes to us from the Southern California desert. We serve them alone, like candy after dinner, or paired with the mandarins, which are available at the same time. The tart flavor of the citrus balances the extraordinary concentration of sugar in the dates.

The oranges start coming to the market in late November, and the season climaxes with the blood oranges that usually start to arrive in mid-December, the California-grown Moros. True to their name, blood oranges have blood-red flesh and their flavor hints of raspberries. This berry character is particularly strong in the Tarocco variety, which ripens from January through April. Blood oranges make lovely juice (which we serve at the bar), and they are also good in tarts with pastry cream, in sherbets, and in ice creams. For special occasions, we love to make Ali Babas, rum babas with blood oranges.

In early spring, when strawberries are still a tantalizing month or so away, we go beyond California and use a few of the tropical fruits from the increasing numbers of organic growers of tropical fruits in Hawaii, Mexico, and Central America. Spring is the best time for papayas, and the beginning of the season for mangoes and pineapples. Poached pineapples make a delicious galette with frangipane. Soon the strawberries do come to market, and the yearly cycle begins again.

Most people will eat chocolate at any time of the year, so we try to have at least one chocolate dessert on the Café menu every day. Besides Lindsey's Chocolate Cake (page 218) we also make chocolate ice cream, custards, cookies, and chocolate mousse.

Chocolate lovers who are also environmentalists should be pleased by recent developments in cocoa bean farming. In the past, many producers of chocolate have ignored the effects of unsustainable agriculture. The conventional practice has been to clear areas of rain forest and plant cacao trees. When production from a plantation declined, from disease or loss of soil fertility, another area of the forest was cleared and planted and the old trees abandoned. Now growers and the big chocolate companies are beginning to realize that not only are we running out of rain forest, but that large, unsustainable cocoa plantations produce a lower quality, less reliable harvest.

The new model emphasizes smaller farms, with the cacao trees intermingled with other rain forest species, closer to the conditions under which these trees evolved. It actually costs less to produce cocoa on these small farms. The more closely the farm environment resembles conditions in the open forest, the better the cacao trees perform. Evidently the greater mix of species reduces insect and disease problems. On such farms, growers spend more time tending each tree, and can spot problems early on, before they spread to all the trees, which is less likely in any case because each grove is small and separated from its neighbors. An important dividend of these growing conditions is the increased numbers and variety of native birds and other animals these farms support.

We feel it best to buy from the smaller growers of just about everything we use. We may get Meyer lemons from someone with a single tree in the backyard, but the owner knows every lemon on that tree and when it will be ready to pick. Other growers, like Al Courchesne in Brentwood, or Ernie Bierwagen in the Sierra foothills, may have fifty or 100 acres, but they still use their own dedicated hands and eyes to keep track of what's going on. With their thousands of acres of crops, large growers, even organic ones, can never achieve the same quality.

AFFOGATO

Affogato—the word means "drowned" in Italian—is a simple and most satisfying dessert. Nothing more than good warm espresso poured over good vanilla ice cream, it is a year-round favorite, and a great way to have coffee and dessert at the same time. It is pretty when served in coffee cups with a little finely chopped candied citrus peel on top.

Makes 2 generous quarts, enough to serve 10 to 12.

VANILLA ICE CREAM
12 egg yolks
2½ cups half-and-half
1 vanilla bean, split lengthwise
1½ cups sugar
4½ cups cold heavy cream

¼ cup hot espresso for each serving

LIGHTLY whisk the egg yolks in a large bowl. Pour the half-and-half into a large heavy-bottomed saucepan. Scrape the seeds from the vanilla bean into the half-and-half, add the bean and the sugar, and warm over medium heat without allowing the mixture to come to a boil. When the sugar is dissolved and the half-and-half is giving off wisps of steam, slowly whisk the liquid into the yolks.

Return this custard to the saucepan and cook over low heat, stirring constantly, until the mixture thickens slightly and reaches a temperature of about 170°F. Immediately remove from the heat and strain through a fine-mesh sieve. Whisk in the cold cream, then cover and chill thoroughly.

Freeze the mixture in an ice cream machine, following the manufacturer's instructions. Transfer to a container and store in the freezer compartment of the refrigerator for several hours or overnight.

To serve, scoop the ice cream into bowls or coffee cups, and pour about ¼ cup freshly brewed espresso over each serving.

Variation: Sprinkle each serving with a pinch of finely ground espresso beans, chopped candied lemon peel, or ground cinnamon, and top with a spoonful of softly whipped cream.

MEYER LEMON ÉCLAIRS

Meyer lemons begin to ripen around the first of November. These lemons are not well known, even in California, where they are a common backyard lemon tree but grown commercially by only a handful of growers. They are special favorites of ours. They suggest a cross between an orange and a lemon, rounder in shape than other lemons and a deep yellow orange color when completely ripe. They are less acid than other lemons, and their skin is intensely perfumed. We use them not only for this recipe but also to make lemon curd tarts, ice cream, and sherbet. The candied peel is particularly distinctive and flavorful.

Makes 40 finger-sized eclairs; serves 10 to 12.

LEMON CURD
½ cup Meyer lemon juice
1 tablespoon tart lemon juice (from ordinary lemons)
Grated zest of 1 Meyer lemon
½ cup sugar
8 tablespoons (1 stick) unsalted butter
¼ teaspoon salt
3 whole eggs
3 egg yolks

PÂTE À CHOUX
8 tablespoons (1 stick) unsalted butter
¼ teaspoon salt
1 teaspoon sugar
1 cup flour
4 eggs

WHIPPED CREAM FILLING
1¼ cups heavy cream
1½ tablespoons sugar
¼ teaspoon vanilla extract

Powdered sugar for dusting the éclairs

To make the lemon curd, combine the lemon juice, zest, sugar, butter, and salt in a heavy-bottomed nonreactive saucepan. Stir gently over low heat until the butter is melted. Put the eggs and yolks in a bowl and whisk briefly. Whisk half of the hot lemon mixture into the eggs, then slowly whisk the egg mixture back into the remaining lemon mixture. Cook over low heat, scraping the bottom constantly, until the mixture thickens, about 5 minutes. Do not allow to boil. Pour the thickened curd through a fine-mesh sieve into a bowl. Refrigerate until cold and firm.

To make the pâte à choux, preheat the oven to 425°F. Measure 1 cup water, the butter, salt, and sugar into a large saucepan. Bring the mixture to a boil over medium heat. Add the flour all at once and stir quickly with a wooden spoon until the mixture pulls away from the sides of the pan. Continue to cook for 1 minute to dry out. Transfer the mixture to a bowl and beat in the eggs one at a time (an electric mixer works best). With each addition, make sure that the dough is smooth and glossy before adding the next egg. Using a pastry bag fitted with a ⅓-inch round or star tip, pipe the éclairs onto a parchment-lined baking sheet in finger-sized strips about 3 inches long. Bake at 425°F. for 15 minutes, and then turn the oven down to 350°F. and bake for about 20 minutes more, until the pastry is golden and dry.

To make the whipped cream filling, whip the cream into soft peaks with the sugar and vanilla extract.

When all the elements are ready, cut the éclairs in half lengthwise and separate the tops and bottoms. Fill the bottoms with lemon curd and then pipe on the whipped cream using a pastry bag fitted with a small star tip. Place the lids on top and dust the éclairs with powdered sugar. Serve immediately.

COMICE PEAR CRISP

Among the pear varieties, we prefer the silky, juicy flesh and slightly winy flavor of Comice pears for eating, and they are exceptionally good in this crisp. (For poaching and in tarts, good Bosc pears have the right texture and body.)

Serves 4 to 6.

CRISP TOPPING
½ cup walnuts or almonds
1 cup all-purpose flour
3 tablespoons brown sugar
2 tablespoons granulated sugar
⅛ teaspoon ground cinnamon
A pinch salt
6 tablespoons (¾ stick) unsalted butter

FILLING
6 ripe pears (about 2 pounds),
    peeled, cored, and
    cut in ½-inch dice
¼ cup sugar
2 tablespoons flour

PREHEAT the oven to 375°F. Toast the nuts until fragrant, about 7 or 8 minutes, and chop them medium-fine. Combine the flour, brown sugar, granulated sugar, cinnamon, and salt in a mixing bowl. Cut the butter into small pieces. Work it into the flour mixture with your fingers until crumbly. Add the chopped nuts and mix well—the topping should hold together when squeezed. (The topping can be prepared up to a week ahead and refrigerated.)

Put the diced pears in a large mixing bowl. Add the sugar and taste; adjust if necessary. Sprinkle the flour over the pears and mix gently. Turn the mixture into an earthenware dish just large enough to hold the fruit, slightly mounded at the center. Spoon the topping over the pears, pressing down lightly. Place the dish on a baking sheet to catch any overflow and bake on the center rack of the oven for 40 to 50 minutes, until the topping is dark golden brown and the juices have thickened slightly. Serve warm with ice cream or Armagnac-flavored whipped cream.

Variations: Other fruits may be substituted with the same general proportions, but some fruits require more or less sugar and flour, depending on their natural sweetness and juiciness. Rhubarb, for instance, requires more of both; apples require no flour at all.

PANNA COTTA

This pure white, lightly sweetened custard made without eggs disappears on the tongue and is a perfect accompaniment for fruit. Its Italian name means "cooked cream." Nancy Silverton, of Campanile Restaurant and the La Brea Bakery in Los Angeles, gave us this recipe, which has become one of our favorites. Panna cotta is delicious with peaches and with berry compotes. In the winter it can be served with cookies and a glass of Sauternes.

Serves 8.

One ¼-ounce package unflavored powdered gelatin
Almond oil (or a flavorless vegetable oil)
1-inch piece vanilla bean
3 cups heavy cream
1 cup whole milk
¼ cup sugar
Zest of ¼ lemon, removed with a vegetable peeler
    or citrus zester

Put 3 tablespoons cold water in a small stainless steel bowl, sprinkle on the gelatin, and set aside to soften. Lightly brush eight 4-ounce ramekins with almond oil and chill them while proceeding with the recipe.

Slice the piece of vanilla bean lengthwise, scrape out the seeds, and put the seeds and bean into a 2-quart saucepan with the cream, milk, sugar, and lemon zest. Bring to a simmer and cook for about 1 minute.

Remove the pan from the heat and let the cream mixture cool, stirring occasionally, for about 10 minutes, until the temperature falls to 130°F., about the temperature of hot water from the tap. Pour about 1 cup of the mixture over the softened gelatin. Stir until the gelatin is completely dissolved, rubbing with your fingers to feel any hard bits of gelatin. When the gelatin is completely dissolved, pour it back into the remaining cream mixture, stirring well. Strain through a fine-mesh sieve. Fill the ramekins and refrigerate for 4 hours or overnight. To serve, run a knife around the sides of the ramekins and turn upside down onto dessert plates. Gently tap, and ease the panna cotta from its mold.

LINDSEY'S CHOCOLATE CAKE
WITH SICILIAN SABAYON

One of our favorite cakes is this very rich chocolate one developed by Lindsey Shere, the founding pastry chef at Chez Panisse. To mitigate the intensity of the chocolate flavor, we sometimes serve this tender and rich cake with lightly sweetened whipped cream, flavored with vanilla or Chartreuse, or an ice cream such as Cognac or vanilla. However, it is especially good with this slightly spicy, creamy Sicilian-style sabayon.

Serves 8 to 10; makes about 1 quart sabayon.

CAKE
½ pound plus 2 tablespoons (2¼ sticks) salted butter
7½ ounces bittersweet chocolate
1½ ounces unsweetened chocolate
6 eggs, separated, at room temperature
1 cup plus 2 tablespoons sugar
6 tablespoons cake flour
½ teaspoon cream of tartar

SABAYON
3 tablespoons golden raisins, coarsely chopped
½ cup plus 1 tablespoon Marsala
6 egg yolks
5 tablespoons sugar
1 cup heavy cream
¼ teaspoon ground cinnamon

BUTTER a 9-inch cake pan and line the bottom with a round of parchment or waxed paper. Butter the paper and dust the pan with flour, shaking out the excess. Preheat the oven to 350°F.

Place the butter in a mixing bowl and heat over barely simmering water. While the butter melts, chop the chocolate into small pieces. Add the chocolate to the butter and stir occasionally until the chocolate is melted and the mixture is very smooth. Remove from the heat and cool slightly.

Whisk the egg yolks with a wire whisk until just blended and beat in the sugar until just mixed. Whisk the yolks into the warm chocolate mixture, and fold in the flour.

In a separate bowl, beat the egg whites until frothy. Add the cream of tartar (if you are not using a copper bowl) and continue beating until soft, rounded peaks form. Fold the egg whites quickly into the chocolate mixture, taking care not to deflate them.

Pour the batter into the pan and bake for 45 to 50 minutes. The cake is done when the sides are set but the center of the cake is still soft. Remove from the oven and cool completely in the pan. The cake will develop cracks in the top as it bakes, and more will appear as it cools, but this is normal. When the cake has cooled to room temperature, you may cover the pan tightly with foil if you are not serving it right away. It will keep for a day or two.

To make the sabayon, combine the chopped raisins and 1 tablespoon of the Marsala in a small bowl and set aside to soften. Have a stainless steel mixing bowl ready in an ice bath. Warm the remaining Marsala over low heat in a heavy-bottomed nonreactive saucepan. In a medium bowl, whisk the egg yolks with the sugar until the yolks are very pale in color and form a slowly dissolving ribbon when the whisk is lifted. Whisk in the warm Marsala and return the mixture to the saucepan. Continue beating constantly over low heat until the mixture thickens and wisps of steam arise from the surface, about 5 minutes. Immediately pour the mixture into the bowl on ice. (Be careful not to scrape any coagulated egg from the bottom of the saucepan.) Whisk until cool.

In another bowl, whip the cream just until soft peaks form. Fold the whipped cream into the egg mixture. Add the raisins and cinnamon. The sabayon may be refrigerated, but should be used within a couple of hours.

To serve, unmold the cake, peel off the paper, and place the cake on a plate, the more presentable side up. Dust with powdered sugar and serve with the sabayon.

HONEY-PISTACHIO BRITTLE ICE CREAM
WITH LAVENDER SAUCE

This is a wonderful summertime dessert, reminiscent of sun-drenched afternoons in Provence when the air is heavy with the scent of lavender in bloom. We get lavender fresh from the backyard garden of Alan, our dessert chef, and hang it up to dry at the restaurant.

If you wish, some of the pistachio brittle can be chopped fine and folded into the ice cream, and the rest roughly broken up and served on the side. This brittle is best when made thin.

Serves 4 to 6; makes 1 generous quart ice cream.

HONEY ICE CREAM
⅓ cup sugar
1 cup half-and-half
6 egg yolks
2 cups chilled heavy cream
⅓ cup honey

PISTACHIO BRITTLE
Vegetable oil or canola oil
4 cups sugar
2 tablespoons honey
2 cups finely chopped pistachio nuts

LAVENDER SAUCE
½ cup sugar
¼ cup honey
¼ cup dried crumbled lavender
A few drops lemon juice

HEAT the sugar and half-and-half in a small nonreactive saucepan. Whisk the yolks just enough to break them up. Pour some of the hot liquid into the yolks and whisk. Pour all back into the saucepan. Stir constantly over low heat until the custard coats the spoon. Strain the mixture into the cold heavy cream. Heat the honey slightly and stir into the custard. Chill thoroughly.

While the ice cream mixture is chilling, make the pistachio brittle. Generously oil the backs of 2 cookie sheets or jelly roll pans and 2 large pieces of parchment paper. In a medium nonreactive heavy-bottomed saucepan, heat the sugar with just enough water to make a paste. Wash the sugar crystals off the sides of the pan with a clean pastry brush dipped in water. Allow the sugar to melt and caramelize without stirring, and continue to dissolve sugar crystals on the sides with the wet pastry brush. When the sugar begins to turn a light mahogany color, add the honey and pour the caramel onto the oiled sheets. Sprinkle each pan with 1 cup of pistachios. Place the parchment paper on top of the brittle, oiled side down. With a rolling pin, spread the mixture toward the edges of the pan. When the brittle is rolled out to a thickness of about ¼ inch, let it cool. If the brittle cools off too quickly before it is rolled thin enough, remove the parchment paper, put the cookie sheets in a 325°F. oven for a few minutes, and repeat the rolling process.

Remove the large piece of brittle to a cutting board and break it up with a heavy knife into roughly 2-inch pieces. (If you wish, chop a handful of the brittle pieces very fine and fold into the chilled ice cream mixture.) Freeze the ice cream in an ice cream maker.

To make the lavender sauce, heat the sugar and 1 cup water in a small heavy-bottomed saucepan. When the sugar is dissolved, add the honey and lavender. Boil until the temperature reaches 235°F. on a candy thermometer. Let the syrup cool and strain out the lavender. Add a few drops of lemon juice to taste. Keep at room temperature until ready to serve.

Serve the ice cream with a spoonful of lavender sauce and a plate of pistachio brittle on the side.

CHERRY CLAFOUTIS

By mid–April, there will be cherries from Lagier Ranches in the Central Valley: big baskets of cherries still covered with dew to put out on the tables in the Café and to use for cherry tarts, cherry ice cream, and cherry clafoutis. The traditional French clafoutis is a dish of unpitted sour cherries baked in a batter. The pits infuse the dessert with an almond flavor. In this version, with sweeter, pitted cherries, the addition of almond extract enhances the flavor and makes it taste more like the French original.

Serves 4.

1 pound sweet cherries (preferably Bings), washed and pitted
2 teaspoons fresh lemon juice
¼ teaspoon grated lemon zest
A pinch ground cinnamon
⅓ cup sugar
2 eggs, separated
3 tablespoons sugar
2 tablespoons flour
1 teaspoon vanilla extract
¼ teaspoon almond extract
⅓ cup cream
A pinch salt
Powdered sugar

Preheat the oven to 350°F. Lightly butter a baking pan large enough to hold the cherries loosely in a single layer. Prepare the cherries and arrange them in the pan. Sprinkle with the lemon juice, zest, cinnamon, and sugar. Bake until the fruit is tender, about 15 minutes, stirring once or twice.

Raise the oven temperature to 375°F. Butter another gratin dish large enough to hold the cherries in a single layer, or use four individual gratin dishes. Drain the cooked cherries, reserving their juice in a small saucepan. Arrange the cherries in the bottom of the baking dish. Beat together the egg yolks and sugar until well blended. Beat in the flour, vanilla, almond extract, and cream.

Beat the egg whites with a pinch of salt until they form soft peaks. Stir a little of the whites into the batter, and then carefully fold in the rest. Pour the batter over the fruit in the baking dish, letting a little fruit show through the top.

Bake in the upper third of the oven for about 20 minutes, until the batter has puffed and browned. While the clafoutis is baking, reduce the fruit juices to a thin syrup. When the clafoutis is done, dust it with powdered sugar and serve warm with a drizzle of the syrup.

ANGEL FOOD CAKE

This very American dessert is ideal with perfectly ripe midsummer berries. Its light airy texture doesn't interfere with the freshness and sweetness of the berries, as a richer, buttery cake would.

Serves 10.

1½ cups egg whites (about 12 large eggs)
½ teaspoon vanilla extract
2 teaspoons lemon juice
Optional: ¼ teaspoon orange flower water
1 cup cake flour
1½ cups sugar
½ teaspoon salt
1 teaspoon cream of tartar

PREHEAT the oven to 325°F. Carefully warm the egg whites in a large stainless steel bowl over barely simmering water, stirring constantly, until they are at body temperature. (You get more volume from egg whites if they are whipped warm.) Measure 1 tablespoon water, the vanilla, lemon juice, and orange flower water (if using) into a small bowl and set near the mixer. Sift together the cake flour, ½ cup of the sugar, and the salt, and set aside.

Begin whipping the egg whites at medium speed until they appear frothy. Add the cream of tartar and the measured liquid ingredients. Continue whipping until the whites hold a very loose peak. At this point begin adding the remaining cup of sugar, ¼ cup at a time, whipping briefly between additions. Continue beating the whites until they hold a softly stiff peak when the beater is lifted from them. They should not pour easily, but form soft mounds when scooped, and appear glossy and meringuelike but not dry.

Sift half of the dry ingredients over the whipped whites, folding in by hand with a plastic pastry scraper or a rubber spatula. Sift the remaining dry ingredients over and quickly fold them in. Turn the batter into an ungreased 10 × 4-inch tube pan. Smooth the top evenly.

Bake until the top is golden brown and the edges have begun to pull away from the sides of the pan, 40 to 45 minutes. The cake should spring back when gently touched. Invert the pan onto a cooling rack, or, if the cake has risen to the very top of the pan, hang the pan by the center tube over a large bottle. Inverting the cake helps prevent it from sticking or deflating. Cool completely. Run a knife around the inside of the pan and around the center tube. Gently tap the cake out of the pan, using the knife to guide it out if necessary. Place on a serving plate. To cut the cake, use a sharp serrated knife dipped in water, dipping after each cut. This helps prevent the cake from sticking to the knife.

Variation: Rose water or finely chopped orange or lemon zest can also be added to perfume the cake. This is especially nice if you are serving the cake plain with afternoon tea.

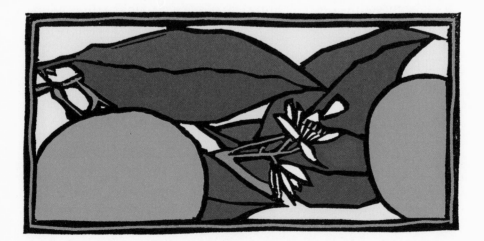

PLUM AND PLUOT GALETTE

Our plum season begins in June, when sweet-tart Santa Rosas appear in the farmers' markets. It peaks in July and August, when dozens of flavorful varieties are available, and ends in early fall with the last of the very sweet prune plums. Recently, more and more orchardists are including pluots in their plantings. A pluot is a cross between a plum and an apricot. The fruits look like big plums, and may be green, purple, or a speckled combination of both. They have the intense perfume of a plum, and some of the flavor and texture of an apricot. Our favorite variety is the aptly named Flavor King. It has a beautiful purple skin, reddish orange flesh, and a voluptuous flavor. This galette is very nice made with plums and pluots, but will be delicious with only one or the other.

We sometimes serve this tart with bitter almond ice cream and drizzled with plum caramel sauce.

Serves 8.

10 ounces Galette Dough (page 227), rolled into a 14-inch circle
1¼ pounds ripe plums and pluots, unpeeled
About ¼ cup sugar, plus additional for sprinkling
1 tablespoon flour
1 tablespoon ground almonds
1 tablespoon butter, melted
Optional: 2 tablespoons plum jam

PREHEAT the oven to 400°F. Remove the pre-rolled dough from the refrigerator or freezer and place on a buttered or parchment paper–lined baking sheet.

Cut the plums and pluots in half and gently twist the halves to separate them. Remove the pits and cut the fruit into slices about ⅓-inch thick. You should have about 5 cups of sliced fruit.

Mix 2 tablespoons of the sugar with the flour and ground almonds, and sprinkle the mixture over the pastry, leaving a 2-inch border. Arrange the fruit slices on the dough in barely touching concentric circles, again leaving the 2-inch border. Sprinkle the fruit evenly with 2 or 3 tablespoons of sugar, depending on the sweetness of the fruit.

Trim away most of the 2-inch border, leaving about ½ inch of pastry. (Save the trimmings to make little sugar cookies.) Finish the tart by folding the exposed border over on itself, crimping to make a narrow pastry rim around the fruit. Brush the rim generously with melted butter, and sprinkle with sugar.

Bake in the lower third of the oven for 45 to 50 minutes, until the fruit is tender and the crust is well browned and its edges slightly caramelized. Let the galette cool for 20 minutes. If you would like to glaze the tart, brush it with a little gently heated plum jam. Serve the tart warm, with vanilla ice cream.

GALETTE DOUGH

This dough is one we learned to make when Jacques Pépin visited us several years ago. The only trick to making it is getting the pieces of butter in the dough to be the right size. This recipe makes enough for two single-crust tarts or galettes, with some dough left over that you can bake into little cookies. We prefer fruit galettes with more fruit than crust.

Makes 20 ounces dough, enough for 2 galettes or tarts.

2 cups all-purpose flour
1 teaspoon sugar
¼ teaspoon salt
6 ounces (1½ sticks) unsalted butter

COMBINE the flour, sugar, and salt in a large mixing bowl. Cut the butter into ½-inch pieces. Add half the butter to the flour mixture and work it into the flour with your fingertips, until the dough has the texture of coarse oatmeal. Add the rest of the butter and quickly work it into the dough until the biggest pieces are the size of large lima beans. Dribble about ½ cup ice water into the dough in several stages, tossing and mixing between additions. Don't try to dampen all of the dough evenly. It should look rather ropy and rough. Stop adding water when there are still a few bits of dry flour remaining in the bottom of the bowl. Gather the dough into 2 balls and wrap each tightly with plastic wrap, pressing down to flatten each package. Refrigerate several hours or overnight before rolling. (Dough may be frozen for a few weeks.)

Roll each flattened ball into a 14-inch circle on a lightly floured board; the dough will be a little less than ⅛ inch thick. Refrigerate the rolled-out dough for at least ½ hour before using. (The rolled-out circles can be frozen and used the next day.)

CHOCOLATE ESPRESSO CUSTARD

This rich custard is meant to be served at room temperature, so bake it no more than four hours ahead of time, until it sets perfectly, and do not refrigerate it when it comes out of the oven. The unbaked custard mixture, however, can be made a day or two ahead and kept in the refrigerator.

Serves 6.

1 cup heavy cream
1 cup half-and-half
5 tablespoons sugar
¼ cup espresso beans
4 ounces bittersweet chocolate
½ ounce unsweetened chocolate
6 egg yolks
1 teaspoon Cognac

PREHEAT the oven to 350°F. In a heavy-bottomed saucepan, warm the cream, half-and-half, sugar, and espresso beans over medium heat. Cook just long enough to dissolve the sugar, taking care not to let the mixture boil. Let the mixture steep for 30 minutes or so, off the heat, to infuse with espresso flavor. (For a more intense espresso flavor, steep longer.) Set aside.

Melt the chocolates slowly over warm water in a double boiler, stirring occasionally, for about 10 minutes, until smooth and glossy.

In a large bowl, beat the egg yolks lightly. Rewarm the cream mixture gently and whisk it gradually into the egg yolks. Add the warm chocolate and the Cognac, stirring well. Strain the mixture through a fine-mesh sieve. At this point, the custards may be baked, or the mixture may be refrigerated for a day or two.

To bake the custards, fill six 4-ounce ramekins and place them in a deep ovenproof dish. Pour in enough hot water to come halfway up the sides of the ramekins. Cover tightly with foil and bake 25 to 30 minutes, until the custards are just set, the centers slightly soft when jiggled. Remove the ramekins from the hot water bath and cool to room temperature. Garnish with a spoonful of softly whipped cream and chocolate curls, if desired.

Mulberry Sherbet

We get our mulberries from one source—the giant mulberry tree in Charlie Grech's backyard in Sonoma. Inside the tree, Charlie has built a makeshift scaffolding that he uses to climb up into the upper branches early in the morning to pick only the ripest mulberries, filling small handmade wooden crates with these tiny jewel-like fruits. By mid-morning, when we come to pick up the mulberries, his gray-white hair, clothes, and weathered hands are all stained mulberry purple. If you can find mulberries, they should be used like this, in a way that accentuates their unique flavor.

Makes 1 quart.

4 cups mulberries
¾ cup sugar
Kirsch to taste

IN a heavy-bottomed nonreactive pan over medium heat, warm the berries slightly until they begin to give up their juice. Purée the warm mulberries 1 cup at a time in the food processor. When all the berries have been puréed, pass this mixture through a medium sieve to remove most of the seeds. Heat the sugar with 1 cup of the strained purée in a small saucepan, stirring until the sugar dissolves, and add to the rest of the purée. Add a few drops of kirsch to taste. Cool the mixture in the refrigerator. Freeze in an ice cream maker, following the manufacturer's instructions.

Variations: This recipe can be adapted to use with raspberries, blackberries, or boysenberries.

PLUM UPSIDE-DOWN CAKE

In late spring, many small farmers start coming to the farmers' market again. We are always eager to hear if the weather has been good to them or not. A good winter will bring full-flavored fruit in the summertime. Two of our favorite plums are the Santa Rosa, which has a great tangy flavor, and the Elephant Heart, which is large, deep red–fleshed, and milder. A combination of the two varieties makes a beautiful and delicious cake.

Serves 8.

TOPPING
4 tablespoons (½ stick) unsalted butter
¾ cups brown sugar
6 ripe plums (about 1¼ pounds), preferably
    3 Santa Rosa plums and 3 Elephant Heart plums

BATTER
8 tablespoons (1 stick) unsalted butter
1 cup sugar
1 teaspoon vanilla extract
2 eggs, separated
1½ cups all-purpose flour
2 teaspoons baking powder
¼ teaspoon salt
½ cup whole milk
¼ teaspoon cream of tartar

OVER low heat, melt the butter in the bottom of a 9-inch round cake pan, stirring in the brown sugar until it dissolves. Swirl the pan to coat the bottom, then remove from the heat and cool. Cut the plums into ¼-inch-thick wedges and arrange them neatly over the brown sugar mixture, covering the bottom completely. Set the pan aside and prepare the cake batter.

Preheat the oven to 350°F.

With an electric mixer, cream the butter with the sugar until pale, light, and fluffy. Add the vanilla extract and beat in the egg yolks one at a time, scraping the bowl to make sure all the butter is incorporated. Sift together the flour, baking powder, and salt, and add them to the batter alternately with the milk, beginning and ending with the dry ingredients. Whisk the egg whites with the cream of tartar until they are stiff enough to hold a slight shape. Fold the whites into the batter a third at a time. This helps to lighten the batter before all the egg whites are incorporated. Pour the batter into the prepared pan and spread it evenly over the plums. Bake for 25 to 35 minutes, until the top is browned and the cake pulls away slightly from the edges of the pan. Let the cake cool for 15 minutes before turning it out onto a cake plate. Serve with slightly sweetened whipped cream, flavored, if you wish, with a plum eau-de-vie.

Variations: This cake is very versatile and can be made with pears and peaches, but it is better made with a slightly acidic fruit like cranberries. Cranberry upside-down cake is not only beautiful in appearance but the berries' tartness serves as a counterbalance to the sweet topping.

APPLE AND BRANDIED CURRANT TART

The summer's bounty of fruit is intoxicating, but the first new-crop apples in the fall are seductive in their own way, heralding cooler weather and a whole new season of autumn recipes. One of our favorite apples is the crisp, juicy, and tart Sierra Beauty from Mendocino County's beautiful Anderson Valley. Ripening in September and October, this handsome red-striped, yellow-green fruit is excellent for eating fresh or cooking.

Serves 8.

3 pounds baking apples, quartered, peeled, and cored,
     skins and cores reserved
½ cup plus 2 tablespoons Calvados or brandy
1 cup currants
10 ounces Galette Dough (page 227), rolled into a 14-inch circle
4 tablespoons (½ stick) unsalted butter, melted
¾ cup sugar

GLAZE
Reserved apple skins and cores
1 cup sugar

Preheat the oven to 400°F. Peel and core the apples, reserving the trimmings. Slice the apples about ¼ inch thick and toss with 2 tablespoons of the Calvados. In a small saucepan, warm the currants with the remaining ½ cup Calvados and ½ cup water over medium heat. Bring to a simmer; remove from the heat, and leave to plump up.

Remove the pre-rolled dough from the refrigerator or freezer and place on a buttered or parchment paper–lined baking sheet. Leaving a 2-inch border, arrange the apple slices over the pastry, mounding the fruit to a thickness of 3 or 4 slices at the edges. Trim away most of the 2-inch border, leaving about ½ inch of pastry. (Save the trimmings to make little sugar cookies.) Finish the tart by folding the exposed border over on itself, crimping to make a narrow pastry rim around the fruit. Brush the edges of the tart with the melted butter. Sprinkle the buttered edges with a tablespoon or so of sugar and sprinkle the remaining sugar directly on the apples.

Bake in the lower third of the oven for 30 minutes, rotating the pan several times to make sure the edges are browning evenly. Drain the currants and scatter them over the apples. Continue baking 20 to 30 minutes longer, until the apples are soft and the pastry edges have begun to caramelize. Slide the tart directly onto a cooling rack and allow to cool slightly.

While the tart is baking, simmer the apple skins and cores with 1 cup of water and 1 cup of sugar until a thick rosy syrup is achieved, about 20 minutes. Strain the syrup and drizzle it over the tart just before serving. Serve with vanilla ice cream or crème fraîche.

APRICOT BREAD PUDDING

This is a comforting, warm, substantial finish to a meal. In fact, it is often too substantial after a rich meal. However, in this version, the acidity of the apricots tempers the richness.

Serves 6 to 8.

1 cup dried apricots, sliced, or 8 fresh apricots,
   cut in small wedges
1¼ cups sugar

PUDDING
7 egg yolks
⅓ cup sugar, plus additional for sprinkling
2 cups half-and-half or whole milk
2 cups cream
Grated zest of 1 orange
¼ teaspoon salt
1 teaspoon vanilla extract
¼ teaspoon almond extract
⅛ teaspoon nutmeg
1 tablespoon kirsch
Optional: 4 ounces good-quality almond paste,
   cut in pea-size pieces
About 1 pound brioche, pain-de-mie, or good day-old
   homemade white bread, cut into ½-inch cubes (about 5 cups)

IN a small saucepan, simmer the apricots in 1 cup water and ¼ cup of the sugar. Poach the fruit until tender, about 12 minutes for dried, 5 for fresh. Drain the fruit, saving the liquid, and set the fruit aside to cool. Return the poaching liquid to the saucepan and add the remaining 1 cup sugar and ½ cup water. Boil this mixture, and when it begins to brown, swirl the pan so that it caramelizes evenly. Cook to a medium amber color. Very carefully pour the hot caramel into a 2-quart gratin dish or divide it evenly among 6 small ramekins. Cool.

Whisk the egg yolks in a large bowl. Slowly add ⅓ cup sugar and mix well. Whisk in the half-and-half or milk and the cream. Add the orange zest, salt, vanilla and almond extracts, nutmeg, and kirsch. Gently fold in the poached apricots, the almond paste, if using, and the bread cubes. Transfer the pudding mixture to the gratin dish or ramekins. Let rest at least 1 hour or refrigerate overnight.

Preheat the oven to 375°F. Sprinkle a little sugar over the top of the pudding. Place the gratin dish or ramekins on a baking sheet to catch any overflow. Bake until nicely browned, about 55 minutes. Serve warm or at room temperature.

Variation: Substitute prunes for the apricots and Armagnac for the kirsch.

Peach Leaf Crème Brûlée

Peach leaves steeped in red wine lend a herbaceous, fruity almond flavor to vin de pêche, the traditional French homemade peach wine. They also add their wonderful almond flavor to ice creams and custards like this crème brûlée. We get our peach leaves from a small organic peach farm. If you know someone who grows organic peaches in your area, you may be able to procure a few handfuls of fresh peach leaves.

Serves 8.

1½ cups heavy cream
1½ cups half-and-half
½ cup sugar, plus more for the caramel topping
1 cup crushed peach leaves
6 egg yolks

Pour the heavy cream into a medium bowl and refrigerate. Warm the half-and-half with ½ cup sugar in a nonreactive saucepan over medium heat, stirring occasionally, until the sugar dissolves. Off the heat, add the peach leaves and let them steep for 5 to 10 minutes. Taste the mixture; it should be faintly floral and somewhat almond-flavored. Beware—if the leaves steep too long the infusion can become bitter. Remove the leaves and let the mixture cool slightly.

Whisk the egg yolks lightly in a medium bowl. Gradually add the half-and-half mixture to the yolks, stirring constantly until the yolks are thoroughly incorporated. Strain through a fine-mesh sieve into the bowl of cold heavy cream and stir well. Refrigerate for up to a day, or proceed with the recipe immediately.

Preheat the oven to 350°F. Fill eight 4- to 5-ounce ramekins with the crème brûlée mixture, and place them in a shallow baking dish. Fill the baking dish with warm water to reach halfway up the sides of the ramekins. Cover tightly with foil and bake for 30 minutes. Open one corner of the foil and check the custards. They should be completely set except for a small dime-sized spot in the center. To test for doneness, jiggle the ramekins, protecting your hand with an oven mitt. When done, remove the finished custards from the water bath and cool them for several hours or overnight in the refrigerator.

Just before serving, sprinkle the top of each custard evenly with 2 tablespoons of sugar. Using a small propane torch (available in hardware or kitchen supply stores), caramelize the sugar, moving the flame back and forth over the sugar until it bubbles and browns, and tilting the ramekins to even out the caramel. The caramel will stay crisp for about an hour.

Variations: Infuse other flavors into the custard—black currant tea is another favorite. Or flavor the crème brûlée in the traditional way, with half a vanilla bean split lengthwise and its scraped-out seeds.

WOOD OVEN–BAKED FIGS WITH RASPBERRIES

Our wood oven gives these figs a wonderfully smoky, roasted flavor, but similar results can be achieved in a hot oven at home. These figs get caramelized around the edges and have a great aroma from the honey and sweet wine. If you use more than one variety of fig, this dish is even more beautiful. Heating figs can transform less-than-perfect fruit—figs that are a little tough or slightly over- or underripe—into a delicious and savory dessert.

Serves 4 to 6.

10 medium-size figs, about 1½ pounds
¼ cup sweet wine, such as Beaumes-de-Venise,
    vin santo, or Sauternes
⅓ cup honey, warmed
1½ tablespoons sugar
½-pint basket raspberries

Preheat the oven to 425°F. Remove the stem ends of the figs and cut each fig in half. In an earthenware baking dish, place the halves skin side down, lining them up so they all fit evenly. Pour ¼ cup water and the sweet wine into the bottom of the dish. Drizzle the figs with the warm honey. Sprinkle the sugar over the figs, making sure each fig gets a tiny bit of sugar.

Bake the figs in the upper part of the oven for 15 minutes. Baste with the water and wine mixture and bake for another 5 minutes. When the figs are starting to caramelize at the edges, add the raspberries, tucking them into the spaces between the figs. Save any extra berries to garnish the dish. Bake for another 5 minutes just to warm the raspberries through. Serve the figs warm with vanilla or honey ice cream.

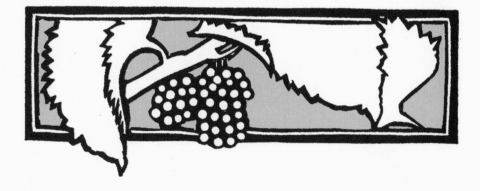

Chilled Papaya with Lime

Lime and papayas make one of those flavor combinations so good they seem predestined. The melting, too-sweet flesh of a perfectly ripe papaya is enlivened by the bright perfume and acid of a squeeze of lime. Lime suits many other fruits, especially mangoes and watermelon.

Although found now in all parts of the tropics, papayas are native to the West Indies, where they ripen year-round. They are especially welcome in late winter and early spring, when they are at their most prolific and citrus seems to be the only other fresh fruit around.

Papaya with lime is one of the few exceptions we make to our focus on local produce. Thanks to Bill Fujimoto at Monterey Market in Berkeley, we have access to large, perfectly ripe papayas from an organic producer in Mexico. Our limes come from a number of organic growers in Southern California and Mexico.

Papayas are oval in shape, the stem end blunt, the other end pointed. Ripe papayas will have a yellow-orange skin, sometimes streaked with green. They should give gently when squeezed, but they should not have any soft watery areas on the skin. They will continue to ripen when kept at room temperature, and should be eaten soon or refrigerated once they are soft.

The papayas we get from Mexico weigh several pounds and are the size of small watermelons! More commonly available are the smaller grapefruit-size papayas from Hawaii. Look for those that are not treated with fungicide before shipment. The color of the flesh depends on the variety, but it ranges from pale orange to salmon red.

To serve papaya, chill for several hours in the refrigerator or in a bowl of ice. Cut the fruit in half lengthwise. Scrape out the seeds, which look like big shiny grains of caviar, dark gray to black in color. There may be few or many, but save some to serve with the fruit; they have a refreshing peppery flavor much like watercress. Cut the fruit into wedges ½ to ¾ inch thick and peel off the skin with a small knife.

Served with wedges of lime and a sprinkling of papaya seeds, this is a treat after a rich dinner. Papaya with lime also makes a sublime breakfast.

FAVORITE CAFÉ COOKIES

Cookies are baked every day in the pastry kitchen. We try to bake cookies that have distinctive flavors and crisp texture to contrast with the desserts they are served with, and that aren't too sweet or too buttery. These recipes have been adapted from the contributions of our friends and pastry cooks over the years. My personal favorite is Cats' Tongues: I could eat a platter of them with a Faye Elberta peach.

PAIN D'AMANDE

Makes 4 dozen cookies.

2⅓ cups flour
¼ teaspoon baking soda
¼ teaspoon salt
8 tablespoons (1 stick) unsalted butter
½ teaspoon cinnamon
1½ cups raw washed Hawaiian sugar
1 cup sliced almonds

SIFT together the flour, baking soda, and salt. In a small saucepan, heat the butter, cinnamon, and ⅓ cup water until the butter is just melted. Remove from heat and stir in the Hawaiian sugar. Stir in the flour mixture and the almonds. Put the dough on a large piece of plastic wrap and form into a bar 3½ inches wide, ½ inch thick, and 9 inches long. Freeze the bar. Slice the cookies about ⅛ inch thick and bake on parchment paper–lined baking sheets at 350°F. for 10 minutes, or until golden. Store in an airtight container.

BUTTERSCOTCH BATONS

Makes 25 to 30 cookies.

½ cup light corn syrup
½ cup brown sugar
8 tablespoons (1 stick) butter
¾ cup flour
½ cup finely chopped pecans
¼ teaspoon salt

Melt the corn syrup, brown sugar, and butter together over low heat. Stir in the flour, pecans, and salt. Drop teaspoon-sized dollops onto an ungreased baking sheet about 5 inches apart—they will bubble and spread out quite a bit.

Bake 8 to 10 minutes at 350°F. Remove from the oven and cool just enough to be picked up with a spatula. Quickly roll each cookie into a finger-sized cylinder. If they harden before you have formed them all, put them back in the oven for a moment to soften them again. Once they are cool, store them in an airtight container to keep them crisp.

Variation: Instead of rolling them, mold the cookies while still warm over inverted small bowls or ramekins to make cookie cups for ice cream or berries.

Chocolate-Almond Cookies

Makes 30 cookies.

12 ounces bittersweet chocolate
4 tablespoons (½ stick) unsalted butter
¼ cup brandy
1 cup ground almonds
½ cup plus 2 tablespoons cake flour
¾ teaspoon baking powder
¼ teaspoon salt
3 eggs
½ cup sugar, plus extra for rolling
Powdered sugar

Melt the chocolate and butter together in a bowl. Stir in the brandy. In another bowl, mix together the almonds, cake flour, baking powder, and salt. In a third bowl, beat the eggs with ½ cup sugar until pale yellow. Add the chocolate mixture and stir until just mixed. Fold in the flour mixture. Chill the dough. Roll into 1-inch balls. Roll the balls first in granulated sugar, then in powdered sugar. Bake on a parchment paper–lined baking sheet at 325°F until the tops are cracked, about 10 minutes. The cookies are done when they lift easily from the sheet. When cool, they should be slightly chewy. Do not overbake or they will be dry and hard.

CATS' TONGUES

Makes 28 cookies.

4 tablespoons (½ stick) butter, softened
⅓ cup sugar
2 egg whites
½ cup minus 1 tablespoon flour
¼ teaspoon salt
⅛ teaspoon almond extract
¼ teaspoon powdered ginger
Optional: 1 teaspoon cocoa powder

BEAT the butter and sugar together. Beat in the egg whites and fold in the flour. Add the salt, almond extract, and ginger, and mix until the batter has a smooth consistency. Refrigerate. Spread with a spoon into very thin ¾ × 3-inch rectangles onto a parchment paper–lined baking sheet. Bake at 350°F. until the edges are golden, about 7 to 10 minutes. While the cookies are still warm they may be manipulated to hold a shape: drape them over the handle of a wooden spoon, or twist them from both ends. When cool, store in an airtight container to keep them crisp.

Variation: For a marbled effect, mix cocoa into a small amount of batter and spread a little bit onto each cookie before baking. For a more whimsical-looking cookie, make them twice as long, or use this batter to make homemade fortune cookies.

ORANGE-CURRANT COOKIES

Makes 6 dozen cookies.

10 ounces (2½ sticks) butter
1½ cups sugar
1 large egg
1 teaspoon vanilla extract
2½ cups sifted flour
1 teaspoon salt
½ cup currants
½ cup finely chopped candied orange peel

CREAM the butter and sugar until light and fluffy. Add the egg and vanilla, and mix well. Stir in the flour and salt. Finally, stir in the currants and orange peel. Form the dough into 2 logs, each about 1½ inches in diameter. Wrap in plastic and freeze. Slice into ¼-inch rounds and bake at 350°F. on parchment paper–lined baking sheets until the edges of the cookies are golden, about 12 minutes.

Sources and Resources

The Center for Urban Education About Sustainable Agriculture
41 Sutter Street, Suite 1744
San Francisco, California 94104
510–524–3863
sfpmc@igc.org
Information about CSAs and farmers' markets in California.

Community Alliance with Family Farmers
P.O. Box 363
Davis, California 93617
530–756–8518
caff@caff.org
Nonprofit organization for family farmers and the general public;
information on CSAs in California.

Corti Brothers
5810 Folsom Boulevard
P.O. Box 191358
Sacramento, California 95819
916–736–3800
Aged balsamic vinegar, Catalan anchovies, organic olive oils.

Fairview Gardens
598 North Fairview Avenue
Goleta, California 93117
805–967–7369
Publicly owned historic organic farm; sells produce locally; provides
educational services for schools and communities nationwide.

The Gardener
1836 Fourth Street
Berkeley, California 94710
510–548–4545
Gardening supplies and housewares; importer of the Tuscan Grill
for fireplace and outdoor grilling.

International Slow Food Movement
    Via della Mendicità Istruita, 14
    12042 Bra (Cuneo)
    Italy
    Toll-free: 877–SLOWFOOD (877–756–9336)
    www.slowfood.com
    Supports and protects sustainable agriculture and traditional small food
        producers and promotes the pleasures of the table.

King Arthur Flour Co.
    P.O. Box 876
    Norwich, Vermont 05055-0876
    800–827–6836
    www.kingarthurflour.com
    Baking equipment and ingredients (including some organic flour).

Mothers and Others for a Livable Planet
    870 Market Street, Suite 654
    San Francisco, California 94102
    415–433–0850
    40 West 20th Street
    New York, New York 10011-4211
    212–242–0545
    Toll-free: 888–ECO–INFO
    www.mothers.org/mothers
    Promotes agricultural sustainability and environmental health
        for women and families.

Mozzarella Company
2944 Elm Street
Dallas, Texas 75226
800–798–2954
Fresh mozzarella and handmade cheeses.

Niman Ranch
1025 East 12th Street
Oakland, California 94606
510–808–0330
www.nimanranch.com
Naturally raised beef, sausages, and bacon.

The Sausage Maker
177 Military Road
Buffalo, New York 14207
716–876–5521
Sausage-making ingredients and equipment.

Seed Savers Exchange
3076 North Winn Road
Decorah, Iowa 52101
319–382–5990
www.sse@salamander.com
Organic heirloom seeds.

Seeds of Change
P.O. Box 15700
Santa Fe, New Mexico 87506–5700
505–438–8080
Certified organic heirloom seeds.

The Spanish Table
1427 Western Avenue
Seattle, Washington 98101
206–682–2827
Organic Spanish oils, smoky paprika (*pimentón de La Vera*) and other
   Spanish ingredients, and cooking equipment.

Straus Family Creamery
   P.O. Box 768
   Marshall, California 94940
   www.strausmilk.com
   Certified organic dairy; milk, cream, butter, and eggs.

Tomales Bay Foods and the Cowgirl Creamery
   P.O. Box 594
   Point Reyes Station, California 94956
   415–663–9335
   www.cowgirlcreamery.com
   Local organic cheeses and imported cheeses, including a selection
      from Neal's Yard Dairy in England.

Zingerman's
   422 Detroit Street
   Ann Arbor, Michigan 48104-3400
   734–769–1625
   Toll-free: 888–636–8162
   Organic olive oils, cheeses, honey, and pomegranate molasses.

THE CHEZ PANISSE FOUNDATION

TOWARD a more humane and sustainable future, The Chez Panisse Foundation supports youth and community projects that teach people the interwoven pleasures of growing, cooking, and sharing food, inspiring them to respect and care for the land, their communities, and themselves.

1517 SHATTUCK AVENUE
BERKELEY, CALIFORNIA 94709
510–843–3811

BIBLIOGRAPHY

Andrews, Colman. *Catalan Cuisine*. New York: Random House, 1988.

Bayless, Rick. *Rick Bayless' Mexican Kitchen*. New York: Scribner, 1996.

Bertolli, Paul, with Alice Waters. *Chez Panisse Cooking*. New York: Random House, 1988.

Braker, Flo. *The Simple Art of Perfect Baking*. New York: William Morrow, 1985.

Bugialli, Giuliano. *The Fine Art of Italian Cooking*. New York: Times Books, 1977.

Creasy, Rosalind. *Cooking from the Garden*. San Francisco: Sierra Club Books, 1988.

Cunningham, Marion. *The Fannie Farmer Baking Book*. New York: Alfred A. Knopf, 1984.

Daguin, André, with Anne de Ravel. *Foie Gras, Magret, and Other Good Food from Gascony*. New York: Random House, 1988.

David, Elizabeth. *Elizabeth David Classics*. New York: Alfred A. Knopf, 1980.

Field, Carol. *The Italian Baker*. New York: Harper & Row, 1985.

Gray, Patience. *Honey from a Weed*. New York: Harper & Row, 1987.

Grigson, Jane. *The Art of Charcuterie*. New York: Alfred A. Knopf, 1967.

Kasper, Lynne Rossetto. *The Splendid Table*. New York: William Morrow, 1992.

Kennedy, Diana. *My Mexico*. New York: Clarkson N. Potter, 1998.

———. *Nothing Fancy*. New York: The Dial Press, 1984.

Knickerbocker, Peggy. *Olive Oil: From Tree to Table*. San Francisco: Chronicle Books, 1997.

Larkcom, Joy. *The Salad Garden*. New York: Penguin, 1984.

Madison, Deborah. *Vegetarian Cooking for Everyone*. New York: Broadway, 1997.

Olney, Richard. *Lulu's Provençal Table*. New York: HarperCollins, 1994.

———. *Provence the Beautiful Cookbook*. San Francisco: Collins, 1993.

———. *Simple French Food*. New York: Simon & Schuster, 1974.

Peel, Mark, and Nancy Silverton. *The Food of Campanile*. New York: Villard, 1997.

Pépin, Jacques. *The Art of Cooking*. New York: Alfred A. Knopf, 1987.

Ratliffe, Kate. *A Culinary Journey in Gascony*. Berkeley, Calif.: Ten Speed Press, 1995.

Roden, Claudia. *Mediterranean Cookery*. New York: Alfred A. Knopf, 1987.

Sheffer, Nelli, and Mimi Sheraton. *Food Markets of the World*. New York: Abrams, 1997.

Shere, Lindsey Remolif. *Chez Panisse Desserts*. New York: Random House, 1985.

Silverton, Nancy. *Desserts by Nancy Silverton*. New York: Harper & Row, 1986.

Waters, Alice. *Chez Panisse Menu Cookbook*. New York: Random House, 1982.

———. *Chez Panisse Vegetables*. New York: HarperCollins, 1996.

———, with Bob Carrau and Patricia Curtan. *Fanny at Chez Panisse*. New York: HarperCollins, 1992.

———, with Patricia Curtan and Martine Labro. *Chez Panisse Pasta, Pizza, and Calzone*. New York: Random House, 1984.

Wells, Patricia. *The Food Lover's Guide to France*. New York: Workman, 1987.

Wise, Victoria. *American Charcuterie: Recipes from Pig-by-the-Tail*. New York: Viking, 1986.

Wolfert, Paula. *Couscous and Other Good Food from Morocco*. New York: Harper & Row, 1973.

———. *Mediterranean Grains and Greens*. New York: HarperCollins, 1998.

———. *Paula Wolfert's World of Food*. New York: Harper & Row, 1988.

ILLUSTRATIONS

Headcheese: *Dandelion*
Country Terrine with Pistachios: *Pistachios*
Prosciutto, Spring Onion, and Artichoke Antipasto: *Artichoke*
Smoky Garlic Sausage with Kale: *Kale*
Catalan-Style Sausage and Clams: *Clams*
Crépinettes with Swiss Chard: *Chard*
Long-Cooked Pork Shoulder: *Chili Peppers*
Simple Cured Pork Chops: *Allspice*
Brine-Cured Pork: *Allspice*

CHAPTER SIX: LAMB
Chapter Title: *Red Clover*
Spicy Lamb Sausage: *Paprika*
Lamb Braised with Tomatoes and Garlic: *Bay Leaves*
Grilled Boneless Lamb Leg with Olive Sauce: *Olive*
Lamb Couscous with Turnips, Carrots, and Harissa: *Turnips*
Braised and Grilled Spring Lamb: *Onions*
Warm Lamb Salad with Pomegranates and Walnuts: *Pomegranate*

CHAPTER SEVEN: POULTRY
Chapter Title: *Poultry*
Shaved Foie Gras and Rocket Salad: *Hazelnuts*
Pigeon Salad with White Bean Toasts: *Pigeon and Beans*
Warm Duck Breast Salad with Green Olive Relish: *Green Olive*
Duck Confit with Baked Figs: *Fig Branch*
Duck Rillettes Croûtons with Chicory Salad: *Chicory*
Duck Legs Braised in Zinfandel: *Grape Leaves*
Polenta with Duck Sauce: *Corn*
Grilled Quail with Bread Crumb Salsa: *Quail*
Grilled Chicken Breasts au Poivre: *Grapes*
Pollo al Mattone with Lemon and Garlic: *Lemon Branch*
Chicken Ballotine with Chanterelles: *Carrot*

CHAPTER EIGHT: SWEETS
Chapter Title: *Honeycomb and Honeysuckle*
Meyer Lemon Éclairs: *Lemon Slices*
Lindsey's Chocolate Cake with Sicilian Sabayon: *Cocoa Flower*
Honey-Pistachio Brittle Ice Cream with Lavender Sauce: *Lavender*
Cherry Clafoutis: *Finch and Cherries*
Angel Food Cake: *Oranges and Orange Flowers*

Mulberry Sherbet: *Mulberry*
Plum Upside-Down Cake: *Plum Branch*
Apple and Brandied Currant Tart (at head of recipe): *Apples*
Apple and Brandied Currant Tart (endpiece): *Peels and Cores*
Apricot Bread Pudding: *Apricot Branch*
Peach Leaf Crème Brûlée: *Peach Branch*
Wood Oven-Baked Figs with Raspberries: *Mulberry*
Orange Currant Cookies: *Flower*

SOURCES & RESOURCES
Slow Food: *Snail on Leaf*
Chez Panisse Foundation: *Sheep on Hillside*

Index